EAST ENDERS

Family and community in East London

Katharine Mumford and Anne Po

The POLICY
P P
PRESS

First published in Great Britain in April 2003 by

The Policy Press
Fourth Floor, Beacon House
Queen's Road
Bristol BS8 1QU
UK

Tel +44 (0)117 331 4054
Fax +44 (0)117 331 4093
e-mail tpp-info@bristol.ac.uk
www.policypress.org.uk

British Library Cataloguing in Publication Data

A catalogue record for this book is available from the British Library

ISBN 1 86134 497 X paperback

A hardback version of this book is also available

Katharine Mumford was Research Officer in the ESRC Centre for Analysis of Social Exclusion (CASE) at the London School of Economics and Political Science, before leaving to start a family. **Anne Power** is Professor of Social Policy and Deputy Director of CASE.

Cover design by Qube Design Associates, Bristol.

Front cover: photograph kindly supplied by www.third-avenue.co.uk

Printed and bound in Great Britain by Bell & Bain Ltd, Glasgow.

Contents

List of tables, figures and boxes

Tables

Figures

Boxes

Acknowledgements

This book represents three years of intensive visiting in the London boroughs of Hackney and Newham. We would like to thank the hundred families and the many local organisations, including schools, health workers, local authorities, police, park staff, community organisations and churches who helped us so generously and offered warm hospitality.

We would also like to thank the research organisations who helped us to set up the study and whose work gave us a firm basis, including: the ESRC who funded the research; the Centre for Analysis of Social Exclusion at the London School of Economics and Political Science; the Joseph Rowntree Foundation; the Institute of Community Studies; the Centre for Neighbourhood Research; One Plus One Marriage and Partnership Research; and the Nuffield Foundation. Several individuals helped us with language interpreting during interviews.

We owe a particular debt to Ruth Lupton, whose work on area change formed the original basis for this study. She has provided invaluable background material for this book. Helen Bowman (based in Leeds) extended this research to the North, and her comments and suggestions gave extremely useful insights. Bani Makkar (based in London) has continued the interviewing in Hackney and Newham, and her findings have strengthened and extended what we were able to say. Liz Richardson's work with community organisations (within the Centre for Analysis of Social Exclusion, LSE Housing) gave us additional insights. Tom Sefton helped with research approaches and analysis. Caroline Paskell was an invaluable researcher, tracking down literature and statistics. Abigail McKnight generously shared her knowledge and experience in the field of work, helping us to identify trajectories and to classify the work histories of the families. Penny Mansfield advised us on our overall research approach and supported our work very generously. Geoff Dench at the Institute of Community Studies also advised us on setting up the study. John Hills made many useful comments and suggestions on at least two drafts. The Policy Press helped direct our study. We drew heavily on the work of Roger Burrows at the University of York, and owe a great debt to him for introducing us to 'the geography of misery'.

We must also thank Jane Dickson and Lucinda Himeur for their constant help with producing, checking and correcting the text. The final work was down to the hard work, care and commitment of Nicola Harrison.

Most importantly, several local workers in Glenridding, including Robert Teasdale and Anne Sharman of Sharmans, Lisa, Sonica and Laura at the Inn on the Lake, made sure that the many pages of this work moved between Katharine Mumford, who went on maternity leave just as we were finalising the text, and Anne Power, as she tried to start her summer holidays! Electronic communication was simply not up to the job in the last stages and we had to rely on people.

During all this period Tom Hanss and John Hills provided unstinting support and advice. We owe them both an unpayable debt of thanks.

Finally, we offer our deep gratitude to Michael Young (Lord Young of Dartington) whose work inspired us, whose advice proved invaluable until shortly before he died last year, and in the footsteps of whose work this book follows.

Material from the Survey of English Housing is Crown Copyright; it has been made available by the Office for National Statistics (ONS) through the Data Archive and has been used by permission. Neither the ONS nor the Data Archive bear any responsibility for the analysis or interpretation of the data reported here.

ONE

Getting the inside view

"I don't know no different. I just like living here. I wouldn't want to live anywhere else." (Tina)

"Mixture of old and new, and old and new ways. It's becoming a bit cosmopolitan." (Peggy)

This book is about two low-income areas in the East End of London and the lives of a hundred families who live there. The families tell us about the impact of poor neighbourhood conditions on family life, why neighbourhoods matter to families on a low income, how family life is inextricably bound up with neighbourhoods, and how families help determine the future of neighbourhoods. The families tell us about their homes, their children, their work, their schools, their neighbours and relations, their sense of belonging, and their fears and anxieties about the future. All the families have children. It seems particularly important to understand how neighbourhood conditions affect both parents and children. We visited the families twice before we wrote this book, usually in their homes, over a period of two years; we almost always talked with mothers although fathers, grandparents, friends and children sometimes joined in. So the insights into neighbourhood life are usually reported through the eyes of the mothers. We are still visiting the families and have a lot more to tell than can fit here, but this book begins the story of the lives of East End families today. They shed light on today's urban problems, on the significance of family and community relations, and on economic and social changes at the bottom of the hierarchy of neighbourhoods.

We chose the East End of London as part of a much bigger study of poor neighbourhoods throughout the country (R. Lupton, interview with police inspector, West-City Police Station, 17 May 1999; R. Lupton, discussion with author 4 June 2001; Lupton, forthcoming). The East End has by far the biggest concentration of poverty in the capital. The families are Londoners, but their day-to-day experiences and attitudes reflect much wider patterns of neighbourhood life, as many works in this field show. There is a much broader urban neighbourhood and community debate, of which East Enders is a part[1].

From our evidence, and from other studies, we know that living in an inner-city neighbourhood is a daily struggle for families, particularly for those with young children. It is expensive and you don't have much money. So many things fall outside your control – often even your own home, but particularly if you are a tenant, which most families in these areas are. There may be talk of demolition. You may need more space but there are more urgent cases. You can't move because you can't afford to buy, and the council won't help you, or they say that they can't. You get on well with your neighbours, but feel worried about letting your children play out because you see lots of 'rough' behaviour. There are also many things you like about where you live.

In traditional communities, social links and families connect people together in a pattern that changes slowly over time – in ways that allow people to develop a sense of belonging. This was certainly true of the East End families in Michael Young and Peter Willmott's famous book of the 1950s, *Families and kinship in East London*. In inner-city neighbourhoods today social relations are far more uncertain – many people are new, from 'outside', and move frequently. The 100 families from the study talk about how these changes affect them. People who regard themselves as 'locals' sometimes can't live near parents, sisters, friends or other 'locals' because 'outsiders' are seen to take priority. Newcomers may have more children, be actually homeless or be fleeing from a civil war. Many longer-term as well as newer residents are from overseas, of different races, cultures and creeds. But people from different racial and ethnic backgrounds have often been born and bred in the East End. Who is or isn't an 'outsider' is itself no longer clear in many inner-city neighbourhoods.

Families generally 'rub along' quite well together, despite problems and differences, but there are many unresolved strains. Crime and threatening behaviour are more common because there are more strangers, fewer controls, less of a common sense of belonging, and more agitation and aggression (Power and Tunstall, 1997). In smaller, more settled communities, where people move less, it is often more difficult to 'step out of line'. There are more informal controls. So who belongs in large inner-city communities? Who copes and how? Is there any sense of community ownership? By whom and of what?

Our book is about the experiences of 100 families bringing up children in dense and 'difficult' urban areas. The mothers have a particular perspective on life in the city. Many small-scale, local and immediate concerns shape and pressurise their lives. The large volume of writing about women's perspectives on neighbourhoods and their specific caring role forms a rich backdrop to our findings[2]. The day-to-day encounters of families with neighbourhood conditions offer crucial insights for policy makers, particularly in social policy. For neighbourhoods are where women spend much of their time. They shape their children's life chances, as mothers explain to us. The mothers tell us what it is like to care for their children in such an uncertain environment.

Parents talk about their strong sense of community, their need for good neighbours, and their links with relatives and friends. They talk about relations between races, about neighbourhood services and amenities, about opportunities for employment. They have many fears and worries for their children and often want to move away because of their lack of sense of control within the area. It is a contradictory story that helps us understand how some neighbourhoods have come to be so deeply troubled and depleted, yet so valuable. For they are also home to people who care; families who need to live somewhere and who want the best for their children; mothers and fathers who want to help their neighbours and contribute to society. Most families struggle with little money and many social pressures, but accommodate big community changes, accept newcomers and believe in an ideal of inter-racial understanding, tolerance and community spirit. We try to capture the views of the 'most present' parent, giving an inside, ground-level view of some of the most significant issues facing cities, as played out where the impact of change is harshest and therefore may be the clearest (SEU, 1998a).

Most of the families are tenants, not homeowners. This means that they have less levers over conditions, with little sense of ownership or direct control. They are far more dissatisfied with their accommodation, their living conditions and services than people in better neighbourhoods, and they are far more worried about crime, disorder and social breakdown. Who is in charge of these neighbourhoods? Or responsible for their conditions? Who do they belong to? Why do the people in them feel so worried about the future, insecure and unable to control conditions at their own front door? And who can make a difference? Certainly no individual family or group of neighbours felt that they could, even though they often wanted to.

People do not just give up in the face of such difficulties. Most of the families help out in some way or other, and believe that a sense of community matters a lot. They try to make their community work although they may feel ground down by the daily struggle of their lives. But can they make a critical difference to their neighbourhoods and to their own lives? If so, why don't they want to stay? Most recognise that they cannot move, so there is a pent-up dissatisfaction and a strong urge to do something about it.

This book is about the actual lives of families, rather than the broader structural problems of society, although the connections are clear and we aim to highlight them. We recount what people have to say for themselves, rather than the wider academic debates of a more theoretical nature about regeneration and community relations[3]. We believe that it is the very detail of life experiences that can help us understand broader trends and establish a firmer basis for interventions to improve conditions.

The families' feelings and reactions to life in their neighbourhood are described in four parts. Readers can miss out the sections that interest them less. Each chapter has a concluding summary to make this easy.

• **Community and race relations:** why does community matter and where can it be found? Who do people rely on, and what are their links with their family? How do they see their neighbours and how involved and connected are they with local activity? In rapidly changing neighbourhoods, what tensions and conflicts are there between different groups? What advantages do mixed neighbourhoods offer? How do people from different backgrounds and ethnic groups get on with each other and what do different racial groups think about race relations? The families' experience of ethnic mixing indicates a higher potential for cohesion than is often believed possible.

- **Mothers in work or staying at home:** what jobs have mothers done up to now? How does it combine with family life? Do mothers who work enjoy it? Can they juggle family, home and work? Do they work nearby or in the city? Mothers who don't work outside the home see things differently. Do they intend to go back to work and do they have similar work backgrounds to the mothers in paid work? How ambitious are they? Casual and part-time work, frequent job changes, low wages, welfare dependence, being a lone parent are all things that affect a mother's ability to work. What job prospects do these mothers have? The attitudes of mothers to their home, their children, their employment and income prospects affect their decisions about staying at home or going out to work.

- **Neighbourhood conditions – the threat of breakdown:** how do public services, such as schools, the neighbourhood environment, leisure, transport and so on work? Which ones work badly? How do poor services affect neighbourhoods and family life? How do these neighbourhoods compare with others? The condition of open spaces and parks shows how poor services lead to decay and neglect, resulting in less people using public areas, more disorder and eventually loss of control. Is anti-social and 'rough' behaviour more common and more disturbing in these areas? Are children more out of control and are they under more pressure as a result? Is fear a big factor in people's lives? Does social breakdown threaten the future of these neighbourhoods? There is a tug of war between things that are going better for the families – such as schools – and things that feel out of control – such as drug-related crime. We explore the risks that parents feel they're running with their children's lives.

- **How change affects families:** are the neighbourhoods getting better or worse? In what ways? Can both happen concurrently? What are the prospects for inner-city neighbourhoods and for the families living in them? How do these neighbourhoods and these families fit with wider patterns of change? These neighbourhoods are among the very poorest in the country, and we know that our families broadly reflect the neighbourhoods they live in; 45% are lone parents; more than 50% are from ethnic minority groups; 75% are social housing tenants; 41% are entirely dependent on state benefits. The pace of change among the people who live there, the high proportion of families who say they want to leave the area, the close proximity of extreme wealth in the city and the struggle to survive of these families all create a sense of uncertainty and anxiety in mothers, particularly. But almost everyone we spoke to identified good as well as bad things about living in the East End of London.

The questions we address fit within major academic and political debates about whether poor areas are significantly different and suffer greater pressures and disorder; whether neighbourhoods themselves affect people's life chances, particularly those of children; whether regeneration attempts and other government interventions make a difference or are simply a waste of money; whether families are surviving and whether the critical role of mothers can withstand the multiple pressures of child-rearing, home responsibilities, employment and community roles; what significance people attach to the idea of community in modern cities; whether people's housing – who owns and runs it, how this constrains people's freedom – affects family life and relations; what social pressures are created by more mixed populations and incomes; whether different racial and ethnic groups want to mix or prefer to live separately; whether individuals see themselves as on their own or as part of a community. We try to remain true to the families' accounts of their lives, and answer these important questions largely through their own words.

The book has several crucial messages. Community matters much more to the families in these neighbourhoods than to the average person. Race relations are generally good and a majority of families believe that living in a multi-racial area is positive. But some people experience racial harassment, including severe intimidation and physical attacks. Some people (from all races) are worried about the number of refugees, which creates even more competition for housing, pressure on schools and sometimes fuels racist behaviour. A large majority of the families are linked in to their neighbourhoods through voluntary activity, community organisations or local jobs, yet many still want to move. Half the mothers work and half are at home caring for their children. Many work locally, the majority in low-skilled service jobs, but many are upgrading their skills and progressing into valuable, if not underpaid, new service jobs. Many services are good. Transport links, leisure facilities and shops are more accessible in these city neighbourhoods and therefore more useful. But neighbourhood environments are much worse. Most families have a mixed view of their neighbourhoods' prospects, believing that physical conditions are getting better but social conditions are getting worse, particularly with regard to aggressive and anti-social behaviour.

Parks and open spaces are a litmus test of neighbourhood progress for they matter greatly to our 100 families. They provide critical links within the neighbourhood to the world outside the home. They also reflect a wider attitude to public and communal assets. Public spaces play a critical role in cities, as many studies show[4]. The withdrawal of front-line services, the disappearance of people from the street who have a caring, custodial role is the greatest threat to the stability of these neighbourhoods. By the same token, familiar faces in a custodial role offering careful supervision of neighbourhood conditions would make many mothers and children feel safer, happier, more confident and more likely to stay. It is not outside our control as a society to make unstable, highly pressurised and seriously poor neighbourhoods work better. These neighbourhoods are a vital housing resource for low-income families. As such they provide an essential building block for cities as a whole.

Our findings should help politicians and policy makers, for they come straight from the groups who are least heard, with the least power to shape what happens, yet have the strongest interest in shaping neighbourhood conditions. Our families occupy spaces that offer a vital resource for the future of cities.

Our earlier work on neighbourhood problems shows not only UK-wide patterns of neighbourhood distress, but strong parallels with urban experience in Europe[5]. The work of William Julius Wilson, of Harvard University, and colleagues, underlines the value of family accounts from within neighbourhoods in understanding what is really happening and why it matters to the future of cities. It helped shape an American rebirth of interest in cities (Katz, 2002). Without families, it is unlikely that urban communities will flourish, or government attempts at regenerating inner-city neighbourhoods will work.

A large representative group of families within two of the most difficult areas of London try hard to make their own corner work. But they are unable to manage the wider problems, and will not stay long enough to make an impact unless we rethink our approach to neighbourhoods and see them as the essential building blocks of successful cities in the future. So who is actually responsible? Who do these neighbourhoods really belong to? And who can take control and make them work? By the end of the book we hope to answer some of these questions – based, of course, on the lives of our 100 families.

Notes

[1] This book probes the value and form of 'community' in relation to the neighbourhoods of the study – where 'neighbourhood' is understood as the area residents recognise as their 'local area'. Relating 'community' to 'neighbourhood' fuses social networks with geography, suggesting the existence of shared interests and/or identity in shared space (Goffman, 1972; Halperin, 1998; Bourdieu et al, 1999; Bridge, 2002). It is in neighbourhoods, places of day-to-day association, that casual encounters give rise to common interests, concerns and identity, or to conflict and exclusion (SEU reports, 1998-2001; CASE, 1997-2002: http://sticerd.lse.ac.uk/case). The Joseph Rowntree Foundation has supported extensive programmes of research on neighbourhoods, community and social exclusion. The most important of these are listed in the References (JRF, 1998-2002; see www.jrf.org.uk).

[2] In disadvantaged areas residents' social interaction and participation in local activities, service provision and decision-making structures are linked to women's distinct roles (Frazer and Lacey, 1993; Gatens and MacKinnon, 1999; Weissberg, 1999). Women have denser local social networks than men (Jarvis, 1999; Russell, 1999), are more frequently involved in local activities, have higher rates of service uptake and involvement with formal decision-making structures. This has been linked to women's more extensive childcare responsibilities (Drew et al, 1998; JRF, 2000d) since childcare can serve as a conduit both for local social interaction (Jarvis, 1999) and uptake of local services. This informal engagement can provide both opportunity and motivation for taking a more

formal role in the local area. Women's perspectives on their local area, and the relative significance women attach to local services and conditions, are significantly different from men's (Bourdieu et al, 1999; JRF, 1999b) – a difference that is reflected in their higher rates of involvement with local self-help initiatives, service provision and locally focused decision-making structures (McLaverty, 2002). The gendered nature of local engagement is an element in the debate over the existence and form of 'social capital' in local areas (Putnam et al, 1993; Dasgupta and Serageldin, 2000; Putnam, 2000; Schuller et al, 2001).

[3] Whenever there are relevant studies of a wider nature that lend support to what the families say about their experiences, we make that connection clear. We draw extensively on the wider work of the Centre for Analysis of Social Exclusion at the London School of Economics and Political Science within which this study is based, on the neighbourhood and regeneration studies of the Joseph Rowntree Foundation, the Economic and Social Research Council Cities and Neighbourhoods programmes and the Social Exclusion Unit. Our own studies of acute neighbourhood decline and recovery have helped us frame this work and to put it in context (Power, 1987, 1991, 1996, 1999; Power and Tunstall, 1995, 1997; Power and Mumford, 1999; Mumford and Power, forthcoming).

[4] Jan Gehl, the renowned Danish architect and urban planner, has detailed in two important studies the role of public space in the social life of cities. Originally using Copenhagen as a live experiment for his ideas, and monitoring impact over 30 years, he has now studied similar initiatives in cities worldwide, showing that traffic-calmed, people-orientated, cared-for streets, squares, parks and gardens humanise cities and encourage people to participate. Peter Rowe, in *Civic realism*, creates a clear theoretical framework for understanding the centrality of urban public space in helping us to share space amicably and positively. With Richard Rogers, we have explored and documented in detail the way social life is enhanced or hampered by the way society treat the public realm (Gehl, 1996; Rowe, 1997; Rogers and Power, 2000; Gehl and Gemzoe, 2001). These ideas are now widely recognised by government (DETR, 2000; HM Treasury, 2002).

[5] Studies of urban neighbourhoods across Europe – and in practice of urban problems worldwide – detail these common patterns (van Vliet, 1990; Jacquier, 1991; Harloe, 1995; van Kempen and Ozuekren, 1998; UNCHS, 2001). Our earlier work on marginal European estates and on the development of housing policy in Europe exposed both the extreme social conditions parallel to our families' experiences, and multiple initiatives to combat the worst effects of these problems (Power, 1993, 1996, 1999).

TWO

Investigating neighbourhood life

"When it comes to the area itself, like renovation, it is getting better. But then again, we've got this pack ... a new pack ... I used to know them when they were little and they've grown up. Now they are big boys of about 14 or 15 years old. I'm terrified of these because I knew them as babies, and now I'm terrified of seeing them. They are so big and tall and in these packs.... Every time I come from work, before I come into that lift, my heart is thumping and I'm thinking 'God I'm going to get mugged before I can even press for the lift'."
(Cynthia)

The two East London areas that we chose for our work are among the most deprived neighbourhoods in the country. Inner London has many low-income neighbourhoods despite its economic prosperity. It houses only 5% of the total population of England and Wales, yet 11% of all the people in England and Wales who live in high 'poverty areas' live in inner London (R. Lupton, interview with Police Inspector, 17 May 1999).

'West-City' in Hackney and 'East-Docks' in Newham[1] are in different East London boroughs, with some different housing patterns, ethnic make-up and histories. We can thus gather a wide picture of family life in the East End since our aim is to understand how low-income families with children cope with the problems of the inner city and with other pressures. But both areas are within the East End, near to growing local economies – one is on the doorstep of the City of London, the other in 'Docklands', the Thames Gateway and within sight of the Millennium Dome. The big up-turn in the economic prospects of these areas have not as yet had much impact on the overall deprivation of the neighbourhoods we studied. Both neighbourhoods are generally very poor and have a reputation for crime and other social problems. Yet there is great potential within these neighbourhoods, and our families wonder whether they may or may not be the beneficiaries (Mumford, 2001). We concentrated on the East End in order to give a coherent and local focus to the families' views. To avoid specific distortions, we drew the families from two neighbourhoods within that part of London. In focusing on a single city and particular areas within it, we follow the example set by three important neighbourhood family studies: Young and Willmott (1957), John and Elizabeth Newson (1968, 1976) and William Julius Wilson (1996 and forthcoming). The East End has long been studied as a high poverty area, which has given us invaluable background. It is also now experiencing rapid change in a global context – this provides new information on which to base wider conclusions.

James Joyce claimed that in the small detail we understand the universe. We hope that this is true of our work, as it was of its famous predecessor *Family and kinship in East London*. First produced in 1957 by Michael Young and Peter Willmott, it documented family and community relations in the East End in the post-war period of rapid social change. Their findings reflected the view of families from one part of London, which did not prevent the findings from having an international resonance. We believe that the same holds true for families today. Many of our ideas for this study drew on that earlier landmark work with East Enders.

Our focus in this book is on how families interact with their neighbourhoods and how family life is shaped or troubled by neighbourhood conditions, rather than on how kinship patterns and contacts are sustained within urban communities (we examine this question in later rounds of the study). We look closely at community relations because we, like Young and Willmott, found that social relations linked to housing tenures and structures could make or break a family's sense of community as they coped with the 'outside' world of the neighbourhood. Our aim is for this study to build on and add to existing work on racial and ethnic problems, mothers and employment, community networks and social capital, neighbourhood regeneration and neighbourhood management, education, crime and other current issues.

The neighbourhoods

Each area houses approximately 20,000 people. We use the term 'neighbourhood' to describe the area, even though they are in fact much larger than what would normally be considered to constitute a neighbourhood. They could better be described as 'mega-neighbourhoods' (F. Furstenburg, meeting with author, 8 May 2000). We use the term 'neighbourhood' because it conveys a sense of 'home' and because people talk about their very local part of the area as being where their neighbours live and where they identify 'home'. Inevitably, area definitions are not fixed and people have different views (Chaskin, 1997). Families showed us on street maps where their neighbourhood or 'home area' was. It was usually within a 10-minute walk or half a mile of their front door, although most families used some shops and facilities that were further afield. 'Home areas' were a series of overlapping spaces, creating our 'mega-neighbourhoods'.

All the families were recruited from within the neighbourhoods. But London is a complex city and people are pulled into neighbouring areas through community networks and for specific services. Some of our families lived just outside our boundaries. We contacted people through local services and by word-of-mouth. People living nearby but using the neighbourhood services offered important insights into links with the wider area of East London and so we included them. The wider area has similar income levels and social conditions even though there are some local differences. Thirteen families lived just outside the West-City boundaries we drew, and 18 outside East-Docks, eight of these in one neighbouring ward. We checked the interviews to see whether there was a different pattern of responses from families living in this other ward near East-Docks. Any differences were very slight. The figures below show the location of all the families interviewed.

Figure 2.1: Map of East-Docks

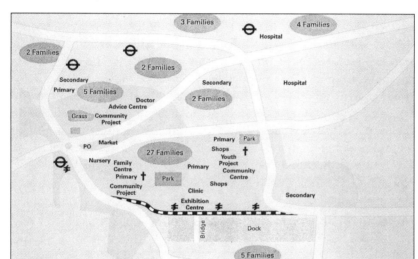

Figure 2.2: Map of West-City

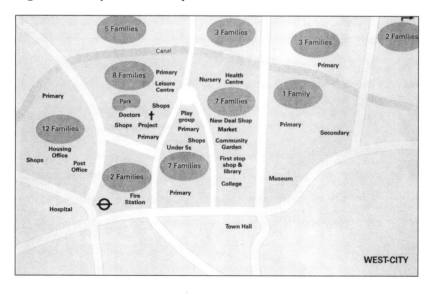

The research approach

All the visits and interviews were carried out by Katharine Mumford. Anne Power has worked in both areas and lived with her own family as they grew up on the edge of Hackney. In the book we combine these perspectives, drawing on close experiences of the neighbourhoods.

Getting to know the area and contacting families started right at the beginning of the study in February 1999, while we were still devising the interview schedule. We learnt much more about the neighbourhoods once the family interviews were underway. In order to build up a clear picture of the neighbourhoods, we made contact with council-based officers, such as the assistant director of education, head of research, directors of primary care, and community paediatricians. We also met with researchers experienced in family research, and with national organisations such as the Department of the Environment, Transport and the Regions (now the Office of the Deputy Prime Minister), the Basic Skills Agency and MORI. We also contacted as many organisations as possible within the areas and these contacts built up over time. Sometimes it was individual families who told us about local organisations, such as the playgroup. Table 2.1 lists the locally based people and agencies who helped us.

Table 2.1: Meetings with local people and organisations (February 1999-February 2000)

West-City	East-Docks
• Community worker – specific estate	• East-Docks Single Regeneration Budget
• Community worker – West-City	• Community development officer, community project
• Tenants' association Chair and activist	• Under-8s worker, large community project
• Residents at an Area Forum (part of New Deal for Communities)	• Community Involvement and Research Organisation
• Private housing management contractor	• Community project specialising in work with refugees
• Head, Primary School	• Head, Primary School
• Two New Deal for Communities 'master-planning meetings'	• Head, Secondary School
• Community Nurse Team Manager	• Head, Nursery School
• Playgroup	• Director, Family Centre
• Patch meeting, Primary Care Group	• Local vicar
• Refugee Women's Association conference	• Locality Manager, Health Clinic
• Parent support group	• Health visitors team meeting
• Under-5s Project	• Social services
	• Community organisation providing adult education and youth activities
	• Community paediatrician and colleagues in the Community Child Health Department

In West-City we attended resident meetings as part of the planning for New Deal for Communities. In East-Docks, we held a focus group with pupils at a local secondary school, and another with parents at a primary school, to begin to find out about people's experiences of the area.

In both areas, we were warned about people's possible reluctance to take part, a concern which we tried to take on board by making the research useful to residents and to people running services locally. The residents' forum in West-City was particularly interested to hear about the views of younger members of their community. The first residents interviewed in East-Docks also responded positively – one father commenting that he thought it was good that we were taking the trouble to go and talk to people in their own homes. In both neighbourhoods, local organisations offered us a local office as a base between interviews.

In East-Docks, local professionals warned us of possible dangers in the area. They were concerned at the idea that a female interviewer would be walking around the area alone, and interviewing unknown families in their own homes. We thought about the safety issues very carefully, and sought different views. We took certain precautions before starting interviewing – basic ground rules such as our office always knowing the interviewer's whereabouts; ringing in after each interview from a mobile; not interviewing men in their home alone; occasionally being accompanied by interested volunteers (mainly LSE students). Almost always we were made very welcome.

We decided that it was important to visit people in their homes if the families were willing – not to be unduly influenced by stereotypes of the areas as unsafe places. Unsurprisingly, people treated the interviewer as a guest in their home, rather than as an intruder. They were helping us with our work and had invited us in (M. Smith, meeting with author, 22 June 1999).

The questions in the first interview covered:

- Basic information about the family, including tenure, household composition, ethnic background, marital status, occupation, qualifications, income, access to car and telephone.
- Questions about the area: housing history, reasons for moving to the area, satisfaction with the area as a place in which to live and as a place in which to bring up children, likes and dislikes, likelihood of moving, changes in the area, regeneration attempts, area image.
- Schools: satisfaction with schools, reputation, contact with teachers, reasons for choosing primary and secondary schools, thoughts about future schools (where pre-primary or pre-secondary children), how children were getting on at school, help with children's reading and homework. We also included a short section on childminding and babysitting arrangements.
- 'Community': existence of 'community spirit', location of friends and relatives, contact with neighbours, participation in local groups, and feelings of involvement in the local community.

• The future: hopes for the family, thoughts about children's destination on leaving school, degree of optimism and concerns about obstacles, what would most help the area and the family, and whether the area was getting better, worse or staying the same.

The second questionnaire asked more detailed questions about community and race relations, local services and conditions, crime and disorder, and change and prospects for the neighbourhoods. Table 2.2 shows the way that the second round of questions developed from the first.

We used questionnaires with a mixture of open-ended and more structured questions with response options. It was important that we did not impose on the families and that we did not probe about personal details of their lives other than basic facts. We explained that the interviews would be kept anonymous, that we would not identify individual families. We asked the families if we could come back and they all agreed. In the second interviews, we took up the most interesting and important issues that the families had brought up in the first round. We tried out the first and second round questionnaires with five families to check the length of each interview (aiming for a maximum of one hour), the

Table 2.2: The second round questions and how they link to the first round

Core Round 1 Findings	Development in Round 2 Questions
Families had a wide mixture of views on their area; a range of likes and dislikes, views on services and area image	Checklist of the quality of key services and the existence of potential area problems, drawn from the Survey of English Housing to enable national comparison
Crime, drugs, insecurity and fear are some of the main reasons for families wanting to move and/or feeling that their children are having restricted childhoods	Pinpointed families' actual experience of crime and drugs, and the way in which they harm family life
Parents are concerned that their children have less freedom than they did	Children's play, with a particular focus on families' use and opinion of parks
The majority of the families raised the issue of race	Asked all the families for their views on the changing ethnic composition of their neighbourhood, race relations and living in an ethnically mixed area
There was a lot of optimism about the direction of neighbourhood change	Asked families for their current view on area change, to enable us to explore whether improvements had been sustained and built on
There was a strong feeling that community spirit was important, and a real sense of missing it when it was not there	Exploration of why community spirit matters, what signs of it there are, how people get involved locally

New topic Questions on jobs, including people's work histories, their current job, and (if not currently working) whether they would like to be working and what barriers they had encountered

---

clarity of the questions and the relevance of the topics. Our five pilot families helped us a lot and their views are included in the study.

Minimising the chances of losing contact with families was very important. We did this by:

- following simple courtesies – sending thank you letters and Christmas cards;
- keeping people informed of our progress by brief letters and summary reports;
- taking a note of mobile phone numbers or contact details of a friend or relative who we could contact if families were likely to move;
- occasionally using permission slips to trace the family's new address through the local education authority.

Ten families had moved by the time we visited again, although we interviewed four of them in their new homes (all remained local). We were not able to re-interview six of the families who had moved, although we hope eventually to be able to interview some again. Two other families could not do the second interviews. One family was about to become homeless; the other was too busy. In all, in the second round we interviewed 92 of the original 100 families.

During the visits and the times spent walking round the area, we recorded observations at different times of the day and evening: using public transport, going through subways, walking through parks. We recorded the number of smashed cars, and amount of litter, graffiti and damage to property. We noted different housing forms, and took photographs of blocks, streets and open spaces. We spent time in doctors' waiting areas, schools, nurseries, churches, other local statutory and voluntary services and also on the streets, balconies and landings, waiting for families. This gave us crucial additional information and a strong sense of how the neighbourhoods 'ticked'. We used our evidence from the observation to back-up what the families said. There was a strong correlation between the two.

Finding families

The most unknown element of the study was whether people would be willing to take part. How would we find them? Could we achieve a mix of families broadly representative of each neighbourhood's population? What language difficulties might we encounter?

We ruled out some potential routes for recruiting families at the outset. Random door-knocking can be a successful method (J. Barnes McGuire, meeting with author, 9 June 1999). However, the small target size of our sample and our need to reflect the ethnic make-up and family types within the neighbourhood made us decide to recruit through local networks, using a snowballing method where families referred us on to other families they knew. In order to make sure that we matched the general make-up of the areas, we recruited from several different sources. If too many families of one ethnic group or one family type came forward, then we recruited elsewhere.

The snowballing method proved particularly helpful in recruiting families with young children, families from ethnic minority groups and lone parents. We also wanted to reflect the range of families with and without employment. A small number of the families came from higher income brackets. We explore this more in the chapters on work (Chapters Five and Six). The purposive method of sampling means that our findings reflect the views of the particular family groups we targeted rather than the population as a whole. The tables in the text present information from the families. We found it useful to set the families' views in the context of national, London and borough statistics.

We make some comparisons between our families' responses and national survey results. To do this we included some questions from wider surveys in our interviews – for example, from the Housing Attitudes Survey (Hedges and Clemens, 1994), and the Department of Transport, Local Government and the Regions' (DTLR) residents survey in seven Single Regeneration Budget areas (Whitehead and Smith, 1998), which also included questions from the 1999/2000 national Survey of English Housing. Although we took great care to ensure that our families were broadly representative of the neighbourhood populations, our small sample size means that we use the findings with caution. However, the national figures place our families' experiences in a wider context and, by providing a 'benchmark', help illustrate the gulf that often exists between conditions in these neighbourhoods and an 'average' living environment. Where possible we also cite neighbourhood-level data – such as crime rates, levels of work poverty, household survey data – and compare these with national data. This gives a much stronger basis for interpreting and contextualising what the families say.

To find the families, we went to the places that families use, and spoke to them in person about our work. This face-to-face contact was generally successful, although it varied between different places and even different days or weeks. We asked the families we interviewed whether they knew of anyone else who might be prepared to talk to us – this helped us reach further into the neighbourhoods and involved people who would not necessarily have responded to the other recruitment methods we had used.

The health authority's ethics committee allowed us to start recruiting from doctors' waiting areas from January 2000. The doctors' waiting areas brought together a greater range of families than most other places, from both very low and higher income households. The local surgery seems to be the one place in the neighbourhood that all income groups use. The health visitors working from the surgeries introduced mothers who might otherwise not have taken part. In one of the West-City surgeries a Turkish advocate attending the mother and baby clinic helped recruit Turkish and Kurdish families on our behalf. A Turkish interpreter also helped us at the primary school parents' evening in

West–City. The under-5s project helped with both Turkish and Punjabi speaking families.

Figure 2.3 shows how all the families came forward over time, through many different routes. The first interviews began in June 1999 and the last was completed in mid-February 2000. The second visits ran from May 2000 to January 2001. Appendix 1 gives basic information about each family, using invented names.

Figure 2.3: Locating the 100 families

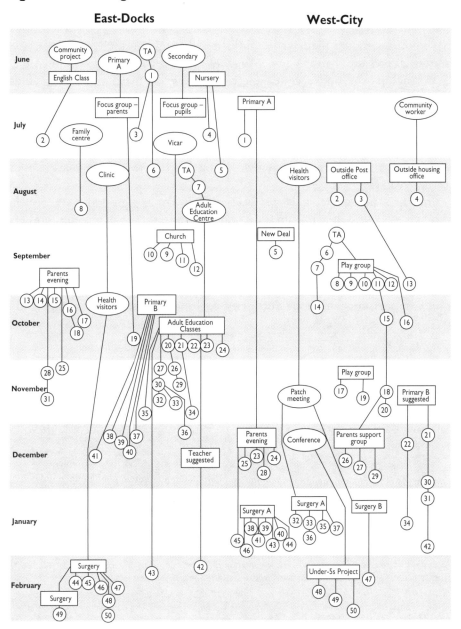

We use these names in attributing quotations, except in the few instances where the specific details would then identify the family. By allowing the reader to trace almost all the quotes we use to the actual 100 family sources, we show the range of family sources we rely on. Virtually every family is quoted somewhere in the book.

The make-up of our 100 families broadly reflects the composition of the neighbourhoods, although a higher proportion of our lone parents work than might have been expected. However, employment rates have risen since 1991, which may in part account for the difference. Figure 2.4 shows this match and the contrast with the rest of London and the country. Our families, neighbourhoods and their surrounding areas have much higher levels of need and social pressure than the city. (Appendix 2 gives a detailed breakdown.)

Throughout the book, we use the term 'family' to mean an adult or adults living together in the same home with children aged 18 or under. There are, of course, many different kinds of families who do not have children living with them, but we chose to focus specifically on the experiences of bringing children up in the inner-city neighbourhoods. The interviewee was nearly always the mother because families usually rely on the mother (or other key female member) as the organiser.

Our main point of contact was places where families go, and it was usually mothers who were present. On the whole, therefore, this book presents mothers' perspectives of family life in the neighbourhoods. In Appendix 1 we indicate where fathers also contributed significantly to the interviews, and where

Figure 2.4: Characteristics of the neighbourhoods, families interviewed, and comparisons with local authority, regional and national averages

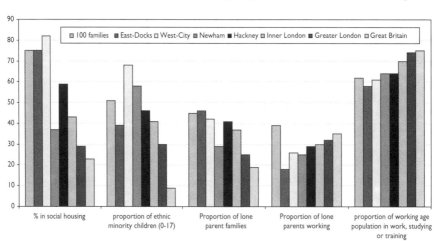

Note: In this figure we use the 1991 Census definition of ethnic minorities. But 16% of our families came from other minority groups, (eg Turkisk, Kurdish) that the Census classes as white.

Sources: A West-City figures are based on the 1999 NDC 10% sample, unless specified. East-Docks figures are based on the 1991 Census for three wards, unless specified. The national tenure figure is from Malpass and Murie (1994). All other figures are based on the 1991 Census

occasionally grandmothers or teenagers were the interviewees. Six fathers joined in the interviews with their wives, one father was on his own, and five families included relatives and friends in the interviews.

Are these neighbourhoods different?

In many ways both neighbourhoods are reflective of most inner-city areas. They have gone from being the hubs of the first industrial revolution to being abandoned by some of the richest investors in the world. Today they are becoming a true melting pot on the very edge of one of the world centres of the second industrial revolution, high-tech, high value and high skill.

Here we set out briefly the neighbourhoods' genesis and their very different conditions today. Our work in these two neighbourhoods is set within a much more comprehensive, national study of area change, based on 12 representative low-income areas, of which East-Docks and West-City are two. The wider study is briefly described in Appendix 3. The survey of 100 families in East London is happening over eight years. There is a sister study, for which we are responsible, following 100 families in two Northern cities, Sheffield and Leeds. Appendix 3 briefly explains the Northern families study.

West-City

West-City was originally a 'place of rural retreat'. Even in the mid-18th century there were still relatively few buildings, and market gardening was a major activity. The area has long been associated with the arts – theatres were established there in the 16th century. From the late 1700s, West-City grew very rapidly, and its population more than doubled between 1821 and 1851 as industrialisation made its mark (see Table 2.3). Most of the housing built during this time was in two-storey terraces. The rich gradually migrated outwards and the area gained a poor reputation (Mander, 1996). However, during the 1990s the population began to grow again – increasing by 3.4% between 1991 and 1998 (Lupton, forthcoming).

The main sources of employment were the gasworks, and manufacturing industries, linked to the canal. Furniture and shoe manufacturing were two key trades – with both large and small firms. This industrial

Table 2.3: West-City's population (1801-1991)

Year	Population
1801	34,766
1821	52,966
1851	109,257
1861	129,364 (peak)
1891	124,553
1901	118,637
1921	104,248
1931	97,042
1951	44,871
1991	26,765[a]

Note: [a] This represents the population of the four electoral wards containing West-City (as currently defined by the NDC), based on the 1991 Census. The area boundaries are unlikely to be completely consistent with those used for the previous periods' figures, so caution should be exercised in making a direct comparison.

Source: Mander, 1996 (1801-1951 figures) and Lupton, 2000 (1991 figure[a])

activity is now largely a thing of the past. The last gasworks was destroyed by a bomb in 1944, as were many local businesses. Manufacturing shrunk with advancing technology: from 1965 many older businesses closed – a large shoe firm went bankrupt in the 1970s (Mander, 1996). However, some old factories still make clothes in the 'sweat shop' tradition of the area and a few small workshops have survived.

Depopulation began in earnest between the wars and was caused not only by job losses, but also by slum clearance and council redevelopment, which started in the inter-war years and continued after the Second World War. For example, the redevelopment of one pocket in 1938 displaced 2,400 people, 1,000 of whom were rehoused outside West-City (Mander, 1996).

West-City in 2002

West-City is on the fringe of the City of London. It is a mixed area in many ways – mixed income, mixed ethnic make-up, businesses, shops, and market stalls. Parts of West-City have become very trendy. New cafes, restaurants, a cinema, theatres, and clubs are thriving. But there are still traditional, inexpensive cafes and shops. There is a sharp divide between the fast gentrifying traditional streets and the large council blocks.

Most of West-City is dominated by a large number of medium-size, council-owned, mainly post-war flats and tower blocks. A total of 82% of the people in West-City live in social housing (West-City New Deal Trust, 1999). The estates on the whole are quite dilapidated, in serious need of care and repair. Many communal entrances to blocks of flats are without any security systems in place. In some of the blocks, most residents have fitted iron bars in front of their doors. New Deal for Communities is funding secure door entry systems to open communal entrances. However, there are still many pressing problems.

Part of the canal, West-City

Mixture of street properties and flats in West-City, varying tenure

House prices are very high throughout the area, even for ex-council properties. From the mid-1990s house prices rose noticeably, as buyers who could not afford rapidly increasing prices in more popular parts of inner London looked to previously less popular areas, such as West-City. Strong media interest in the area and its 'housing revolution', including conversion of warehouses to flats, continued to push prices up. Between 1996 and 2001, house prices rose by 153%, to an average price of £221,000 – far beyond the reach of anyone on a low or middle income, and even higher than the Greater London average of £202,000 (Lupton, forthcoming). However, the dominance of council housing in the neighbourhoods means that three quarters of the families rent from a local authority or housing association.

This helps explain why, despite the local boom, unemployment is a serious problem. Unemployment has been falling recently and figures from 1996 show that the reduction in West-City's unemployment has been broadly in line with the Hackney average. But in April 2000, Hackney's unemployment rate was still 9.8% – much higher than the national average of 3.8% (Lupton, forthcoming). West-City is the lowest income area in Hackney, which is London's second poorest borough. A total of 59% of households with children receive Housing Benefit or Income Support (West-City New Deal Trust, 1999).

West–City is ethnically very diverse. During the 1950s the population gradually became more mixed, with migration from the West Indies and Asia (Mander, 1996). Until the 1980s the population of the area was still mainly white, and there were many reports of hostility towards people from ethnic minority groups; however, since then the area has rapidly diversified. By 1991, white people made up less than three quarters of the population and this fell to under two thirds by 1999. White residents tend to be older and 73% of children in the area have black and ethnic minority parents (West–City New Deal Trust, 1999).

Activities and services

West–City offers many facilities, including a nearby hospital; a thriving market; a recently built community college; a new library and 'First Stop Shop'; a large leisure centre (which some families cannot afford); seven primary schools (some denominational); good public transport links in most of the neighbourhood; playgroups and other clubs and community groups for children and older people; small playgrounds within *some* estates; several active churches; a museum; two modern, attractive doctors' surgeries; post offices; night clubs and eating places.

However, the area lacks a large supermarket, bank or building society. The only secondary school in the area is an all-girls' school. Meanwhile New Deal for Communities is injecting significant sums of money into parts of West–City.

There is an Underground station at the corner of the neighbourhood boundaries. This tube link is generally very helpful, although some people in the area live a good 15 minutes from it and have to cross dark, unfrequented side streets and estate paths to get to it. West–City is also linked by bus to many different places, including the centre of Hackney, Islington and the City. Bus journeys, even in the middle of the day, can be unreliable and slow because of the heavy traffic in this and neighbouring areas.

Families described the area in many different ways (see Box 2.1).

Box 2.1: Families' descriptions of West-City

"Exciting, there's a real buzz about it. Very cosmopolitan."

"It's fine to live in. The good thing about it is you're in the middle of London. You're near to the shops and the market. It's comfortable. You've got a mixture of people round here."

"It is a community – it is a little urban village within London – it's warm and friendly."

"I just liked it from the moment I arrived. I just walked up the road and thought 'I like it here'."

"Friendly people. But it's all down to whether you make an effort. There are people in this block that you don't know anything about – they keep themselves to themselves."

"It's really coming up now – with more shops, the college, more businesses opening up. It's a bit livelier than it used to be."

"It would be marvellous if they sorted out the drugs and housing."

"It's a good area, good people here, it's quiet. But they should look after buildings. I don't know what they do in their office – only stay there."

"I'm here because I came years ago and my family are all here, but I would never advise anyone to move into it. This place went downhill when West-City was put in together with Hackney. All the problems from up there came down here."

"Scum, rotten, the down and outs, the low life. Not everyone's like that. But you don't seem to know anybody anymore. They move in and out. They get in and shut their door and don't want to know."

"Stark – all concrete."

"Dump! Run-down but they are trying to build it up."

"There's no atmosphere in any of the pubs now. No community spirit except in the market – that little elderly clique are the last bastion."

East-Docks

Like West-City, the areas around East-Docks were a rural retreat for the wealthy between the 1500s and the early 1800s. Marshland had been reclaimed for arable farming and market gardening (Padfield, 1999). East-Docks itself began to be settled in the early 1840s (Bloch, 1996). At its peak in 1921, the population of the old county borough containing East-Docks was 300,860. It then fell to just a third of that total (Aston Community Involvement Unit, 1996). But, like Hackney, East-Docks has seen an increase in its population over the 1990s – up by 6% between 1991-98 (Lupton, 2003 forthcoming).

The development of the docklands from the middle of the 19th century transformed East-Docks into a busy industrial hub. This group of docks represented "the largest area of impounded dock water in the world" (Bloch, 1995). As well as the docks, jobs arose from the new industries that sprang up around them. A large gasworks nearby was also a major source of work.

Row upon row of terraces were built to house the workers. A lot of the work was casual and so unemployment and poverty were major features of the area. The population was very mixed. Black seamen settled in the area before and during the First World War, and East-Docks had the largest black population in London in the 1930s (Bloch, 1995). Racial tension was strong, with street violence against the seamen in 1919 (Aston Community Involvement Unit, 1996).

The housing, docks and associated industries were badly bombed during the Second World War. The docks and many of the factories did recover from this damage – although some industry was re-sited as the area was 'slum cleared' and redeveloped. But they soon received another huge blow in the form of changing world trade patterns and advancing technology. Many of the long-established factories moved away, reduced their workforces, or closed completely during the 1960s and 1970s. The gasworks and docks closed down between the late 1960s and the early 1980s. "A way of life had gone forever" (Bloch, 1993).

East-Docks in 2002

East-Docks is on the edge of the 'new' Docklands, and housing and commercial developments are being extended eastwards all the time. Physical isolation, lack of resources, redevelopment of 'slum' housing after the extensive wartime damage, led to the area having a tough reputation. The predominantly white working-class community (now changing) acquired a reputation for hostility to 'outsiders' (Cattell and Evans, 1999).

House prices rose significantly in recent years, increasing by 188% between 1996-2001 to an average price of £124,000. This was much lower than prices in many other parts of London, and was almost half the West-City average, but just above the national average of £120,000 and still beyond the reach of many families. They continued to rise in 2002.

The new pedestrian bridge in East-Docks seen from above and below with flats in the background, in East-Docks

A major exhibition centre has been built alongside a nearby dock. A mixed development of private and housing association homes now occupies the other side of this dock as a new 'urban village'. A bold new pedestrian footbridge links East-Docks to this new area – although the lift is often out of order.

The area is dominated by social housing, with over two thirds of it council housing and 7% owned by a housing association (East-Docks SRB Partnership, 1996). The council estates are a combination of post-war tower blocks, terraced houses, and small walk-up blocks of flats and maisonettes. The private housing in the neighbourhood consists of a few rows of old terraces and small new estates.

A major dual-carriageway brutally splits the area, with six lanes of fast, heavy flow traffic. The main shopping centre is north of the road. There are subways but these can be quite dark, even in the daytime. South of the road, East-Docks is somewhat cut off.

The area is quite rundown, but a lot is happening nearby, land values are increasing and some blocks of flats have been refurbished. Any recovery is still in the early stages, however, and there is now a threat of renewed demolition to some of the council estates, which is creating a lot of anxiety. This plan is part of the local council's attempt to diversify and upgrade the area.

Unemployment became a major problem as jobs declined rapidly following closure of the gasworks, docks and other industries. Jobs fell by a further 30% between 1992 and 1995 during the long recession. By 1996, 12% of retail units were empty and 26 hectares of land vacant or underused (East-Docks SRB Partnership, 1996; R. Lupton, interview with police inspector, West-City Police Station, 17 May 1999). Both East-Docks and Newham as a whole have experienced recent falls in unemployment near the national average. But unemployment in the area was falling from a much higher point, and at April 2000 Newham's unemployment rate of 11.7% was nearly four times the rate for England and Wales (3.8%) (Lupton, forthcoming).

East-Docks is still less diverse than the rest of Newham, but is becoming much more ethnically mixed. Nearly 40% of pupils at five primary schools and two secondary schools serving the area are now from ethnic minority backgrounds (Newham Education, 1999).

Facilities

East-Docks is less well served than West-City. The shops are basic, there is a small supermarket, and the local market is popular. A nearby High Street has a range of small shops and there is a large shopping centre at Stratford. There is also a post office and MacDonalds.

A number of active community groups, including one of the original settlements, a parent support group, youth projects, a community project working with refugees, a community education service, and a community-led project in a converted church which houses a labour hire agency, doctors, and a rent-a-desk scheme for small businesses, provide quite a range of local activities. In addition, there are churches, parks and open spaces. A leisure centre and cinema complex are quite close, but not within the area itself.

There are several primary and secondary schools within the area, including a newly built secondary school which opened in the autumn term of 1999. There is also a new university on a brand new campus nearby, although it is struggling to recruit students. An Education Action Zone is making measurable improvements to local school performance, and Sure Start is targeting families with under-fives in parts of the area. There is a Health Action Zone, and a Single Regeneration Budget programme is nearing completion.

Until recently, transport links were poor. This has changed significantly with the development of the Docklands Light Railway and, even more recently, the extension of the Underground to this area and improved bus services. East-Docks has had a tube station since 1999, in an impressive new station where the Docklands Light Railway, Silverlink services and a variety of bus services also stop. It takes under 25 minutes to get from East-Docks into central London on the tube or the train. City Airport is nearby. Some families live closer to other train stations. Some are not in easy reach of any train station and rely instead on buses.

Families living in and around East-Docks expressed a wide mixture of views about their area (see Box 2.2).

Box 2.2: Families' descriptions of East-Docks

"Friendly. I feel as though I can be myself: I don't have to wear Gucci clothes. I feel comfortable walking the streets."

"Quite a good environment to live in, very peaceful, very safe ... there are no burglars."

"Very family-oriented. Close knit community for the people that originate from East-Docks."

"Neighbours are friendly."

"I've been here for many years and this Close is a bit better – everyone looks out for each other. I haven't heard about all the bad things happening here in the Close – things like people breaking into houses and clearing people out."

"No one really interferes with anyone else. Not really a lot of vandalism. People here have domestics, but it's just amongst themselves."

"It has improved. Before, there was a lot of racism. Now that has gone down."

"Don't live in Newham! The whole of Newham really now is crap. It's changed over the years so much, it has lost all its reputation. We're losing all our history."

"Very deprived, gloomy. It has lost its character."

"Drugs, crime, sad. It's just sad."

"The bad thing is that racism is really high."

"I don't think Newham is one of the best places for educating your children."

"Boring! There's nothing for my age group. The nearest club is in Ilford."

Table 2.4: Neighbourhood environment

Problems	Potential
Both	
Bare neglected parks and green spaces	Canalside and dock waterfronts
Heavy traffic and air pollution	Open spaces with potential for more green areas and safer walking
Poorly maintained communal areas – litter and graffiti	New developments, more diversification, pressure for better services
West-City	
Insecure entrances to blocks of flats	NDC creating secure communal entrances
Dog mess	Management contract delivering more intensive care
East-Docks	
Derelict buildings including five empty pubs	Houses with front and back gardens
Many smashed abandoned cars	Generally lots of space for development

Shared problems

There are two major factors undermining the social cohesion and economic prospects of both areas – crime and disorderly behaviour, and the neighbourhood environment – or the public realm, as Richard Rogers calls it (Rogers and Power, 2000). Both undermine the stability and prospects of the areas and shape the attitudes of families to where they live. Table 2.4 highlights the main problems and potential of the neighbourhood environments.

Both Hackney and Newham are very high crime areas. Hackney is 66% higher than the London average, and Newham is 29% higher. Hackney's crime rate is *double* the national average. The two neighbourhoods are among the most deprived in their boroughs and we discuss later how seriously crime affected the families. Even more seriously, the fear of crime and the lower level disorder that usually goes with it made many of our families worry a lot about bringing up their children in these areas. Figure 2.5 shows these problems starkly.

Figure 2.5: Index of recorded crimes per head of population (July 1997-June 1998)

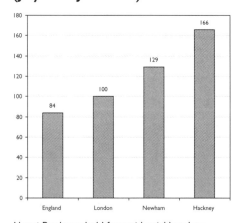

Note: [a] Per household for residential burglary.

Average crime rates for the whole of the Metropolitan Police District (London) were set at 100. Each borough's figures are then expressed in relation to this index.

Summary and conclusion

The two neighbourhoods are very distinct, despite many common elements. West-City, dense and full of traffic, is almost in the centre of the city, run-down, yet bursting around its edges with new and renovated buildings, adventurous new enterprises and extreme wealth. The area feels very pressured. East-Docks, in contrast, feels very spread out, with old, decayed blocks and facilities. The busy main roads and abandoned spaces make it feel much more empty. The new buildings have not yet filled these spaces so the area feels almost 'left over'. However, East-Docks is also experiencing knock-on effects from the booming London economy – including steep house price rises.

We found 100 families with children through many local channels – schools, doctors, churches, community centres, their own friends and relatives. They agreed to help us try to understand the interaction between family life and neighbourhood conditions. Although we had things we wanted to ask them about their children, housing, work, local services and conditions, we took our cue from them and followed up on things that mattered most to them – such as race relations, fears for their children, unsupervised play areas, parks and social breakdown.

Although much of the East End has a decayed, run-down feel to it, and it has serious problems of high crime, poor school results and high levels of unemployment, it also has some assets – often casually abandoned in the 'second industrial revolution'. Some of these are now being reclaimed. What will happen to families under the huge economic and social pressures that these changes are generating?

The neighbourhoods and the families that live in them are really different from most other places – with lower incomes, greater diversity of ethnic backgrounds, and more social pressures – how does that affect families' feelings about their neighbourhoods, their community, their children, their future? First we look at 'community', since this idea dominated much of what families told us mattered to them about their neighbourhood.

Note

[1] These are invented names to try to prevent stereotyping of the actual neighbourhoods.

Part I: Community and race relations

Community spirit

"When you've got children it would be quite sad to live in a place that didn't have community spirit. It would be sad. I know quite a few on my estate; it makes you feel good." (Sarah)

"When you see people doing things together, organising activities together. Dealing with issues like making sure the elderly are not bored sick at home, making sure the women are not battered, the children have somewhere to play. Making sure that everyone's OK, no noisy neighbours. It's very important." (Aminia)

Introduction

Overwhelmingly in these neighbourhoods, families feel that community spirit matters. It is the crucial element in creating a sense of community. Parents have many views on what community itself means and why it is important. People say that a sense of community creates a friendly atmosphere, a sense of trust and reciprocity, a link to neighbours and to local activity, a helping hand, mutual support, a sense of responsibility and it is these things that reflect community spirit, a more ephemeral feeling about social relations. Mothers often use the terms interchangeably and we try to explore their meaning.

There is a real sense of people missing community spirit when they feel it is not there. Two thirds of the families in both neighbourhoods feel that community spirit exists in their area, but almost everyone – 90% – feels that community spirit matters; this is much higher than the national average (57%) (Hedges and Clemens, 1994). We explore in depth the idea of community because of the significance that families attached to it when we first visited them.

The almost universal support for the notion of community spirit makes it one of the most critical factors in whether people feel happy in their neighbourhoods. So what do people mean by community and community spirit? How do they explain its importance in their lives? What signs do they see of it? Do they feel a part of it? These are some of the questions we explore in this chapter.

Why does community spirit matter?

> "If you've got that community spirit, people do things for each other. My neighbours next door, I do quite a bit for them. I just think it is nice." (Alice)

The top three reasons families gave for community spirit mattering were:

- friendliness between local residents generally enhances quality of life;
- community spirit results in informal help and a sense of people being there for each other;
- community spirit brings different people together and contributes to a better understanding between people of different cultures.

These three aspects of community spirit are informal and intangible. They are based on unstructured, local relations that are the basis for social networks, social support and social control. More organised aspects of community were also mentioned as being important, such as campaigning for area improvements, but fewer families raised this. There were very few negative views about community,

Table 3.1: Families' views on why community spirit matters (of the 83 families who thought it did)[a]

	West-City	East-Docks	Total
Friendliness/makes you feel better/enhances quality of life	12	13	25
Support/informal help/means you have someone to rely on, people looking out for you	11	10	21
Brings people together, means people live well together, acceptance, tolerance	10	9	19
People would be lonely/isolated without it	6	4	10
Gives ownership/responsibility in your area; common goal to improve area; having a say	5	4	9
Makes you feel safer	6	1	7
Helps challenge bad behaviour/maintain order	1	3	4
Leads to organised help by the community as a whole/planning activities	2	2	4
Should be able to trust people	1	2	3
Enables information/knowledge to be shared	2	0	2
Other reason[b]	0	3	3
Warning that community can be too close	0	2	2
Total comments	56	53	109

Notes: [a] This table classifies comments the families made in response to an open question 'Why does community spirit matter?', asked of people who had already answered that it did matter. It is possible that more families would have agreed a certain aspect of community spirit mattered if we had asked them about this aspect directly. [b] The other reasons, each mentioned by one family only, were: 'maintaining traditions', involvement in school, somewhere to go.

only a lament for it not being as strong and binding as families feel they need. One worry concerned the possible narrowness of communities.

Here we explore the top six reasons why families felt community spirit mattered.

Community spirit as a friendly feeling

The main reason why families felt that community spirit mattered in both areas was because they felt that it would lead to a better quality of life. Families talked about how it was better to feel a friendly atmosphere between people living nearby, how it made them feel happier. They described how this could be just a smile, or exchanging a few words; it was not necessarily about actual friendship. For example:

> "I would say that there needs to be a few people within your setting, your community, that you can talk to, or everyone would just walk round with glum faces and it would make it difficult to live in those kinds of surroundings. You don't have to speak to everybody in your community but it is nice, and I do speak to quite a lot of people round here. Just even saying so much as a 'hello', it is really nice." (Flowella)

> "If they can speak to each other, share something with each other, even if it is to have a moan, it does give encouragement and a bit of hope." (Diane)

> "You need to live in a nice, happy environment. If you go out the door – you know what I mean don't you – you want to go outside and see a smile." (Emily)

Community spirit not only helps people feel happier; it makes the area more attractive and makes people feel a part of where they live. People seem to identify community as meaning positive but fairly intangible social relations.

Community spirit as informal help

The second most important reason that community spirit mattered (given by 21 families) was connected with informal help. It meant having someone nearby that you could turn to, a sense that neighbours were looking out for you and your children and you were looking out for them in turn.

> "In case you get in trouble, you know you can rely on someone." (Rose)

"If something is wrong, you are there for the other people around you. You know that you can turn to people here." (Barbara)

"Because everybody likes to live in an area where they look forward to going home – where if they're locked out or need a cup of sugar, they can knock on someone's door. But we don't live in each other's pockets." (Linda)

Being able to rely on neighbours for small favours makes people more confident, more secure and makes them feel more helpful themselves; a sense of mutual dependence. Such help could be particularly important for people newly arrived in the area.

"Especially if you're new in this area – you need community spirit to get things going. It can be make or break if someone says 'hello'. And you can find out where your nearest post office is, where you can get your fruit and vegetables, where to get advice." (Oni)

Community spirit as living together well, with acceptance and tolerance

A total of 19 families felt that community spirit mattered because it would bring people together and help increase different people's understanding of one another. Families often talked about it in connection with positive inter-racial contact. The following quotes are typical:

"Just so that people live together well, and there's that acceptance." (Madeleine)

"If there is no community spirit, people will be arguing." (Miriam)

"It matters if it's in a positive way – people being supportive irrespective of your colour, your gender – sincere support." (Frances)

"Just respecting one another really, and letting people have their own space, being friendly." (Natasha)

"With our community group, we're there to give help and advice to anybody, no matter what their race and beliefs." (Kate)

"It brings about a better understanding of other cultures and their beliefs." (Ellie)

"Because when we're in such a multi-racial area, if there wasn't then there would be friction wouldn't there?" (Tina)

People relate a sense of community directly to where they live, and therefore, in a multi-racial area, it implies creating a sense of belonging across different ethnic groups. The need for and importance of community in part reflects the desire of families with children to make where they live harmonious across racial boundaries. We explore inter-ethnic community relations and their impact on communities further in Chapter Four. A narrower and more enclosed view of community is often suggested by communitarians and their critics (Etzioni, 1993; Tam, 1998).

Community spirit matters because otherwise people would be lonely or feel isolated

Ten families described how community spirit mattered because it linked people together:

"Because there are quite a few people that haven't got close family living nearby. For the older generation as well – a lot of people are on their own. It's nice to know you've got a good community behind you and things going on to be involved in." (Rachel)

"Because I think people are lonely and purposeless without it. I think everybody needs networks of relationships." (Joanne)

"Because you can't be on your own. You need someone to talk to." (Desiree)

Community in this sense underlines the importance of social links in preventing exclusion. Some people can manage without links to others, but many families could not imagine surviving without them. They saw people living all alone – which none of them actually did – and worried about it.

Community spirit means a stake in the local neighbourhood

Nine families saw community spirit as having a sense of ownership and pride in where you live, taking responsibility for things working out in your community. They thought that it was important because it implied having a say, having a shared goal with other residents to improve things. This sometimes resulted in collective action.

"I think it gives you a bit of ownership and a bit of responsibility in where you live. It gives pride. Without it, you've got this 'why should we give a damn' attitude." (Joyce)

There was a sense that you couldn't achieve things for your neighbourhood on your own – a feeling of powerlessness alone as opposed to strength through common interest.

"Community spirit is integral; to make the community work, stick together and be strong. Shared responsibility, shared ownership. If you try to impose solutions they never work." (Alan)

"In order to develop our area, to have a better area, have a common goal together if there's anything we wanted to improve upon." (Audrey)

"I think [community spirit] is the way that you get your voice heard as a group, rather than an individual. As an individual, I don't think you can get that far." (Cynthia)

The families articulated the reason why all official programmes targeted at low-income areas now at least pay lip service to community representation and involvement. Local community action can, in fact, change things for the better. It goes beyond money to people's understanding, commitment and time. It implies taking responsibility so that things are not done *to* you, but *with* you and at least in part *by* you. This makes people feel differently about where they live and whether they really belong.

Sense of security

Six families in West-City, and one in East-Docks, specifically said that community spirit mattered because it made them feel safer:

"I think community spirit leads to a friendliness and a more secure feeling in the area. You feel you can walk around if you know people. It builds up a network of people who know each other in different ways." (Jane)

"Knowing your neighbours helps you feel more secure." (Kathleen)

There were many more general points about living in a friendly place, people getting on together, and helping newcomers settle in. These links can enhance people's sense of security, and enable people to associate and develop confidence. This is one of the reasons why our families felt that community spirit mattered so much – it helped overcome some of the insecurity generated by crime and anti-social behaviour, which we discuss later.

A much higher proportion of our families – 19% in West-City and 13% in East-Docks – said that they felt 'not very secure' in their own homes compared with the London average of just 5% and the average for English families of 6% (Burrows and Rhodes, 1998). The sense of familiarity and trust, of having a stake in, and being part of, a wider social network creating a sense of cohesion, were all elements of community that were prized as counterweights to these negative feelings, experiences and fears.

Signs of community spirit

> "Just the way you see people reacting to each other. In the street, round the school, you see people getting on. Like with my neighbour, when she was having problems, I looked after her baby. At school concerts you see all the mums getting on – black and white." (Ellie)

A total of 62 families saw some sign of community spirit existing even if they did not feel directly involved (see Table 3.2). They identified two main ways in which it existed: through informal, unstructured links, generally 'getting along' with other people living in the neighbourhood, and through organised community activities and groups. Some families highlighted the visible signs of people cooperating with each other and informally helping their neighbours.

Table 3.2: Signs families saw of community spirit (among the 83 families who thought it mattered)

	West-City	East-Docks	Total
People in the area talking to each other, getting on, mixing, tolerance	11	13	24
Organised community activities and groups	12	10	22
Active cooperation, informal help	6	8	14
Specific ethnic community links eg Turkish	4	1	5
Campaigning/involvement	2	2	4
When there is a tragedy or crisis	0	3	3
At church	3	1	4
In the market	2	0	2
Other signs of community spirit[a]	2	4	6
Total families identifying signs of community	29 families (42 signs)	33 families (42 signs)	62 families (84 signs)
Don't know/not recorded	5	2	7
There are not many signs, if any	7	7	14
Total	41 families	42 families	83 families

Note: [a] Other signs mentioned by no more than one family in each area included: among white people only, in school, through 'continuity', translation of written material, people reporting things to the police.

And some identified a more specific community spirit existing within certain minority ethnic communities, such as the Turkish-speaking community in West-City.

There is a strong overlap between why community matters and what signs there are of its existence. In this section we concentrate on what people do or witness as evidence of community. While they clearly match people's views on the significance of community, they root it in actual experience, making the idea of community a reality rather than an idealised concept. Many critics of the notion of community challenge the idea that people identify with their local communities, based on the realities of fast-track modern lifestyles (Kleinman, 1998). However, there is evidence that people's sense of security, their sense of 'being at home and feeling comfortable' in modern cities, derives from small signs and signals of familiarity and friendliness that these families call community (MacDonald, 1999).

People in the neighbourhoods talking to each other, getting on

The main way in which people saw community spirit existing was in a level of contact between people living in the neighbourhoods (identified by 24 of the families). Families talked about having a chat, greeting each other, passing the time of day, respecting each other's differences and wanting to get on together, rather than any deep involvement in each other's lives. This corresponded with the main reason that families felt community spirit mattered; to make them feel better, more at home.

> "A lot of our neighbours care for each other. I ain't talking parties in each other's houses, but just standing out the front. Involving each other in little ways instead of coming out the door and not having a word to say to each other." (Diane)

> "A lot of people seem to know each other. Walking down the road, people say 'hello' – that's really nice." (Madeleine)

> "Where I am now in the block it's really good. Everyone is really pleasant – say 'hello', but don't pry into what you're doing. That's a really good start." (Natasha)

> "You see people talk to each other which is a good thing – otherwise you just live a life of loneliness." (Clare)

> "The way people greet each other, sit down and chat, share jokes. I see quite a few of them down at the pub. I think we're trying to help each other in a way." (Andaiye)

Social contact, in other words, is a way of helping each other feel better. People clearly need that kind of direct contact and communication to feel comfortable where they live.

The families from our study were much less likely to feel that their neighbourhoods were unfriendly places than is usually the case in London, and nationally. None of our families thought that their neighbourhood was 'not at all friendly', and only 2% in East-Docks and 6% in West-City said it was 'not very friendly', compared to 11% in London and 7% among families nationally (Burrows and Rhodes, 1998). Figure 3.1 shows this comparison.

> "[It's a] close community, people are very kind to you, always say 'hello', which is nice." (Alice)

> "The neighbours are all friends, all through the block, so it's really nice." (Linda)

> "We've got many OAPs here. People hold the door open for you when you've got a pushchair." (Shushan)

> "Neighbours are very friendly, everyone I know. You get to know a lot of people in the area when you work in a school. They know your face. You usually get the children down the road calling out my name." (Peggy)

> "Very friendly. Always saying 'hello'. [I] meet people at school.... It's very cosmopolitan as well now – a lot of new people have moved in since the new flats have been finished." (Said)

Figure 3.1: Levels of unfriendliness

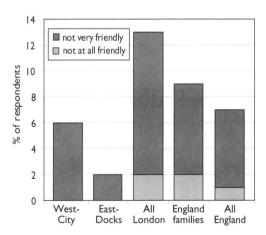

Source: Round 3 interviews, 1994/95 Survey of English Housing in Burrows and Rhodes (1998)

It is possible that residents in low-income neighbourhoods tend to spend more time in the immediate area, work nearer home, have less money for commercial entertainment, travel less and therefore have more chance of social contact locally, families with young children particularly so. Not only do they need and rely on social contact and a sense of community more than the average, they put in more time to secure it. It is possible that families in higher income areas used to have this degree of local social contact too, but with fewer mothers staying at home with their children and television taking up a much greater amount of people's time, society has tended to become less 'social', at least at neighbourhood level (Putnam, 2000).

Organised community activities and groups

Although most families felt that community spirit mattered for 'informal' reasons, such as feeling better about where they live, one of the main signs people saw of its existence was locally organised activities and groups such as tenants associations, adult education or neighbourhood watch schemes. These groups might be campaigning for improvements or working towards a definite goal, but they were also seen as an important way in which local people made links with each other. And, even if a family didn't attend the local tenants' association themselves, they sometimes still cited its existence as a sign that community spirit was present in their area:

> "A lot of local people are involved in these tenants' associations – getting ideas together to improve the area. And the community school round the corner offers a lot of courses – getting people together." (Rachel)

> "The neighbourhood watch thing: I've seen signs." (Audrey)

> "The trip [to Southend for the estate residents] is one sign; 1½ coaches full." (Carrie)

The community project in the former town hall, East-Docks

"What I see as community spirit is where the people are arranging all the outings and they get together and have a good time. There was a party. Not everyone went, but it was really nice – there was no sort of racial or age barrier. It was really, really good. You get a lot of people going to the community centre for weddings and birthdays. It's really nice." (Sarah)

Cooperation and informal help

The third sign of the existence of community spirit was informal mutual aid, a long-running buttress of survival in low-income areas (Thompson, 1990). The families gave examples both of how they received help and how they gave help to other people living locally. And they described how they witnessed examples of their neighbours helping each other:

"The man next door will get the bread for me when he goes to the bakers. And if the baby's asleep, there are two or three people I could ring to watch her while I pop over the school." (Lesley)

"When I had a problem with my ex, the Ugandan community all came to me; talk to me; find out what is wrong. Despite me being [from a different African country] still I had support from them." (Yinka)

"Here in this block; people will take the dog out [for me], they will feed the fish if we go away. If my neighbour goes away, I put her letters on the table." (Linda)

"You see people helping people off the bus with shopping and buggies. Or just being patient if an old person is taking their time to get down the steps." (Grace)

It was striking just how many of these examples emerged, of the normally unobserved and uncounted supports people had. Only when a local neighbourhood disappears – in a regeneration scheme for example – do people normally articulate these otherwise hidden connections (Konttinen, 1983). Yet they are so clearly part of the fabric of everyday life in communities that people can readily cite them. Particularly in low-income communities where people often run up against real shortages or real trouble, the ability to invoke acts of sharing and reciprocal help are very important. Informal support is a resource that people rely on and value immensely.

Few or no signs of community

Of the 83 families who felt community spirit mattered, 14 could see very few, if any, signs of it. Nine of the 14 were 'white' UK/Western European, three were 'black', and two were 'white' with mixed race children. They felt that people were very much left on their own to cope:

> "It does matter if you have got a good community where you can go and everything, but there just isn't that round here. People just can't be bothered, don't want to know. They've got community centres that do things, but it is mainly for the elderly people." (Gillian)

> "Not really. People keep to their own. A couple of people are alright. The rest kind of keep themselves to themselves." (Emily)

People themselves often cannot overcome the hurdles of participation. This may apply particularly strongly to families from ethnic minority groups.

> "When we first came, we tried to go and be confident in the other cultures. We couldn't do it. It's easier to communicate with our people and we have special days. But in this country, the people like to live individual. In Turkey, the people go to neighbours like they do to relatives." (Narin)

> "It's not like what I'm used to – coming from back home, everybody knows everybody. Here I could say I'm friendly with a couple. There is some [community spirit], but everyone's got their own clique. It doesn't spread, it's not universal." (Shushan)

One black mother commented that community spirit existed between white people; black people were not included:

> "It's white to white. If something happened to a white person, you will see how people rally round them." (Frances)

Clearly the issue of community can make some people feel excluded, a problem we return to later. However, some black families commented on positive, helpful relations they had with white neighbours:

> "We've all become friends – both black and white. They call my son the little black boy with white grandparents. They are all nice." (Hannah)

We explore community relations in the two neighbourhoods in more detail in the next chapter.

Feeling part of the community

> "I speak to loads of people and because I've lived here for so long now, I know all the people in the shops." (Flowella)

We asked the families who thought that community spirit existed whether they felt a part of it or not. Three quarters (48) did feel a part of it, and a further three families sometimes did. Two families in West-City said that they felt a part of the Turkish-speaking community, but not the wider community:

> "There is definitely a community spirit in the Turkish-speaking community. But it doesn't matter does it, because living in England, we should be mixing with English! I wish we could be part of the English community – it's probably mainly due to language." (Kezban)

Another mother also described how not feeling part of the 'wider' community was mainly due to language restrictions:

> "I have [never] been in that community. I am [from a] different country. They are not my people. I don't speak very well." (Snejana)

Some families had other reasons for not feeling a part of the community spirit they could see in their neighbourhood. One family put it down to laziness:

> "Apathy on my part! It's all there to use if you want to." (Rachel)

For another, it was connected with the pressures of becoming a parent:

> "Once you've had a child, you see people less." (Sophie)

Of course, community spirit means something different to each family. Some people would define networks of local friends and family as 'community', but one mother saw community as something separate from and wider than that. She commented that she didn't need 'the outside'. Community spirit was a good thing but she didn't feel a need to be part of it:

> "I think it's nice, but I don't need that sort of thing. Because I've got enough around me – my family and my friends – I don't need the outside. Whereas I suppose someone on their own would appreciate that sort of thing." (Jessica)

These families all recognised the basic notion of community as reflecting a sense of belonging locally. Contact and communication are pivotal and therefore language barriers and lack of time can prevent people being a part of this local sense of belonging.

Not being 'too close'

Some families articulated the fine balance between the benefits of living in a friendly place, where people know you and look out for you, and the problems that can arise from local networks that become too intense:

> "You can go to an extreme where you get too close a community, don't allow other people in. [Where] people are very, very close, it can cause friction. A wider community [helps], but a very intensive community [can cause] damage." (Madeleine)

> "A lot of community spirit can end up in gossip. It's who you choose to – you just have to be very careful – but it's like that in every area." (Jackie's friend)

> "I try to [get involved in the community]. I try not to get involved in all the aggravation, but I try to be approachable." (Marilyn)

> "I believe you should know people only to what you want to … not get too involved." (Clare)

These reservations about the power of communities over people's lives are possibly a sign of changing attitudes. People have a freer, less constrained attitude to association and they do not want local links to intrude on their private lives. Many families talked about just getting on with their lives, but knowing people were there for them as the epitome of a good community. Minding other people's business, judging others by your own standards and interfering were *not* what people wanted, and clearly it was a delicate line to tread. Some reacted by staying outside local networks, or at least not getting too closely involved. Despite this, many families who did not identify a strong sense of community or feel part of it, had local friends and knew their neighbours – a common view of community in the eyes of some families.

The ways in which families did feel a part of the community

The main reason for families feeling part of the community was that they knew neighbours or had friends living locally, as Table 3.3 shows.

Table 3.3: Why people felt a part of the community (of the 48 families who did)

	West-City	East-Docks	Total
Know neighbours/have local friends/speak to people	15	10	25
Through locally-based group or activity eg parenting group, playgroup, school, market	6	3	9
Through church	4	3	7
Through local job	1	5	6
Joined 'action' group eg tenants' association, parking campaign	3	1	4
Through attending organised community activity eg day trip, children's party	2	1	3
Have lived there a long time	2	1	3
Have given or received help from local people	1	2	3
Other reason[a]	2	3	5
No reason given	0	4	4
Total comments	36	33	69
	(23 families)	(25 families)	(48 families)

Note: [a] Other reasons given by only one family were: feel a commitment to the area, feel 'fit in' because there's no racial tension, reported suspicious person to the police, 'provide it through the kids', no fear so can go wherever wants.

But feeling part of the community in turn implied doing things to 'bind you in':

> "Most probably because they are neighbours I've known all my life, so they are like family as well. And I do get involved at different things over the school and help out there, so that does make you feel more involved in things." (Lesley)

Going to church locally was another important 'binding' structure:

> "I do on a Sunday [at church]. I don't tend to during the week, just because I'm out so much from the area." (Madeleine)

And local jobs were another point of connection. Several mothers worked at local schools, for example:

> "Round here everyone knows each other and also working at the school you know everyone and everyone knows you. You can walk outside and you'll always see someone you know round here." (Barbara)

Four families said that they felt a part of the community because they had taken part in campaigning/action of some sort (including tenants' associations and neighbourhood watch schemes).

Local links

A total of 85% of the families were 'linked in' to their neighbourhoods in different ways, including, for example, attending local playgroups, churches, and adult education classes. Table 3.4 summarises this.

Table 3.4 suggests an extraordinarily high level of participation in the local community among families with young children. We recruited many of the families through the local organisations shown in Table 3.4, so it is hardly surprising that many are 'linked in'. However, the families reflect the social make-up of the neighbourhoods and did not see themselves as being unusually active. A majority of the families are on low incomes, a high proportion are lone parents or from an ethnic minority background. Many do not have paid work. Nearly all send their children to local schools and are firmly embedded in their neighbourhoods, which are among the poorest in London. Formal attendance at official, organised 'participation' or 'consultation' meetings may be very much a minority activity, judging by Table 3.4, but a majority of families are involved in some local activity. As well as using local services, by the second interview 22 families had at least one 'responsible' voluntary role, sometimes in addition to a local job or other involvement in local activity. This voluntary role involved a regular 'work-like' commitment (such as being a member of a management committee), rather than

Table 3.4: Links between the families and their neighbourhoods in Round I

	West-City families		East-Docks families		
	One-parent	Two-parent	One-parent	Two-parent	Total
Attending church or other religious institution	5	10	14	8	37
Regularly attending local groups such as Newpin, Gingerbread, Tenants' Association	8	15	8	2	33
Employed locally[a]	5	10	7	9	31
Regularly helping with school/ other children's activities	5	9	10	7	31
Attending an 'adult education' course such as basic skills, computers, or post-graduate study	2	5	15	3	25
Responsible voluntary role	2	8	6	4	20
Occasionally attending local group	3	0	0	1	4
Total families linked in[b]	12	28	30	15	85
(% of the sample)	86%	78%	97%	79%	85%

Notes: [a] This is likely to be a slight underestimate because place of work was not a specific question in the interview. [b] The total number of families is less than the number of linkages because families were often involved in several different activities.

Source: Mumford (2001)

a less formal role, such as attending church, helping with reading at schools, or going to other local activities.

People did not necessarily connect taking on a 'responsible local role' with 'community spirit', but these families were making a formal and potentially significant contribution to the resources of the neighbourhoods without being paid. People's willingness to get involved in a community activity was an acid test of the strength of the community. People only commit themselves to an active, recognised role if they think it is worth it, if they believe it will make a difference, and will be welcomed by others. Getting involved implies collective commitment.

We wanted to find out what had prompted these people to freely invest their time and energy in their local neighbourhood. We recorded the roles of other family members as well as the interviewee where possible, to get as complete a picture as possible of family involvement. The roles were very varied, and some people took on more than one. Table 3.5 shows the different roles.

Table 3.5: Responsible voluntary roles taken on by the families

Role	West-City	East-Docks	Total currently involved
School governor	7	2	9
Committee member of local group for children	3	2	5
Church council member/other formal voluntary work at church	1	3 (+1)	4
Committee member of other local group (eg neighbourhood watch)	3	–	3
Committee member of tenants' association	3 (+2)	(–1)	3
Regular volunteers in under-5s project	3 (+1)	–	3
Committee member of group for single parents	–	1 (–1)	1
Voluntary sports coach	–	1	1
Volunteer coordinator of local African organisation	–	1	1
Volunteer in hospital, voluntary classroom assistant[a] or children's escort	1 (–1)	+1	2
Member of Parent/Teacher Association	+1	–	1
Formal involvement in tenant compact	–	(–1)	0
Total current roles	22	11	33
Total families currently with role	13	9	22
	(1 stopped, 3 started)	(3 stopped, 2 started)	

Note: [a] We did not count more casual help with school activities in this table, although we consider it no less important.

Becoming involved

The five main reasons for the families taking on these responsible roles were as follows:

- an explicit desire to get involved in their community;
- an existing personal link;
- they or their children were already users of the service or activity and it was a natural progression to become involved in running the group, or in fundraising to improve facilities and equipment;
- they had gone along to meetings prompted by a specific concern or interest, for example, and then when it came to electing a committee had found there was no one else to take on the role;
- a chance event or something 'turning up' that filled a gap or met a need.

Often the route to involvement was a combination of these reasons. As one new mother who became a committee member of a conservation group described:

> "When I first moved here, I wanted to get involved in something in the community. I wanted to get involved because I knew we had a plan to have this child, so I knew I would be based here. The conservation group came up. [I became a committee member]; we just volunteered ourselves. Nobody else wanted to do it, so I stuck at it for two years." (Felicity)

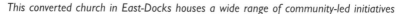

This converted church in East-Docks houses a wide range of community-led initiatives

Some people had actively sought the specific role, as one parent governor described:

> "I just feel it is so essential because I love kids. I became interested when they started their nursery. I thought maybe I could become involved. I heard a lot of people saying you had to go on courses – but I thought 'what's wrong with that?' Because I was part of the church council, I expressed an interest and was nominated. It took two years." (Miriam)

And one mother had felt a sense of duty. People had been asking her to join the church council for some time, and eventually she decided she should agree:

> "[The church council is there] to serve people in the community. We are Christians, reaching out ... but there are people who stay in their houses. There should be things that bring people together. It's difficult because some people don't want to know. We are trying, but we are just small." (Sasha)

A personal link could be an important way in; through friends who were already involved, or by being approached by a head teacher, for example.

One couple are volunteers in a project for parents and children. Two of their friends were working there:

> "And I go see, I like it very much – many different people are coming, using the crèche. And they said 'Do you want to work here like a volunteer?' 'Yes!' More than three years [ago]." (Onur)

Existing users of the service or activity became involved in managing the groups:

> "I was asked to be on the committee years ago, and gradually people moved away and no one was willing to take on the responsibility of chairing things. As I'm much better at that than administrative things, that was how it happened. Word of mouth is the ultimate way that it happened. I was already using the group." (Joanne)

> "I was a face that was always there [at the after-school club], and people just nominate your name." (Sasha)

The theme of there being nobody else to take on the role recurred.

Carrie had just become secretary of her tenants' association: "Unwillingly ... nobody else turned up ... there were only four of us".

Marilyn's husband had recently joined the committee of his residents' association, having been along to a few meetings prompted by concerns about the council's service charge. The elderly people who had been running it stepped down because they were finding it too much. They said "You'll have to get up otherwise it will close". Two women got up to be secretaries, and then they said "We want a man now", so he got pushed into it! But this underlines the sense of community responsibility that certain individuals feel.

Charley was asked to become a parent governor by her friend who was already a parent governor. This personal link, together with her frustration that no one else would stand, prompted her to get involved herself:

> "I got roped into it really! You have to be elected. You can nominate yourself. When I got elected there was no one else standing. No one else wanted to do it – no parent in the whole school, which is quite sad really. I felt really quite upset that no one else could be bothered. It's my child's school, and I want to know what's going on in it. So that's why really."

Some of the school governors commented on the workload and huge responsibility that the job involved:

> "Governors in this country are unsung heroes." (Kathleen)

Often involvement was part of reciprocal help – one favour deserves another:

> "I sign all the cheques for the youth club, and if they need a helping hand, I'll go over and help. They've been good to us – when we didn't have a facility for our sports club, they let us train there until we got something sorted out. They were very, very supportive." (Barbara)

A chance event, at the right time, could also play a part:

> "Their Dad had left and I was sitting here feeling sorry for myself one day. And I saw the organisation on telly. My local group was [in Tower Hamlets] – I went, but it was too far to keep travelling backwards and forwards. They said they had premises nearby and asked me to run it – and I had nothing better to do, and it just went from there." (Kate)

Some people enjoyed having community recognition and a certain sense of power or status. These are important ingredients of social organisation:

> "I quite like getting involved, organising things. Whereas most people get stressed, I can get involved with that quite easily." (Kate)

Stopping involvement

Being conspicuous as a community leader only works if supporters are there to validate your role – not just to hand you 'all the grief'.

Clare had stopped because the tenants' association itself had folded. She got involved originally because "I went to a meeting one day and this other woman resigned and they asked me would I like to. And I suppose for my block's sake, and I don't mind helping new tenants. There's one lady who doesn't speak very good English – I'd always help her out".

But the association folded: "It's really hard – you get these people that come, but you can't expect them to keep coming. You need them there to support you. The lady that was Chair got fed up of the knocks on the door complaining, but they didn't come to the tenants' meetings" (Clare).

Another had been involved in developing a tenant compact (a council landlord's formal service agreement with its tenants), but stopped because she did not want to be associated with something that she did not believe would achieve something concrete:

> "That all sort of fizzled out. It's like everything with the council, it's stage-managed, it looked good, but I haven't been to a meeting since [it was launched]. They do all these things on the surface, but that's where it seems to have ended. I've distanced myself from it again, because I don't want to be part of something that only looks good on the surface." (Joyce)

Sometimes responsible voluntary roles become a major burden, leading to disillusionment and withdrawal. More often they go in waves, attracting active people who like to be involved or who feel they should be involved – a form of informal leadership and representation that keeps a network of organisations as well as informal contacts going.

Information and support

> "I go up me nan – she knows everything and everyone. If it's about the council or the kids – nan. If it's about something to cook – one of my mates." (Linda)

We asked the families where they would generally go for information and who they could turn to if something was troubling them, in order to explore further people's links in the local area. We know that this is extremely important to families, because of their children's needs, their reliance on community, and their feelings of vulnerability if they are lone parents, recent arrivals or from an ethnic minority group.

We asked an open question: 'If you need to find out some information, where do you tend to go to get it?' This was a very wide, general question, and many families pointed out that it obviously depended on what kind of information they were looking for. For example, they would go to the housing office for housing advice, and to friends for other information.

The overall results show the importance of local libraries, the telephone, word-of-mouth, advice centres, and the growing importance of the Internet. Unsurprisingly, given that the vast majority of the families live in council property, the council was also an often-used source of information. Families also got information from schools, colleges, local community groups and from leaflets and newspapers.

The most frequently mentioned information source by West-City families was the library. It contains a 'One Stop Shop' and is a relatively new building, with racks of written material from a huge range of different sources. Many of the families in East-Docks mentioned an advice centre which is a well-established, popular, grassroots organisation, located next door to the main library:

> "I use the local library, which is brilliant, I love it! It's got a lovely atmosphere and is really well set up, and I like the fact that there is a study area downstairs that anyone can use. It is a nice place to be." (Joanne)

> "If it was really important information, I would expect it to be put up in the library." (Natasha)

Many families (19) said they would use the telephone to find out information, having first checked the Yellow Pages, Thompson directory, or spoken to directory enquiries or Talking Pages:

> "I usually phone directory enquiries. I spent a few years walking up and down to offices – I don't bother anymore because it takes so much time. And I can go into the Internet, print out a particular page, and I have it." (Sinead)

The use of the Internet was striking; 16 families said that this was one of their information sources. Of these families, four didn't have access in their own home, but used either the library or a friend's computer. One mother did point out that information overload from the Internet could be a problem:

> "The Internet wastes your time. You don't get what you need because there's so much information." (Aminia)

'Word-of-mouth' via friends, neighbours or acquaintances was an important information source for 15 families, but only three families mentioned family members as a source of information.

However, when we asked about sources of support, with the question 'Who do you see on a regular basis who you could talk to about something that was troubling you?', family members were mentioned much more often[1]. Partners received 11 mentions, other family members 22 mentions, and friends 24 mentions. Who people turn to most often fits with people's idea of community as something very local and quite personal.

One mother would sometimes go to her friends, sometimes her work colleague, and sometimes family. People did not always want to involve family members:

> "Then there's family and all — sometimes you don't want the family knowing everything." (Justine)

> "Sometimes it is my daughter, but if I don't want to involve her because of the worry, it is usually a friend. Or if it is just a light worry, it is usually the friend that I work with, my colleague in the office. I've seen her children grow up, we get along fine, we can talk to each other about worries and we don't divulge." (Peggy)

Sometimes friends had replaced family as the main source of support because family members lived far away – "No family so any of my friends" was a typical comment.

Telephoning both family and friends had become an important link for many, reflecting the greater distances between people, and dispersal of families.

> "[I speak to] one friend on a regular basis. Sadly my other close friends have all moved out of the area, so it tends to be phone calls, rather than seeing people. Four or five people who are very close friends and who lived in this area and now don't." (Joan)

> "My mum. I only see her once a week, but she's there to take my problems. I speak to her every day on the phone though – maybe twice a day." (Clare)

People would go to different people for different reasons:

> "[I talk to] my partner, or I phone my mate. My doctor's quite nice. Different problems – different people. To have a good old moan, get on the phone to one of your mates." (Linda)

> "It depends on the worry. Mum – but she's in Essex – that's only emotional worry. Financial and other problems – I would tend to use the advice centre, or friends." (Rachel)

A total of 11 families said they would talk to local professionals (including their doctor, head teacher, solicitor, or workers in voluntary projects):

> "My doctor, because of my health. He's quite supportive, very caring. If I'm in hospital, he'll make sure I'm alright. He'll come out and visit the children. I make sure I look after him as well – I'm always giving him presents! It's a good GP practice – everything can't be bad!" (Sola)

Sometimes local groups act as a strong support:

> "When serious stuff is bothering me – [I turn to that domestic violence support group]. That's the place in the past two years that have been giving me good advice. They can advise me where to get particular help, or help me get that help. So far that's the only place. They're very supportive. They may not get you directly to where you need to be, but they'll [put you in touch with someone who can]." (Gloria)

The church also emerged as an important source of support for at least five families, and sometimes as the only source:

> "Just church because we get together, discuss things, pray on issues. It's been very helpful." (Yetunda)

A further two families said that their sole source of support was to pray to God:

> "I try not to let anything bug me, but if it does, I pray – I don't ever talk to anyone about it." (Shushan)

Five families, four in East-Docks, said they had no one at all they would talk to about something that was troubling them:

> "You just get on with it yourself." (Gillian)

> "I tend to keep things to myself. There's no one I could really entrust." (Nora)

One other mother said that she usually kept things bottled up. She did have one close friend, but she didn't find it easy to talk:

> "I normally shut it up inside me. I don't let no one know. Or there's a close friend I normally talk to. But he don't do anything, just listen. I'm more of a listener than a talker." (Nicola)

Summary and conclusion

The 92 East End families give us a privileged insight into their views on community. Overwhelmingly they attach great importance to it, even when they feel it is missing. They recognise its core elements as social contact and communication, informal mutual aid and support. They see it as a way of overcoming social and racial barriers, breaking down isolation, making people feel more responsible and creating a sense of security.

In this chapter we have identified why people think community spirit matters, what signs they see of it, and whether they feel part of it. The families have an understanding of the meaning of community and explain it in clear and simple terms: helping neighbours, feeling safe, bringing people together, making people responsible, joining in, making things work, cooperating, overcoming barriers, seeing familiar friendly faces. Given their definitions and understanding of community, it is easy to see why it matters. In low-income areas, mothers with few economic resources and little power to influence major decisions rely heavily on local social relations, contact with neighbours and mutual aid for their survival, security and sense of family well-being. They share this feeling with low-income communities around the world (IIED, 1997-2002).

If these views of community were simply hopes or dreams, most families would experience bitter disappointment, and clearly some do. However, over half the families felt that they were part of their community and 62 saw signs of it existing even if they were not directly involved. The most obvious visible signs were simple, friendly exchanges, but organised community activity also played a big part. A total of 85% of all the families were directly connected with the local area and local activity through work, through helping in schools or with other children's activities, by attending a locally based group, or taking on a representative or official unpaid role in a local group. Community spirit matters because it not only generates friendly relations and greater tolerance; it combats isolation and means that there is someone they can turn to. This high level of engagement and connectedness reflects the strong need felt by women with children to meet with other mothers and share their child-rearing anxieties and experiences. This is found in many similar studies (Young and Willmott, 1957; Mitton and Morrison, 1972; Newson and Newson, 1976).

The surprising level of community activity and linkage by mothers suggests that local community organisations contribute to local well-being and to local attempts at improving conditions in ways that are not normally acknowledged from outside. It is clear that the often invisible social networks that bind people together in low-income neighbourhoods are highly valued from within. They act as a hidden glue, enhancing a sense of harmony, offering practical benefits, helping families to function, and overcoming some of the barriers that pull people apart. However, not everyone experiences this sense of belonging and not everyone finds a role. Some people opt out or drop out. Some feel excluded by others' clear sense of belonging. Despite this, the vast majority of families we spoke to felt a strong need for community and most did participate in some way. Studies of more formal methods of participation and the structures to facilitate it acknowledge the importance of informal networks, particularly among women (Cairncross et al, 1990; Hastings et al, 1996).

A major problem in the public participation debate is the failure to weight sufficiently the role of informal social networks in building valuable community assets (Schuller et al, 2001). This is partly because, as our families show, it is made up of extremely small-scale, highly localised actions across many different activities and small groupings.

Robert Putnam, the American writer who has argued the value of social capital to community well-being, defines social capital as informal social relations based on familiarity, trust and shared values that generate shared goals and cooperative ways of working. This enables people to realise the common goals that will make their neighbourhoods and eventually their cities and regions work better (Putnam et al, 1993). The families we spoke to are not only acutely aware of this, but generally willing to invest in what they define as community and politicians now call 'social capital'. 'Social capital', based on our findings, becomes the strength of community belief in the common good.

The range of local organisations the families belong to, the varied roles and responsibilities they assume, their tangible commitment to helping other people and their need for support suggest a level of social capital in low-income neighbourhoods that is possibly undervalued. It is certainly undermined in the eyes of these families by conditions people feel they cannot change, such as disrepair, poor environments, crime and disorder, and lack of control.

Subsequent chapters look at some of the reasons why local relations in practice are often more fraught than people's ideal of community. We explore why the potential of 'community spirit' as local families know it is often imperfectly realised, and how the multiple pressures on disadvantaged communities can disrupt important social networks, thus undermining social capital.

Note

[1] In further rounds of interviews with the families we are finding out a lot more about how families are linked into social networks. Following the pattern of questions asked in *Family and kinship in East London* we are finding that while there has been a big reduction in extended family contact, most mothers still have frequent contact with their own mothers and particularly mothers who still live nearby. This is very important to the mothers concerned (B. Makkar, correspondence with author, 2002).

FOUR

Race and community relations in changing multi-ethnic neighbourhoods

"Vast change. It's more of a multi-cultural area now. Whereas at first it was white-dominated. You've got all kinds round here now." (Louise)

"13 years ago, it was totally white. Now African people are coming in, settling down, actually choosing to buy in East-Docks." (Madeleine)

Introduction

One of the most direct ways in which the meaning of community is tested, particularly in a global capital city such as London, is in its community relations, meaning in the daily dealings between groups who have different community roots, distinct racial and ethnic backgrounds, but who share spaces. Strong cultural and religious differences divide neighbours and can pull communities apart. The two neighbourhoods where our families live experience these divisions in full force, for they are going through a period of rapid ethnic change. The families we talked to reflected the changing communities of the East End. A total of 46% of the families were black, Asian or of mixed race, and a further 16% had at least one member from another minority ethnic background (including Turkish, Kurdish, or Kosovan, for example). They had much to tell us about the experience of community, as played out in inter-racial contacts and relationships. They share everything that the community holds in common – its schools, shops, parks, play spaces, housing estates, block entrances, doctors' surgeries. Community events and organisations are for everyone, at least officially, and have to be brokered by community members.

Community relations between different ethnic groups loom particularly large in the two East London neighbourhoods because they are conspicuously different in their racial composition from even a generation ago; they are also very different from most areas of the country though less so from other London boroughs. These neighbourhoods form part of a fast changing urban residential pattern in Britain and other European countries (Wilson, 1996; Modood et al, 1997). Not only have minority ethnic populations grown rapidly over the post-war period, they are heavily concentrated in inner urban neighbourhoods, most often the poorer, more run-down areas of cities and towns from which the white population has increasingly moved out (SEU, 2000a). They experience many extra pressures and tensions because of the close intermingling of many groups from very different backgrounds in blocks of flats (Power, 1999).

In areas with fewer resources, the competition for space, for jobs, for a reasonable share of what is available, can be intense. People's sense of identity and belonging can become more fragile under such pressures. The very meaning of community that we showed mattered so much to residents in the previous chapter can be called into question if relations between different ethnic groups are not harmonious and people mistrust or, worse, attack each other on the basis of ethnic identity. So what our families said about their experiences of race underpinned their understanding of community relations more broadly, their sense of control over their lives and of belonging to a community.

Both East End neighbourhoods where the families live are traditionally white working-class neighbourhoods with a reputation for racial antagonism. Sir Oswald Mosley's fascist marches in the 1930s had their genesis on the borders of West-City, and we were warned of the latent violence and racial antagonism in East-Docks. However, both neighbourhoods have become conspicuously multi-racial since 1981.

We did not want to raise the question of race or ethnicity until we knew the families better. However, a majority of families raised the issue of race in the first round of interviews; 28 out of the 50 in each neighbourhood. They brought it up in connection with what they liked or disliked about the neighbourhoods, their concern or praise for schools, their desire to move, their housing and rehousing problems, the image of the neighbourhood, the way the area was changing, and their hopes and fears for their children's future. Negative comments were narrowly outnumbered by more positive or neutral ones – just describing the change, but not expressing an opinion.

The main 'positive' comments were refuting the racist image of the neighbourhoods, describing a reduction in racism, or stating the benefits of bringing children up in a multi-cultural environment. The negative comments included expressing dislike of the changing ethnic composition of the neighbourhoods, feeling that housing allocations were discriminatory, and describing racial harassment and racial tension within the neighbourhoods. Five families expressed concern about racism in society more generally; sometimes when discussing the barriers that children might encounter as they grew up.

Given the importance of this issue to so many of the families, we asked all of the families about it directly in the second round. In this chapter we give their responses to our questions about:

- changes in the ethnic composition of their neighbourhood, and how they felt about those changes;
- whether their children played with children, and they themselves had friends, from different ethnic groups;

- how well they felt people from different ethnic groups lived together in their area;
- what the good and the bad things about living in an ethnically mixed area were;
- whether overall living in an ethnically mixed area was a more or less positive experience.

The 92 families who answered these questions are clearly not fully representative of the neighbourhoods' populations but our sample of families broadly reflects the ethnic composition of the neighbourhoods, with some variation. In particular, white UK families are under-represented in our East-Docks sample, and black families are under-represented in our West-City sample. We often break families' responses down by ethnicity to show variations, although we cannot draw firm conclusions about whether differences in responses are associated with ethnicity. We use four broad categories for the purposes of clear presentation: 'white British and Irish'; 'Euro and others' (which includes Western and Eastern European, Turkish, Kurdish, white American, and families where one partner was from one of these groups and the other was white British or Irish); Black and Asian; and mixed race. For simplicity, we class as mixed race any family where one parent was white and the other black or Asian, and any family where the mother identified herself and/or at least one of her children as being of mixed racial origin (Modood et al, 1997). We used these whole-family descriptions based on what the interviewees told us, rather than individual interviewee ethnic identities, to try to capture the differences between all-white families and those with members from other ethnic backgrounds.

   The quotes are an attempt to reflect the full meaning of the families' views and experiences. Sometimes a combination of prejudice and vernacular usage meant that terms used by the families, such as 'coloured', were out of date and not the term favoured by the groups described. We have not changed the families' words because people generally tried to make sure they were not using hurtful expressions and we wanted to portray their views as accurately as possible.

   We originally chose to have one interviewer conduct all the interviews so that she could become embedded in the neighbourhood and gain a comprehensive understanding of the views of all the families. However, the fact that the interviewer was white may have influenced people's responses. Black people may have chosen to say more positive things through a desire not to offend, although many people did speak openly about problems they had experienced. At the same time, white people may have felt less inhibited, although many were concerned not to be thought racist. The account we present here of the families' insights is shaped by many factors, but families' keenness to discuss this issue and the general openness with which they relayed complicated feelings and experiences make the findings helpful to our understanding of community relations.

The changing ethnic composition of the neighbourhoods

West-City's population became much more mixed over the course of the 1980s. The 1981 Census is based on country of birth and not ethnic group (which the 1991 Census uses), so the two censuses are not directly comparable, but they do give some indication of the change. In 1991 white people represented 72% of West-City's population (the Census definition of white includes Turkish and Kurdish people, an increasingly important minority ethnic group in West-City); whereas 10 years earlier, in 1981, 85% of West-City's population were born in the UK or Irish Republic. Hackney as a whole was already much more mixed in 1981, with 23% of residents born outside the UK/Irish Republic.

The white population of West-City had further decreased to 63% by 1999. There has been an increase in Kurdish and Turkish residents who now form 5% of households in the area. A total of 20% of households speak a language other than English at home. Black and minority ethnic residents have a much younger age profile. Figures derived from the local education authority's ethnicity data in 2000 indicate that only 23% of children at the seven primary schools within the area are 'white UK' (Hackney Education, 2000).

East-Docks is also changing. In 1981, just 7% of East-Docks residents were born outside the UK/Irish Republic. By 1991, 19% of the population of East-Docks was black or from a minority ethnic background, whereas 42% of the population of Newham overall was black or from a minority ethnic background in 1991 (Lupton, 2000a). In 2000, the proportion of 'white UK' pupils at East-Docks primary schools (54%) was more than double the Newham average of 25%.

But East-Docks is continuing to become much more mixed. In 1991, 24% of 0-17-year-olds in East-Docks were from black and minority ethnic groups (1991 Census); whereas eight years later in 1999, 39% of pupils at five primary schools and two secondary schools serving East-Docks were from black and minority ethnic groups (Newham Education, 1999).

Ethnicity data from the schools in each neighbourhood illustrate these changes in more detail, and help fill the 10-year gap between censuses (particularly as results from the 2001 Census are not yet available). The main advantage of these school data is that they close this gap. The main disadvantage is that not all children in a neighbourhood attend local schools. Also, the local schools serve some children who live outside the neighbourhood. However, the primary schools in each neighbourhood appear to have more local catchments than the secondary schools (in fact West-City does not have a secondary school within its boundaries), so we use these data.

Between 1997/98 and 2000, the proportion of 'white UK' primary school pupils fell both in the boroughs as a whole and in the neighbourhoods. West-City, and even more so East-Docks, continued to have a higher proportion of white pupils than the rest of their boroughs, but the rate of change in these neighbourhoods in the past few years has been more rapid than in the boroughs as a whole. Between 1997 and 2000, the proportion of 'white UK' pupils at West-City primary schools fell by 7% to 23%. In just two years in East-Docks, the proportion of white UK pupils fell by 8% to 54%. Figure 4.1 illustrates this.

In both neighbourhoods, the black African population has grown significantly, and is proportionally greater than in the boroughs as a whole. For example, in West-City the proportion of black African pupils increased by five percentage points between 1997 and 2000, from 29% to 34% (compared to the Hackney average of 21%). In East-Docks the change has been even more rapid, with an increase in the proportion of black African pupils of twelve percentage points in two years, from 19% in 1998 to 31% in 2000 (more than double the proportion of black African pupils in Newham as a whole). The black Caribbean pupil population in both neighbourhoods remained constant. The Asian pupil population in each neighbourhood increased very slightly (by one to two percentage points), but remained much smaller than in Hackney and Newham as a whole. Asian children represented just 4% of the East-Docks primary school population in 2000, compared to a Newham average of 36%. In West-City they comprised 8% of the primary school population, compared to 14% of the total primary school population in Hackney. Within the Asian pupil population in West-City, the Bangladeshi population is the largest. Table 4.1 shows these changes.

Figure 4.1: The reduction in white UK primary school pupils (1997-2000)

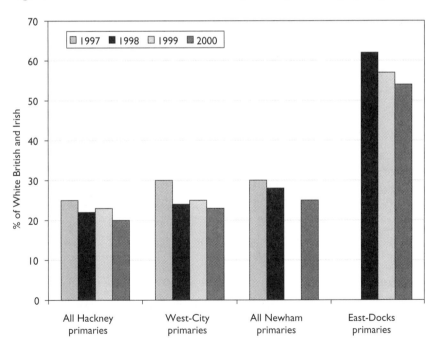

Source: Data supplied by Hackney and Newham Local Education Authorities

Table 4.1: The changing ethnic composition of primary school populations within the boroughs of Hackney and Newham and the neighbourhoods of West-City and East-Docks (%)

	White UK	White Euro/ other	Black African	Black Carib- bean	Asian[c]	Black other/ other	Unknown
All Hackney primaries							
1997[a]	25	12	18	20	15	12	
1998	22	12	18	19	14	16	
1999	23	11	20	19	14	14	
2000	20	13	21	20	14	12	
7 West-City primaries							
1997	30	12	29	13	7	10	
1998	24	10	31	12	8	15	
1999	25	9	35	13	8	10	
2000	23	11	34	13	8	12	
All Newham primaries							
1995	30	2	8	5	41	7	8
1996[b]	27	2	9	5	38	6	14
1997[b]	30	3	11	6	37	14	
1998	28	3	12	6	35	15	
2000	25	4	15	6	36	15	
5 East-Docks primaries							
1998	62	2	19	2	2	13	
1999	57	2	29	3	3	5	
2000	54	2	31	3	4	6	

Notes: [a] Two schools included some of their reception pupils in their ethnicity figures but not in the denominators used to calculate the percentages, which may have distorted the figures slightly. [b] Includes pupils in reception classes. [c] Indian, Pakistani, Bangladeshi and Chinese.

Source: Data supplied by Hackney and Newham Local Education Authorities

Most families were acutely aware of the changes in the neighbourhoods:

"When I moved in, at first I was the only black in this block. It was only my next-door neighbour who would speak to me, the others wouldn't at all. But eventually they all started saying 'hello'. And there are now more black families. We all go to the same church – the church has played a vital role. We all meet each other, we greet each other." (Hannah)

"Drastically. You can only go by the school. When my daughter started there, there was three or four [black children] in her class. When my boy started (there's 3½ years between them), there were 16 coloureds, 13 whites. So they're in a majority now. More coloured people walk past here than whites." (Lesley)

"A lot more mixed relationships – everyone seems to be going with the flow. It's accepted more now; it's the norm. There's a lot more integration." (Nora)

"At first we just had West Indians and they integrated. And then came Nigerians, Africans, Somalians, and then we've got Kosovans and Lithuanian people – really nice families. They have to integrate quickly and that is very hard. There are a lot of things that they don't know and to a lot of white people that is classed as ignorance. I don't think enough patience is given to them." (Peggy)

"There has been a huge difference in the racial mix. It has become much more African – Nigerians and Ghanaians." (Jane)

"Mostly black people live here. You would see mostly middle–aged/ elderly white. As time goes on they reduce, and the number of black families tends to increase." (Delilah)

"I've lived here 20 years now. When I first came it seemed very much white East End families that had been here from way back, and who were very resentful of, probably black Caribbean people at that time. And there was a huge amount of racist graffiti everywhere and I believe the National Front had their headquarters near here, and they used to have a stall in the market handing out leaflets. It was very uncomfortable. But that has changed *enormously*. I don't know who was next to come; probably more African people moved into the area, and then Asian (but there is still not a huge number of Asians), and then a huge influx of Turkish and Kurdish people. Which has changed the place beyond recognition. Just walking round the streets and seeing such a mixture of people. The council has been very tough on the racist graffiti – if it is seen, it is gone immediately. And the National Front aren't here anymore. And although I'm sure there are still undercurrents of [negative] feelings, the general feeling is that there is this much more happy and healthy mixture of people – not the 'them' and 'us' which it was when there were just a few black people." (Joan)

How families feel about the change

People often had mixed views about the radical change in the population of the area. They liked some aspects of their neighbourhood's increasing diversity (for example, the chance to learn about other cultures) yet at the same time were concerned about other aspects (for example, the impact on schools of new children who did not speak English). We counted their positive and negative comments separately, giving a total of 13 positive, 18 neutral and 27 negative ones. A total

Table 4.2: Families' views of the change in ethnic composition of the neighbourhoods

	White British and Irish	Euro, others[a]	Black and Asian	Mixed race	Total
Doesn't bother/affect them: change is a part of life	9	–	6	3	18
Pleased	4	1	6	–	11
Okay	2	–	–	–	2
Total positive/neutral					**31**
Brings some problems eg with housing, schools	7	1	–	1	9
There are too many immigrants; too few whites; should spread the refugees out more	5	–	2	2	9
Incomers are getting priority eg in school, housing	4	–	–	–	4
Now there is segregation	1	–	–	1	2
Other negative	2	–	1	–	3
Total negative					**27**
Not sure	–	–	2	–	2
Not applicable (because hadn't experienced change)	6	9	15	2	32
Total not expressing view of the change					**34**
Not recorded	3	1	2	1	7
Total[a]	43	12	34	10	99

Note: [a] Some families made more than one comment. One family declined the question about ethnicity. They hadn't experienced a change in the composition of the neighbourhood.

of 34 families were not sure what they thought, or said they had not experienced a change in the composition of their neighbourhood, sometimes because they had not been living there for very long.

The following comments illustrate some of the positive views people expressed:

"I think it's lovely." (Madeleine)

"I like it because [before] it was like being in a secluded place. Now you can meet people, some people call me to discuss their problems. It's much better socially." (Hannah)

"A lot of new flats have been built and opened to the public. There's been different members of the community that have moved in – Bengalis, Asians, Africans, whites. A great blend of cultures.... I'm very pleased with it because I get on very well with people of all different races. We all have to be able to get on with people of different races because we'll be living in such a community in the future. I encourage it." (Said)

As well as asking families what they thought about the changing ethnic composition of their neighbourhoods, we asked them for their views on the good or bad things about living in an ethnically mixed area. We focus on problems first, even though a majority of families believe that different races live together quite amicably in these two neighbourhoods. Most people recognise real tensions and underlying problems despite the positive factors. Near the surface lies real fear, influenced by actual experience of sometimes very serious racial attacks.

In addition, people are constantly aware of the threat to community harmony and shared resources of ever more numerous and needy newcomers. The positive relations develop because people have social structures and links through which they meet, cooperate and build constructive contact. If the concentration of particular groups is tipped too far one way, those contacts would shrivel along with the chance to get to know each other and to learn to cooperate (Home Office, 2001).

For these reasons we consider the pressures and problems before looking at the generally positive view that families have of community relations.

A total of 45 families (49%) identified some negative aspects of living in an ethnically mixed area. Their views are shown in Table 4.3. Sixteen further aspects, each mentioned by only one family, are shown in Box 4.1.

Table 4.3: Bad things about living in an ethnically mixed area: the families' views (number of comments)

	White British and Irish	Euro, others	Black and Asian	Mixed race	Total
Racism, harassment,	0	1	7	4	12
Segregation stereotypes	3	0	1	2	6
Tension, disagreements (eg between parents)	4	0	1	0	5
Impact on schools of children with English as a second language	2	0	0	1	3
White people 'feeling hard done by'/ being harassed	3	0	0	0	3
Cultural misunderstandings, different 'standards'	1	1	0	0	2
Children find it hard mixing/separate groups	2	0	0	0	2
Other reasons[a]	10	1	5	0	16
Total bad things mentioned					**49**
No bad things mentioned	11	9	16	4	41[b]
Don't know	1	0	1	0	2
Not recorded	2	0	2	0	4
Total (some families made more than one comment)	39	12	33	11	96[b]

Notes: [a] See Box 4.1. [b] Includes one family who declined the question about ethnicity.

Box 4.1: Range of negative aspects of living in an ethnically mixed area in addition to those in Table 4.4 (each mentioned by one family only)

White British and Irish
- "You accept but will you be accepted?"
- "Some people fear differences."
- "Ethnic minorities have a 'chip on their shoulder'."
- "The woman working in the library is not good with English spelling."
- "Have to learn different languages at school."
- "Have extra days off at school for different festivals."
- "Don't want to live in an increasingly mixed area."
- "Newcomers getting priority, for example, for housing."
- "I don't agree with the mix – white going out with black person – you should go out with your own kind."
- "If everyone started fighting and arguing."

Black and Asian
- "I don't speak English and sometimes don't know what to think of it."
- "people blame newcomers for problems."
- "The smell of food – sometimes you don't agree with it all."
- "A lot of the crime that takes place here is by people who are coming from out of the country – they can't work."
- "You're in a majority here, but in a minority outside the neighbourhood."

European and others
- "Because there are so many people from different backgrounds there is a feeling of insecurity – you don't know what to expect."

The views people gave often contradicted other views about ethnic mixing or about community more generally. Often we picked up the feeling that community mattered more in these neighbourhoods because it was constantly undermined by the pressures.

Black people were directly worried by racism and harassment. The most frequently mentioned negative aspect of living in a mixed area concerned racism, harassment, and people having stereotyped ideas about other cultures. No 'white UK' families mentioned this aspect in answer to this question. Of the 12 black and minority ethnic families who raised it, eight lived in East-Docks:

> "Some of the kids are so racist – it's from [their] home. The boys who egged my windows pick on my son at school." (Hannah)

We explore racial harassment in more detail below.

Some white people were worried by general tensions, poor race relations and a feeling of being 'outnumbered':

> "There's nothing I like because there's nobody getting on with each other." (Rose)

This range of worries suggests that all ethnic groups worry about the sheer scale and pace of diversification. Minority groups feel vulnerable as newcomers make their precarious position in the community more open to challenge. And white people feel ever more in a minority themselves.

When race relations go wrong: segregation, tension, hostility and racial harassment

The danger of segregation

Both white and black and minority ethnic families worry about the fact that ethnic changes may continue until the area becomes 'all black':

> "I don't like it. It should be mixed. When someone moves, you never see a white family come in. It's all changing to black." (Naomi)

This poses a different kind of threat, the danger of segregation. Six families directly raised concerns about segregation. They all lived in West-City; three were white, one was black, two were mixed race.

> "Everybody is keeping themselves to themselves really. Unlike before we could have a chat in the lifts. Now everyone is trying to keep their business away from the other." (Cynthia)

> "We don't always integrate very well. There are pockets of communities rather than one big community." (Debra)

Arguments and conflict between young people often bring racial tensions to the fore:

> "If you've got 10 black youths that didn't know one another and 10 whites … and one starts picking on another, the blacks would stick together, the whites would walk off. That's the difference between the races. When I was growing up, we didn't have that, we all mixed together." (Linda)

> "It seems to be if two people are having an argument, there's always more [black people] stick[ing] up [for each other]. And with gangs –

that's the problem on an estate if you've got more of one [group]."
(Justine)

Cultural barriers can be harder to surmount than strictly racial barriers. Language
and customs can make people feel that it is impossible to create the social links
that then generate harmonious community relations.

> "With my daughter's school, there's quite a lot of kids from Turkish
> and Kurdish backgrounds. It's not a problem, just that they don't
> speak really good English. It's hard to make friends with people from
> that background when they don't speak a lot of English." (Charley)

> "I'm not racialist, I'm really not. I know there's good and bad in
> everyone. But a lot of the ones who are here now are ones that can't
> speak the language and seem to have more of a chip on their shoulder
> than what we do. There are more disagreements between parents....
> If I could move to an area tomorrow where there wasn't so many, I
> would go." (Lesley)

Some white people feel 'uncomfortable', squeezed out

Some people whose main sense of identity is with England, and who feel that by
virtue of being 'born and bred' in London they have a prior claim to belonging,
do not like and are unable to accept people forming a sense of identity that
separates them on racial lines. Lack of integration causes big worries and tension:

> "I'm not a racist person, but I think the blacks are taking over. They're
> going from children to youths and roaming the streets. I find that
> black people stick together. Black people round here have a chip on
> their shoulder. If people have been against them in the past, they
> think it's like that now, and it's not." (Linda)

Some families felt that a fear of being criticised for being racist stopped people
from treating black and white alike:

> "Prime example is that my son likes to play football, and the old boy
> opposite is always on at us, so he isn't allowed to play football out
> there anymore. But if you get the African families with children out
> there playing he doesn't come out. So to me, why doesn't he do it?
> Is it because they are black and he thinks they are going to say he is
> being racist? I think that is unfair." (Gillian)

One parent voiced her opposition to mixed race relationships:

> "I've got nothing against them being with coloured [friends], as long as they keep to their own with partners – blacks with blacks, whites with whites." (Sonia)

Another mother talked about mixed race relationships, based on her own friendships with people from different ethnic groups, and the opinions she had heard them express on the subject:

> "I've got a lot of friends from different nationalities. The people I do know, I can feel at ease [with]. [These friends] wouldn't want their child to come home with a different nationality, they want their child to marry within their culture. That's not wrong, that's not racist. We can be friends without being racist towards each other." (Liz)

Underlying fear and hostility

More seriously, there were many comments suggesting latent aggression towards people of different races. White families were acutely aware of this as well as black, and most of the comments suggested a desire to see this ugly side of community relations tackled:

> "A lot of 'em are racist round here. I've never seen it, but I know there has been physical…." (Rose)

> "There are some individuals that can't accept it and make it obviously known." (Kate)

Some people think that older residents simply cannot adjust and are still influenced by the areas' histories as 'white strongholds':

> "Me personally, I get along with anybody. If they're alright, I get on with them. But you find that, where this area has always been a very white area, it was going back years and years, it was a National Front area I think, you get a lot of old people who have been here years and are stuck in their ways. They look on [racial mixing] as the bad side." (Alice)

Other people think that youth gangs are a bigger problem and that they pull groups apart:

> "The older generation are fine. It's the younger generation – the teenagers – they seem to try and put this 'authority' around, and that's

when it causes trouble. Black children stay with the black children, white with the white, and it's like 'this is our area'." (Jess)

One black family had their windows smashed when they first moved in to East-Docks 15 years ago. Although Louise feels that she has won local people's confidence and overcome any barriers, she is concerned about the hostility that continues to face newcomers:

> "It would be nice to see more people helping out and getting on better – accepting people for the way they are, not for the colour of their skin. There is a lot of racial tension in this area at the moment – it's harder for new people to fit in. It's hard to fit into East-Docks, it really is…. Everyone round here knows me. It's because they know me I feel comfortable. We're a strong family. We're here to stay – people respect you for that. But you shouldn't have to go through it – shouldn't have to put up a fight to stay." (Louise)

Some people see racial barriers as inevitable and there to be coped with:

> "As far as I'm concerned, I think in the UK it's always going to be problems. There's blacks and whites – amongst the blacks there's racial problems, amongst the whites there's English and Irish. I try not to get involved. I say good morning to anyone who's ready to." (Shushan)

A mother with a mixed race background refuses to be pigeonholed by her black friends and simply accepts that she belongs to both groups:

> "Some of them are like – a friend of mine is black – she runs white people down. She's racist. She tries to tell me I'm black – I'm not, I'm mixed. I just laugh at her! My mum is white, my dad is black." (Zoë)

One mother articulated the need for common activities and social gathering points as a way of overcoming the inevitable distance between people who feel strangers to each other, because they do not know each other:

> "I think [people of different races] live side by side and ignore each other! Everyone keeps themselves to themselves. I think that if you belong to some sort of playgroup or nursery or church, when you are sitting there for a couple of hours with the other mothers, you get to understand each other better, and you do feel happy to have a relationship with somebody from another culture. But it doesn't just happen because you live next door to somebody. I think a lot of

people do just keep themselves to themselves and just try and avoid close relationships in order to avoid confrontation." (Joan)

The fear of things going wrong has a strong inhibiting impact on breaking down barriers.

Racial harassment

For many years, the level of reported racist crimes has consistently been higher in Newham than anywhere else in the country, and the level of incidents reported in the part of the borough in which East-Docks is located is higher than elsewhere in Newham (Sampson et al, 2000).

When we asked the families whether they had experienced a crime in the past 12 months, three people described the racial harassment they had experienced (two in East-Docks and one in West-City). One of these families had received such serious threats that they had had to move house since the first interview. In addition, other families, during the first interview and at different points in the second interview, mentioned experiencing racial harassment within their neighbourhood. This included children being harassed at school, food being thrown at their windows, and their cars being vandalised:

> "I did have a really bad [neighbour].... It was a racist problem we are talking about – my husband is West Indian and my children are mixed race and it went on for two years.... It was very, very serious. She kept calling the police to my house, saying we were doing things." (Barbara)

> "I'm stuck here in fear.... My daughter says 'Let's just pray they haven't done anything to the car'.... She asks me 'Mum, what have we done wrong?'" (Frances)

We asked all of the families whether they felt racial harassment was a problem in their area and, if so, whether it was a serious problem. Around three times as many of our families felt racial harassment was a serious problem in their area compared to the London average (4%). Only 1% of families nationally said that racial harassment was a serious problem. Figure 4.2 and Table 4.4 show this.

Figure 4.2: Whether racial harassment is a problem in the area (%)

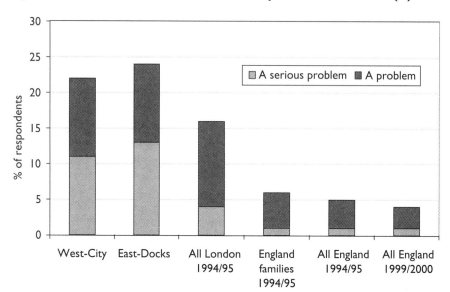

Sources: Round 2 interviews, 1994/95 Survey of English Housing in Burrows and Rhodes (1998) and 1999/00 Survey of English Housing in DTLR (2001). 'England families' comprise lone parents and couples with dependent children. The data was not available for London families only, so we show the figures for all London respondents.

Table 4.4: Whether racial harassment is a problem in the area by family ethnicity (number of families)

	White British and Irish	Euro, others	Black and Asian	Mixed race	Total
Serious problem	4	1	3	3	11
Problem but not serious	3	1	6	0	10
Not a problem	19	9	20	7	56[a]
'Not in that way' (white)[b]	3	0	0	0	3
Don't know	7	0	4	0	11
Not recorded	0	1	0	0	1
Total families	36	12	33	10	92[a]

Notes: [a] Total includes one family who declined the question about ethnicity. [b] These white families felt that they were harassed by black people.

More black and mixed race than 'white UK' families in our neighbourhoods said racial harassment was a problem. Over twice as many families in our neighbourhoods – both white and black – said that racial harassment was not a problem as those who said that it was. People described the latent hostility they encountered:

> "I have had some experience of it – kids – but sometimes kids learn from their parents." (Miriam)

"[There are] those who still have the racist attitude in them – but as long as they know how to live among their neighbours, then fine." (Said)

"It's getting worse. This is a very racist area. I didn't believe it until I lived here myself." (Sola)

"[It's not a problem] for us personally, but there's deep-rooted racism." (Debra)

"I've seen it. And I know quite a few people have a negative attitude towards black and Asian people…. There is inherent racism in people – they will say they have got black friends and they're not racist but [it's there]." (Andrea)

Aziz, who is Kurdish, said that in general he doesn't feel harassed in West-City but there are isolated incidents that come from youth not his neighbours. For example, a year ago, some youths pushed him against his car, saying "Foreigners go back". It is not an everyday thing, but it makes the family feel uncomfortable. Another Kurdish family explained what they saw as an inevitable failure to accept people of different ethnic backgrounds:

"Racism is everywhere because no one wants different people to come and live in their country. They think we are a problem." (Kerim)

A black African mother in East-Docks described an incident where a neighbour's son (of mixed race) was hurt by another boy. When the mother went to complain to this boy's parents, she was told "Get back to your own country, you black…" (Belinda).

Three of the white families we spoke to (one in West-City and two in East-Docks) answered that the problem was "the other way round" – meaning that they were being harassed by black people. Lesley described an incident in which a black child asked if he could play with her white son. Her son said he didn't want to because he already had his own little group of friends. The other boy went to the teacher and accused her son of being racist. The mother took this as a contrived charge:

"It came out that this little boy had been told if he couldn't get his own way to say they was being racist. They are more racialist to us than we are to them." (Lesley)

In Newham, two families talked positively about the efforts they felt statutory agencies were now making to tackle the problem of racial harassment:

"The council's trying very hard to eliminate people being racially harassed. It is still there, but I have read of cases that have been dealt with. In the local newspaper there are now people who've been evicted because they're making the people around [exist] in living hell." (Gloria)

Frances saw the aftermath of the Stephen Lawrence Inquiry as helping to redress racial problems, giving people a chance to be heard:

"I don't like this area because of racism still. The suspected family moved out, but there are still some. But it's a national thing – it's not just Newham. The government is trying their best. Since the death of Stephen Lawrence there's been an improvement. My neighbour – recently there was a confrontation [and] the police had to call me for an interview. They said they had a race department … you are coming out even to listen, it is something. One thing is to listen, the other is to really act. But the fact they are listening is a positive sign. The death of Stephen Lawrence is really doing a positive thing for blacks. At least you're going to be heard anyway." (Frances)

Pressures on resources

One of the strongest causes of racial tension is the competition for scarce resources – particularly school resources and affordable council housing – and the needs of refugees.

School resources

One mother talked about the pressure on school places:

"I'm not very pleased about it. One reason is that people who've lived round here all their life can't get into the school because they don't go to church. Coloureds that haven't been here that long are getting in. It sounds horrible, but I feel that people that have been here all their life are more entitled." (Lesley)

Others were worried that teachers' time was being diverted to helping children who did not speak much English, so that their children were losing out:

"I think they've put too many into the one area. They have concentrated so many asylum seekers, refugees, it's just too much. I think it's affected the schools – they have to concentrate on kids who don't have English as a first language. It's not being racist." (Ellie)

One mother highlighted the tension between positives and negatives – on the one hand, she felt that her children's lives were enhanced by living in an ethnically mixed area, but on the other, she was also concerned about the extra pressures faced by schools when many pupils had English as a second language:

> "In many ways, I'm pleased my children are growing up in a multi-cultural environment. But it does affect the school when there are lots of children with English as a second language." (Jane)

Access to housing

The two neighbourhoods contain a majority of social housing – 82% in West-City and 75% in East-Docks. The estates that dominate the housing in these areas gradually became less popular among younger white families, partly because of the decline in local low-skilled jobs and partly because other, better housing opportunities opened up for more upwardly mobile paid workers. So council housing became harder to let and more unpopular. Both West-City and East-Docks experienced low demand in the 1980s and 1990s (Priority Estates Project, 1980-89).

The dominance of council housing has a significant influence on how access happens. Legislation prioritising homeless families over local residents is often blamed for the rupture of community ties and for the creation of inter-communal conflict. On the other hand, a public resource must be publicly available and

West-City council housing

allocated according to agreed rules. Because affordable housing is in short supply for the most needy in inner London (often minority ethnic families and asylum-seekers), both Hackney and Newham accept disproportionate numbers from these groups for rehousing in council estates. It is here that community consent is vital and has, in fact, been overlooked by public housing authorities.

Inevitably, as more white people moved out, available space went to high priority newcomers, most often minority families. In the eyes of many white residents, minorities have "been favoured" by this process, but in practice they may now form a large majority of those eligible or willing to accept council housing in Hackney or Newham. In this sense, a priority, needs-based public housing allocation system, is bound to put refugees ahead of a settled local family. The potential for racial conflict over this issue is real, and unless handled carefully, could undermine longer-term community relations. Much depends on the pace of change and the transparency of housing allocations. For many it is too fast and too unclear.

People are torn between tolerance and positive community relations on the one hand, and, on the other, awareness of a scarce resource being redistributed away from some groups and towards others:

> "On a one-to-one [people live together] very well – as people. But then you get issues like housing; it really causes a big rift because everyone isn't being treated equally. And I believe that's where the trouble comes from." (Dionne)

> "It doesn't bother me. It doesn't affect me. I feel sorry for English friends who've been on the list for two- or three-bed houses and are getting nowhere. The local people are very angry. They've been on the housing list for years and yet the brand new council houses are given to people who've only been here for two months. They don't come right out and say it, but you can feel it – an underlying resentment." (Sinead)

> "There's many that mind – it's difficult to describe without sounding racist – there's a feeling of being overlooked. Ethnic minorities always seem to come first [eg with housing]." (Rosemary)

> "It's not so much the old races [Caribbean], it's all the new ones that are coming in now, like the Nigerians, the Bosnians. We aren't getting nothing, so even the older ones are getting fed up with it now. I can't get nothing; some of these people coming over now are getting more than I'm getting altogether. This bloke along here after two weeks was given that [flat] straight away. They're getting more than what I am." (James)

"It doesn't really bother me. It seems to bother other people if they see a lot of black people around and they seem to be given downstairs properties. I don't understand the allocations system. I know that deals are done with certain housing officers, but proving it's another matter." (Joyce)

"I think it is good. To me it is really exciting meeting people from other places and I love it when my neighbour comes in and brings me Kurdish food. But I still get the feeling that there are people – well I know there are, because I speak to them – that say 'Why are they here? How can they get a flat when my son, who has just got married, is living on my sofa because he can't get a flat in the area? Born here, educated here, works here, and can't get a flat'. I can understand that, I can." (Joan)

Sometimes council staff talk about the needs of refugees as a way of warding off pressures from other applicants. This obviously has a hugely negative effect on people's attitudes and on the divisions within the community:

"There's just a general feeling of being unhappy with housing and refugees – but I think that's a mood in lots of parts of the country. It can be like that – when you're working your butt off and they're getting everything paid – although you don't know the circumstances – and you haven't got a hope of getting anything better than this. My cousin was told [by the housing office] they had to house 8,000 Turks and Kurds. That's a silly thing to tell the community. It's going to hit a nerve somewhere. You feel so awful saying and thinking things ... but you're fed so much in the papers." (Rosemary)

Dionne was very upset that it was impossible for her to get the transfer she wanted to bigger council accommodation:

"We're moving out soon. We're moving because the council won't give us anything. We can't afford to buy round here. We've got to move 50 miles away from family and friends. But it's alright for everyone else to come in and get what they want. Down the housing office they've said to me off the record that there's absolutely nothing they can do. [The houses are] all going to immigrants. It really gets up your nose, when you've worked 16 years."

Council housing is only available through queuing because there is not enough of it in these areas, but there is a strong feeling in the white population that queuing no longer works. New arrivals effectively 'jump the queue' because they have higher priority. The fairness of a queuing system that never allows you to reach the top of the list even though you have real needs is being questioned among residents. The bigger problem is the method itself of allocating and managing a scarce community resource without any reference to the people affected.

The concentration of refugees

People of all races feel that poor neighbourhoods carry a disproportionate burden of responsibility for extreme need. Sometimes the weight of this responsibility feels too much. For example, refugees are most often housed in large estates in the poorest neighbourhoods, making the areas with least resources and most pressure take on even more. Poor neighbourhoods can become a catch-all for societal responsibilities:

> "In the last one or two years – you just kind of know that when there's a conflict on the television, the immigrants come here – they're always housed in Hackney." (Sinead)

> "I don't understand why more refugees can't go to Chelsea, Westminster, places where they have more money. I'm black myself, but don't you think it's better to distribute the refugees more evenly rather than put them all into Newham? I might be totally wrong ... that's just the way I feel." (Miriam)

There are direct social problems resulting from many refugees having an uncertain status and not being allowed to work. One family mentioned crime:

> "They are doing this petty crime to survive – it's almost understandable." (Shushan)

Other people felt it had made the most pressurised areas too difficult to manage for the authorities:

> "It hasn't really affected me. But in the local paper it's been saying the government's only given Newham so much money and Newham's gone over, and local council tax payers have to make up the difference. But I do know quite a few people are not going to be happy if Newham is used as a dumping ground. It would be nice to have Britain be a simple place, and if we're going to have refugees, spread them all over. It's a big enough place." (Rachel)

People on the lowest incomes often had a sense that they were actually being directly deprived by the constant demands of other groups who they felt had less entitlement:

> "You've got them people that go grovelling for money: the Bosnians. I think it's disgusting to be quite honest, that they let them off the plane in this country and come asking us for my money. I'm on the social – I don't have a lot of money. You think 'how dare you?' It's terrible I think…." (Clare)

Contradictions in some people's views and experiences

Studies of inter-ethnic community relations show that people hold conflicting views of race:

> The relationships between different ethnic groups can be quite complex and simultaneously positive and negative. Thus white people may have black friends, even though they hold racist attitudes. (Sampson et al, 2000)

Many families were concerned not to be considered racist. Clare, who felt very hostile towards Bosnian refugees, was still able to highlight the good things about living in an ethnically mixed area:

> "Just that your kids, you all, grow up to get along with everybody. If you grow up in an all-white area you're bound to be racialist. Nowadays you've got to get on with everyone, you've got to communicate with everyone whether they're black, white, pink or green, otherwise there's no point living in the area. The only ones I disagree with are those who grovel."

Another mother who was very upset not to get rehoused while refugees managed to get ahead of her in the queue tried to explain:

> "Earlier on it sounds as if I'm a bit of a racist, but I'm not. I'm into equality – not different rules for one." (Dionne)

Even though one mother felt very 'swamped' by the rapid increase in black residents and was worried about them 'taking over', she feels that living in a racially mixed area is more positive:

> "Because I think you need to learn about other people – it's ignorant to stay in one thing." (Linda)

The instability and uncertainty of people's attitudes to race relations often reflected an underlying anxiety about whether problems might suddenly bubble over. Rosemary commented:

> "It's positive – but it can quite quickly be not – people are always looking for scapegoats. The balance can quite easily tip."

Another white mother who didn't want to live in an ethnically mixed area said:

> "As long as they keep theirselves to theirselves I don't mind. I would rather it was all white down here – but you can't have that now – can't be prejudiced because we're all equal. They're quite nice.... I've got nothing against them, but I'd sooner be with my own colour." (Sonia)

Sonia's views reflected an increasing awareness of equal opportunities policies, although her underlying feeling was that she didn't like the change. She hadn't chosen to live together with people of different ethnic backgrounds, but realised she might as well get on with it.

Mixed neighbourhoods can work really well

We have explained in detail people's experience of the problems of living in an ethnically mixed area because it is such a live issue and is a genuinely difficult challenge for people. The problems, however, must not overshadow the many positive experiences we recorded. We asked families what they thought were the good aspects of living in an ethnically mixed area. Just 13 families could think of no positive aspects; although some of them could think of no negative aspects either. Thirty-nine families gave as the main reason that people gain from mixing with people of other cultures; they learn from them, it's more interesting, people just *should* mix. The next most important reasons (both mentioned by 19 families) were that it was particularly good for children to mix, and that people "just get on" and "it wasn't a problem". Twelve families identified that it was nice to taste different kinds of cooking, and to be able to buy ethnic foodstuffs locally. Five families said that it made them more flexible and gave them a greater understanding. Views were fairly evenly balanced between racial groups, as Table 4.5 opposite shows.

Table 4.5: Good things about living in an ethnically mixed area: the families' views (number of comments)

	White British and Irish	Euro, others[a]	Black and Asian	Mixed race	Total
People should mix/you gain from others, learn about other cultures	14	7	10	7	39[a]
It's great for children to mix					
— it increases understanding, respect, makes them feel part of the wider society	9	0	4	3	16
— so minority ethnic children don't feel inferior	0	0	0	1	3[a]
In general people get on/fit in better/it's good/not a problem	3	5	10	1	19
Taste different cooking, can get specific foodstuffs	7	2	1	2	12
The acceptance — makes you more flexible/understanding	4	1	0	0	5
Other reason[b]	1	0	4	0	5
No good things mentioned	6	2	2	1	11
Don't know	1	0	1	0	2
Not recorded	2	0	2	0	4
Total (some families made more than one comment)	47	17	35	15	116[a]

Notes: [a] Includes two comments made by the family who declined the question about ethnicity. [b] Reasons given by no more than one family were: having more people of your own ethnicity gives more possibility for mutual help; there's a good street market; the council is evicting people who are racially harassing others; 'it's about the community'; feel more at ease than if it's predominantly black or white.

We will now look a little more closely at what people mean by these assets of positive race relations.

One general view was that it makes life better and more interesting:

"It is really quite nice because you are learning to talk with other people that come from a totally different country. You feel a little bit more in touch with the whole world perhaps. It is a nice feeling. Years ago you wouldn't have dreamt that you would have come home and said 'Oh, I spoke to a Russian today'. That is quite nice." (Peggy)

"I think it's brilliant that all different people can mix together because at the end of the day they've all got to work together, live together." (Refika)

"It's good to live together and make friends. You gain from other people's strong points. You contribute to living together in the area peacefully." (Dominique)

"You're able to share, appreciate people, you're not limited to your own little world." (Aminia)

"Quality of life is brilliant. It is not always easy. But I think that is the future – the world is becoming more mixed." (Joanne)

"I would think of the good things – you learn from other people's beliefs, values, cultures, lifestyle, religion." (Delilah)

"It's more interesting. You see all the different cultures, all the different food stores. The schools – one would have open evenings with all the multi-cultural food. I don't know how to explain it – I think it's more vibrant." (Ellie)

The popular view that it helps children mix, accept and appreciate differences is a strong counterweight to the potential problems families face in bringing their children up in an area which is so heterogeneous:

"Especially if you're going to bring up children – you want to teach them that everybody's the same regardless of colour, so it's very good." (Audrey)

"On the whole, I think it's quite good because then you do know other cultures. It's good for the kids to know they're part of wider society and not just white East-Docks. That's personally." (Rachel)

"The children are exposed to all different cultures and backgrounds. They should learn to become more tolerant of other people. And it makes life more interesting, I suppose." (Nadia)

"I want my children not to be racist." (Jackie)

"From a young age, the children do learn to mix. The younger ones especially, you see it in school; they don't care about colour or race or whatever, it is nice. The older ones have a problem more so than the younger ones but that is changing, because from a young age they've been brought up with it and they don't know any different. 10 or 20 years down the line there will be very little racism at all." (Barbara)

"The good thing is – that's life isn't it? My children are going to have a variety of friends so they get to know everything about everyone … different celebrations in school … so it's not just tunnel vision." (Tina)

"You don't stick out, and when your children go to school they could never point a finger because there are too many!" (Millie)

"I love it. It's good for children growing up as well – they get to know we're all as good as each other. And it doesn't make them feel inferior either." (Annie)

By virtue of living in close proximity, sharing many common elements of life, people learn to accept each other:

"If we just lived in one area and [separated people into different groups], I think that would create more of a divide. I think people realise that we're all men and women and we all do the same things – work, eat, live. I think people realise that people aren't so different from what they are." (Natasha)

People were often struck by the colour-blind relationships they saw:

"In the nursery, they don't even look at colours. People have lived with each other for so long – it's part of life. I don't think my children ever talk about black and white." (Sasha)

And several black and minority ethnic families in both neighbourhoods emphasised how they had not found racism and racial harassment to be a problem in their area:

"I didn't have a problem at all since I moved here." (Snejana)

"I didn't see any racism. I'm happy. Neighbours from Ghana, Jamaica, Irish, Turkish. Different culture, different people. I like it." (Onur)

"I've never encountered that. This is my tenth year in this house." (Sasha)

"It's a very multi-racial area now. Plenty of Africans, Asians, Arabs, whites. We all respect each other. We all take our kids to school – we are always meeting and talking there." (Said)

One of the most striking findings was that more than two families in five found living in an ethnically mixed area an entirely positive experience, with no negative aspects. Forty-one families did not mention any negative aspects of living in an ethnically mixed area at all:

"I don't know about bad ... we have all got different things in our lives. I wouldn't want to say anything bad. We can all give and receive different things from each other." (Joyce)

"If you all try and get on, there really shouldn't be anything bad about people coming together and trying to mix." (Annie)

"You get to learn different ways of life of different people. You then learn how to adapt to the different ways of life. By the time you get close to the person, you realise there's more to the person than his race or his colour, and just live happily with him." (Shushan)

These views, often expressed against a backdrop of serious tensions and problems, bear out some of the optimism people expressed about their community and why it worked for them and their neighbourhood. Could these positive experiences help community relations more generally?

When relations between different ethnic groups go right

Just over half the families in West-City (51%) and 63% in East-Docks – felt that people lived together well. The biggest group said 'okay' and the smallest 'very well'. A quarter of the families in both neighbourhoods explained that people did not live together very well, or did not really 'live together' at all.

Black and Asian families made more positive comments, and were less likely to express problems than 'white UK' and Irish families. A total of 70% of black or Asian families felt that people lived together well or okay, compared with 44% of 'white UK' families. Nearly three times as many 'white UK' and Irish families as black and Asian families talked about problems in answer to this question. Even so, more white families are positive about community and race relations (16) than are negative (14).

Table 4.6: The families' views on how well people of different races lived together

	West-City (%)	East-Docks (%)	Overall %
Total positive	51	63	57
Okay	28	29	28
Fine/fairly good	17	27	22
Very well	6	7	7
Total 'negative'	25	24	25[a]
Not very well/some problems	19	20	20
Badly	0	2	1
They don't 'live together' at all	6	2	5
It depends – some do, some don't	11	4	8
Not recorded	4	9	7
Don't know	9	0	4
Total (= 100%)	47 families	45 families	92 families

Note: [a] Rounded %.

Table 4.7: The families' views on how well people lived together, compared with family ethnicity (number of families)

	White British and Irish	Euro, others	Black and Asian	Mixed race	Declined	Total
Total 'positive/okay'	16	9	23	3	1	52
Total 'negative'/some problems	14	0	5	4	–	23
It depends	3	0	2	2	–	7
Not recorded	2	1	2	1	–	6
Don't know	1	2	1	0	–	4
Total families	36	12	33	10	1	92

Having explored the problems in earlier sections, here we focus on the signs of positive race relations that people identified. Since positive views about how families live together dominate negative views, we relay as fully as we can what people actually said.

The most straightforward and common view was that people live together pretty well:

> "I think very well, considering the area we live in. When we came here 20 years ago, there were very few black people around. It was literally white East-Enders, very few black families, and over the years more and more and more, and the culture has changed." (Barbara)

> "Even the guys that go round doing all these things – they're black and white. It might be crime, but at least they're mixing!" (Miriam)

> "They're doing well. We're not having people cutting off their heads or fighting! Prejudices might exist, but it's not to the fore – nobody notices it." (Dominique)

One important community asset was the often positive relationship between younger black families and elderly white people:

> "There are lots of elderly whites – quite nice people. You can have a problem with someone who's black – it's a strange world. African and Caribbean are so different." (Aminia)

> "Funnily enough, you can hardly count an English person in this block now. Apart from two old ladies, and I met them here when I first moved in. They were the ones who made me feel really welcome. Of course, when I moved in here I was a single parent and they used to see me struggling, going to work and coming in. This one old

lady used to come and say 'I could hear the baby crying, are you alright? If you need any help … if you want to drop her by and go'. Now the rest of the people I don't know half of them. I've seen new families – Asian, Turkish." (Cynthia)

People also reported that community relations were improving. People often attributed this to education:

"It depends how you interact. Some of the people – especially the white people – haven't got friends from different ethnic backgrounds. With the voluntary work, some of them hadn't even spoken to blacks before, but as soon as we begin to interact, we begin to learn from each other. My [white] neighbour is very nice to me … I might meet a white woman who is nasty to me. It's a matter of information and education." (Hannah)

"I think a lot of people maybe years ago would have said something [racist], but they just turn a blind eye [now] because they have to. They'd be too outnumbered to say anything. A lot more people have become educated. They don't use the terminology like 'coloured' anymore; they say 'black people' now. I used to think it was quite insulting when people said 'the coloured person'." (Flowella)

This opinion is belied by the fact that one or two of our families did use the term 'coloured'. Nonetheless it was true that most of the white families consciously tried to avoid any offensive or stereotyping language.

One of the ways that people improved race relations was through direct interaction between ethnic groups – children's play and adult friendships. This reinforces what people said about the sense of community being mainly engendered by social contact. We asked the families whether their children played with children from other ethnic groups, and whether they had friends from different ethnic groups. Apart from families with babies, all but one said that their children played with children from different ethnic groups.

Many parents were very positive about this, and in fact the experience of a multi-cultural childhood was often a particularly positive aspect of the neighbourhood for families:

"From all nations!" (Louise)

"I think it's important for the kids to mix with all types of people … [otherwise] you're not preparing kids for the real life." (Miriam)

> "Oh yes. In fact my daughter – I always tell her not to talk about colour in the house. She has more white friends than black. I educate her to take people for what they are – that we're all the same." (Frances)

> "I'm really glad that my daughter has grown up with all these different cultures around her – I think it broadens her horizons." (Joan)

Parents made a distinction between school friends and playing out on the street or the estate. The only parent who answered 'no' to the question about playing with children from other ethnic groups explained that her daughter did not play in the neighbourhood anyway. Another mother answered 'yes', but said "not on the estate, at school". A few other families commented that their children did not play 'out', but did mix with other children in the school playground. One Kurdish mum said that her children had black friends but not 'English' friends. A mother of mixed race said her son had a mixture of friends, but her daughter was not allowed to play out because of problems with black boys.

The parents themselves were also very likely to have friends from different ethnic groups – 80% of those asked in East-Docks and an even higher proportion – 91% – in West-City.

Two of the mothers in East-Docks who answered 'no' said that they did not have any close friends. One mother in West-City who answered 'yes' commented that they were not close friends. A further five people in East-Docks described having acquaintances or work colleagues rather than actual friends from different ethnic groups. One of these explained her shyness:

> "I am a very reserved person anyway – even with people who come from my area [of Africa]. I have lots of acquaintances, but not to come home. It takes a while to build up a friendship. I go to the shops with people from my block – we talk together." (Aminia)

One mother who had a mixed group of friends commented that not many of these friends lived in her neighbourhood.

There was very little variation between different ethnic groups – of recorded responses, 88% of 'white UK' and Irish, 90% of black and Asian families, and 89% of mixed race families said they had friends from different ethnic groups. The largest 'group' who did not was the broad 'Euro, others' group – three out of ten families asked the question said that they didn't have friends from other ethnic groups. Two were Kurdish and one Kosovan.

People on the whole accepted the fact of a multi-cultural, multi-racial society: "It's just life".

> "Whether you think you want to mix or not, you're gonna have to!"
> (Annie)

"If you don't want any problem, you don't get any problem. You stick to yourself." (Becca)

"I wouldn't say it's good or bad, I would just say it's life. I don't think it's stopping racists from being racist just because they're living in a mixed area." (Emily)

Overall living in a mixed neighbourhood is good

Nearly 70% of the families in both neighbourhoods felt that, overall, living in an ethnically mixed area was positive. Slightly more families in East-Docks (13%) said that it was less positive than families in West-City (9%).

Of the 92 families, 76% of black and Asian families said that living in a mixed area was more positive, compared with 61% of 'white UK' and Irish families. Only one black or Asian family felt that it was less positive. Table 4.8 shows the views of different ethnic groups on living in an ethnically mixed neighbourhood.

The somewhat more positive views of minority families match their more optimistic assessment of how well different races live together. Given black people's open views on the problems, particularly racial harassment, it is unlikely that the interviewer being white is the main explanation. It seems more likely that white people see their position deteriorating under pressure from new incoming groups, while minority groups see their position improving as they gain access to housing and other services.

Should the balance of these communities shift more completely towards becoming 'minority ghettos', a fear expressed by a few families of different races, then people might become far more pessimistic about community relations. One thing that came out clearly from the families' views on community relations was the need for contact, for the chance to meet and get to know each other. In this sense, segregation, particularly along racial lines, is anathema to harmonious community relations between ethnic groups. Conversely, mixing is the bedrock of the better relationships the families most often describe.

Table 4.8: Feelings about living in an ethnically mixed area (number of families, % within ethnicity in brackets)

	White British and Irish	Euro, others	Black and Asian	Mixed race	Total
More positive	22 (61%)	8 (67%)	25 (76%)	7 (70%)	63[a] (68%)
Neither one nor the other	4	1	4	–	9
Less positive	5	1	1	3	10
Don't know	3	2	2	–	7
Not recorded	2	–	1	–	3
Total families	36	12	33	10	92

Note: [a] Includes one family who declined the question about ethnicity.

Summary and conclusions

Within a global city, these neighbourhoods are experiencing rapid ethnic change. With a history of racial antagonism, they are both now experiencing some inter-ethnic tensions. There is competition for housing, worry about pressures on schools and generally mixed feelings. Families saw the dangers of segregation and were three times more worried about racial harassment than the London average.

But 68% of families think that an ethnic mixture is a positive thing, almost all children play together across racial boundaries and 86% of interviewees asked had friends of other races. A total of 57% think that people of different backgrounds live well or were 'okay' together.

The scales are not evenly balanced between the views of different groups about living in a racially mixed neighbourhood. A higher proportion of black and minority ethnic than white families think that different races live well together; and similarly a higher proportion of black and minority ethnic than white families are positive about living in a racially mixed area.

There are several possible reasons for this. Minority families were conscious of having arrived more recently, having overcome initial racial hostility, having broken through into previously inaccessible areas. This contributed to a positive feeling of progress despite the problems. In addition, both areas are undergoing major regeneration and therefore show visible signs of improving. For many residents from minority groups, their situation is improving.

Some white families, in contrast, feel squeezed by the population shifts, particularly on the housing front because of difficulties in gaining a transfer to better housing, wanting but failing to be rehoused near family members because newcomers get priority, or failing to exercise the Right to Buy because they worry that they won't be able to sell or afford the new prices. This was a particularly sore point in West-City where recent valuations put the Right to Buy out of reach of most ordinary families (although some valuations had been successfully challenged, see Chapter Ten). They were also worried about schools where they saw white children rapidly becoming a minority. Their fears about growing segregation and a feeling of displacement were real and clearly articulated. This interpretation, based on what families said, fits with evidence from other parts of the country and from other work (Ratcliffe, 2001; Bowman, 2001; Burnley Task Force, 2001; Home Office, 2001; Oldham Independent Review, 2001).

There appeared to be a serious danger of increasing tension despite the considerable progress in community relations over the last few years, simply by a process of council housing allocation to the most needy (increasingly refugees) and people's worries about minority group-dominated schools. Unless concrete steps are taken to prevent racial polarisation in these two fields of social policy, the positive experiences of families living in ethnically mixed neighbourhoods may disappear, simply because, if present trends continue, they may not remain mixed.

It is not simple racism that causes white families to worry about these things; it is the visible and rapid shift in population, commented on by people of all races. Black families also worried about neighbourhoods becoming 'majority minority', and about large numbers of newcomers putting additional pressure on already limited resources. Council decisions about priorities for housing allocations can make a big difference. The time people have to wait for help can be unduly lengthened by more important priorities jumping to the front of the queue. Often asylum-seekers are used as an excuse for not helping other residents. The scale and speed of change in the ethnic patterns of the neighbourhoods could put too much pressure on fragile social networks and already pressured community resources.

If this happens, a great opportunity will be lost. For both white and black families have many positive things to say about living together. Generally, people feel that the world is going to be ethnically mixed, that it brings richness and excitement, that it helps children grow up with broader minds, and that it makes people feel better about each other. The families went out of their way to emphasise the good experiences, the friendships and kindness, the generally harmonious experiences. The overwhelming majority had friends from different ethnic backgrounds and their children mixed freely. This was only possible as long as the neighbourhoods remained mixed.

One of the most significant contributions to the public debate on community relations since the disorders in Northern towns of 2001 is the analysis by Ash Amin of Durham University of what he calls 'banal encounters'. By this he means the day-to-day casual and informal contacts between people of different races in public places – the streets, buses, libraries, parks, markets, public amenities of all sorts and town centres. He argues that these fine-grained, semi-invisible micro-links of undeclared sociability help diverse groups 'rub along together' and maintain a sense of familiarity and contact (Amin, 2002). This argument is supported by the experience of Northern Ireland where building community cohesion is painstakingly slow and reliant on the shared use of public spaces of all kinds (CRE, 2001; Hanna, 2001). It fits with our theory, based on families' experiences, that community and community relations are made up of very small-scale, barely visible, highly localised actions and contacts, that do indeed weave a positive web of support around the families in their links with their neighbours, often of different races.

Avoiding the levels of racial segregation that have come to dominate many American cities is essential to inter-racial contact and communication. For different ethnic groups to live together harmoniously there must be public and social spaces where people share 'common ground', in the literal sense. Many writers have explored the issues of racial segregation and inter-communal relations within urban communities in great detail, for example, Massey and Denton's impressive study of American apartheid and Jargowsky's detailed study of ghetto expansion (Massey and Denton, 1993; Jargowsky, 1997). We believe that the insights our families shared with us lend new depth to this important subject as they come to be debated more openly in Europe (van Kempen and Ozuekren, 1998).

Thus people's views on race relations, complex, diverse, anxious, but generally positive, reinforced people's sense of community and its importance. Living in a multi-ethnic neighbourhood brought tensions and difficulties, but overall people wanted to get on together, believed that social contact and interaction mattered, thought that inter-racial understanding was helped by this contact, and worried a great deal when things went wrong. They wanted their neighbourhoods – their communities – to be places where people got on, whatever their ethnic background.

FIVE

Families and work: mothers in paid work

"There's just no time. I rush to get home, rush to get up.... I think people feel sorry [for you when] parents don't work. [But] we [working parents] probably need twice as much support. I feel as though I need to be supported even more because I'm not at home to give the children attention some of the time.... I don't go [to the park] that regularly, and the other day my daughter was crying. I just don't have the energy. Half the things that parents that are at home are able to do, I just can't." (Miriam)

Introduction

Neighbourhoods provide the homes, the local services, the framework for people's lives. In Part 1 we showed that for families, social relations are incredibly important, generating as they do a sense of community and harmonious inter-racial relations. But there is another dimension that is possibly as important and for which neighbourhoods often provide the springboard – the world of work.

Around half of the mothers we interviewed were in paid work, and we wanted to understand as much as possible about the kind of work, the work histories, qualifications and work ambitions of the mothers. We were also interested in how wider changes in jobs were affecting the families, and whether the buoyant job market was having any effect in these areas, particularly on women. We know that low pay, low skills, unemployment and poverty, particularly among families with children, are deeply interconnected (McKnight, 2002). We also know that women, young people and people from ethnic minority groups are particularly likely to experience low pay or to be actually out of work. Lone parents are in an especially vulnerable position. Therefore the parents we interviewed gave us useful new insights into changing work patterns, particularly for women living in low-income families within poorer areas.

In low-income neighbourhoods there are many important questions about the world of work. Do men fare differently from women? In what direction are work patterns moving – closer together or further apart? Is the shift to part-time service jobs from full-time manual jobs a dominant pattern? How low actually is low pay and how seriously does low pay undermine a woman's incentive to work? How long a break from work do women take to care for their families? And how difficult is it to go back to work after such a break? How are people's skills developing? What ambitions do mothers have? How mobile are the mothers? How constraining is childcare? What is important to the mothers at home? Do people want to change their current situation by entering or leaving the labour market, or by changing jobs, and what barriers do they face? How is a mother's opportunity linked to whether they are alone or living with a partner? These are some of the questions that our East End mothers helped us to answer.

In this chapter we explore what families, and particularly mothers, do if they work. In Chapter Six we examine the experience of mothers at home. We focus mainly on the mothers because they were the main participants in our interviews. We include information about other family members, including partners, for example, where possible.

The families' overall employment situation

Proportion of families employed, and type of employment

Of the 100 families we interviewed in the first round of the research, one third had no one in work; 24 of these were headed by a lone parent. Each neighbourhood had a similar number of workless households – 16 in West-City and 17 in East-Docks. In East-Docks, lone parents headed 16 out of the 17 workless households, compared to 8 out of 16 in West-City. There were a lot more lone parents among the East-Docks families (62% compared to 28% in West-City).

The 100 families included 169 adults of working age (aged 18-59), parents, grown-up children and extended family members. Of those 169 individuals, 97 (57%) were working (47 in West-City and 50 in East-Docks). A further four 16- and 17-year-olds were also working, three full-time and one as part of an apprenticeship (one in West-City and three in East-Docks). In all, there were 101 workers within the sample 100 families.

There was substantial variation by ethnicity. As Table 5.1 shows, 70% of the 'white British' and Irish adults aged 18-59 were working, compared to 53% of

Table 5.1: Whether adults aged 18-59 were working, by ethnicity (number of adults, % of particular ethnic group in brackets)

	White British and Irish	Euro, others	Black and Asian	Mixed race	None of these/ declined
Adults in paid employment	55 (70)	9 (31)	29 (53)	2 (50)	2 (67)

Source: Round 1 interview with 100 families

the black and Asian adults, and just 31% of adults in the 'Euro, others' group. Nationally, black and people from ethnic minority groups are more likely to be registered unemployed (SEU, 2000a). In West-City, in 1999 the registered unemployment rate for black people and people from ethnic minority groups was 28%, 12 percentage points higher than for the working-age population as a whole (16%) (West-City New Deal Trust, 2000a). In the next chapter we explore some of the barriers faced specifically by the non-working mothers who wanted to enter the labour market.

The distribution of jobs (including apprenticeships) of the 101 workers, classified according to the standard occupational classification, is shown in Table 5.2.

There is a very wide range of occupations and wage levels, with 20% of the workers in both neighbourhoods in managerial or professional occupations. At the other end of the scale, at the time of the first interview, 14% of the East-Docks families and 10% of the West-City families were in receipt of in-work benefits (such as Housing Benefit), an indicator of low wages (Mumford, 2001).

In both areas, the commonest form of employment was in the personal and protective service occupations, which includes jobs relating to childcare, educational assistance, caretaking, catering and security, among other things. Seven women were employed in these service jobs for every man, as Table 5.3 shows. Conversely, four men for every woman were working in manual occupations.

Part-time work

The employed women in the sample were more than twice as likely as the men to be working part-time: 40% of women compared with 15% of men. Even so, a surprisingly high proportion of men were working part-time, nearly double

Table 5.2: Occupations of the working adults in our families (%)

	West-City[a]	East-Docks[b]	Total (%)
Managers and administrators	4	2	3
Professional occupations	10	9	9
Associate professional and technical occupations	6	8	7
Clerical and secretarial occupations	21	13	17
Craft and related occupations	10	17	14
Personal and protective service occupations[c]	27	32	30
Sales occupations	2	2	2
Plant and machine operatives	8	9	9
Other occupations	6	8	7
Not recorded/declined	4	–	2
Total (= 100%)	48 workers	53 workers	100%

Notes: [a] Total of 48 current workers in our sample, of whom 29 were men and 19 were women. [b] Total of 53 current workers in our sample, of whom 25 were men and 28 were women. [c] Personal and protective service occupations include jobs relating to childcare, educational assistance, caretaking, catering, security and related tasks.

Source: Mumford (2001)

Table 5.3: Occupations of the working adults in our families, by gender (% within gender)

	Male	Female
Managers and administrators	6	0
Professional occupations	9	11
Associate professional and technical occupations	7	6
Clerical and secretarial occupations	20	13
Craft and related occupations	20	6
Personal and protective service occupations	7	55
Sales occupations	0	4
Plant and machine operatives	15	2
Other occupations	11	2
Not recorded/declined	4	0
Total (=100%)	54 male workers	47 female workers

Source: Round 1 interviews with 100 families

the national average of 8% (*Labour Market Trends*, 1998). Three women were working full-time for every two working part-time.

We also found substantial variation by ethnicity in the split between full and part-time work. For example, all the 'white British' and Irish male workers were in full-time employment (including one in an apprenticeship), compared to just over two thirds of the black and Asian male workers. 'White British' and Irish working women were also more likely to be in full-time employment (61%) compared to black and Asian working women (50%). Table 5.4 shows the differences.

Comparing the employment situation of lone mothers and mothers living as part of a couple

Female lone parents in the sample were slightly more likely to be in paid employment (45%) than the mothers living as part of a couple (42%), and slightly more likely to work full-time. These proportions are well under the national

Table 5.4: Whether workers were in full-time employment[a], by gender and ethnicity (number of people, % within ethnicity in brackets)

	White British and Irish	Euro, others	Black and Asian	Mixed race	Declined	Total
Full-time paid work						
Male	30 (100)	3 (43)	9 (69)	3 (100)	1 (100)	46 (85)
Female	7 (61)	2 (100)	8 (50)	–	1 (100)	28 (60)

Note: [a] Includes those doing full-time apprenticeships even though they may include a substantial amount of college attendance.

Source: Round 1 interviews with 100 families

Table 5.5: Whether mothers were in paid employment or studying full-time, by 'couple status' (%)

	Mothers in the East London sample		
	Living in couple (%)	Lone parent (%)	Total (%)
Full-time job[a]	24	27	25
Part-time job[a]	18	18	18
Studying full-time	4	2	3
Not working or studying f-t	55	53	54
Total (=100%)	55 mothers	44 mothers	99 mothers[b]
	(23 working)	(20 working)	(43 working)[c]

Notes: [a] Includes self-employment. [b] We interviewed one lone father; he was not working. [c] The total of 43 working mothers is less than the total of 47 female workers because four working women in our sample were not mothers; they were usually adult children living with their parent(s).

Source: Round 1 interviews with 100 families

average of 60%+ of all mothers working, but only just over the national average of lone parents working (Hales et al, 2000, p 32), and much higher than the 1991 Census Hackney and Newham averages of 27% of lone parents working (Mumford, 2001). Table 5.5 shows the distribution of employment in the sample. This pattern does not reflect a random selection of families. We went to places that families use, at different times on weekdays (for example, post office, playgroup, GP surgeries), in the evening (school parent evenings), and at weekends (church). We wanted to make sure that we did not exclude working mothers by only recruiting interviewees through daytime activities. At the same time, we did not especially target working mothers. We were keen to include families with a mix of working and non-working parents. The situation of all the working-age adults (aged 18-59) in the sample is reasonably comparable with the populations of the neighbourhoods and boroughs as a whole. A total of 45% of the West-City adults were not in work, study or training, compared to 39% of the overall working-age population of West-City. The figures for East-Docks were 33% and 42% respectively. A much higher proportion of the adults involved in the study were 'work poor' than the national average. Table 5.6 illustrates this.

Table 5.6: 'Work poverty': the proportion of the working-age population not in work, study or training (% in 'work poverty')

West-City[a]	39 (16+)
50 West-City families[b]	45
East-Docks[c]	42
50 East-Docks families[b]	33
Hackney[c]	36
Newham[c]	36
Inner London[c]	30
Greater London[c]	26
Great Britain[c]	25

Notes: [a] 1999 West-City New Deal for Communities survey. [b] First round interviews. [c] 1991 Census.

Source: Mumford (2001)

Changes over the course of the research

When we talked to the mothers for the second time, we asked those in employment about their current job and their thoughts about future employment. All the mothers in work at the time of the first interview remained in work, although one was now on long-term sick leave. None of the eight mothers who took part in the first round but not the second round of interviews had a paid job. However, the number of employed mothers recorded in the sample increased between interviews, from 43 to 52. Three other mothers expanded or changed their work. These twelve work changes are shown in Box 5.1.

Box 5.1: The changing work position of mothers
• Two mothers returned to work after maternity leave
• One mother got a full-time job in a school
• One mother got a part-time job in a school
• Five mothers talked about part-time work which was not recorded in the first interview
• One mother changed employer (her core job stayed almost the same)
• One mother increased her hours from part-time to full-time
• One mother took on extra evening work in addition to her full-time and weekend jobs

The work position of mothers had thus expanded, whereas the work position of men had generally not improved (see Box 5.2).

Box 5.2: The changing work position of fathers/step-fathers
• Two fathers lost their jobs and were no longer working
• One father was now in and out of work on a casual basis
• None of the fathers/step-fathers who were out of work had gained a job since the first interview
• One father changed jobs
• One father increased his hours from part-time to full-time

In addition, two families had been joined by working partners who had moved in since the first interview.

Men did not seem to be benefiting from the improved London labour market, whereas women did. This relates to the kinds of job changes that have occurred in West-City and East-Docks, documented by Ruth Lupton (forthcoming). Both neighbourhoods lost three quarters of their manufacturing jobs between 1971 and 1991. Even though West-City saw a growth in service sector jobs at the same time, these jobs tend to require low-skilled workers, often part-time and low paid, and often taken by women. As Table 5.7 shows, both neighbourhoods saw male full-time jobs decline between 1971-91; this was particularly marked in East-Docks.

Table 5.7: Decline in jobs in West-City and East-Docks (1971-91) (%)

	Change in manufacturing jobs	Change in service sector jobs	Net job change (all jobs)	Change in male full-time jobs
West-City	−75	+48	−11	−24
East-Docks	−75	−59	−65	−74

Note: Figures based on amalgamated job centre areas.

Source: Lupton (2003, forthcoming)

The 1990s saw job growth across the country (9% between 1991-98). In West-City, jobs grew at a much higher rate than the national average, with a 30% increase over the period, including significant growth in male full-time jobs. The job growth was directly linked to new office developments, media industries, and the increase in cafes and nightclubs for City workers, and was mainly concentrated in one part of the area, closest to central London. At the same time as these commercial developments took place, West-City's refugee population increased. And all of the other residential neighbourhoods in the area saw smaller job growth and a loss of male full-time jobs. East-Docks actually continued to lose jobs between 1991-98, mainly full-time male jobs (Lupton, forthcoming).

The work trajectories of the employed mothers

We looked at the routes our employed mothers had followed to their current job. We found five main trajectories, two of which had a number of sub-categories. Trying to categorise complex human experiences is fraught with difficulties since everyone's life path is unique. Deciding which work trajectory a person followed involved difficult judgements about job aspects, such as wages, security and prospects, and based on limited information. However, the groupings help us to grasp the large range of experiences that the mothers described to us.

The women's work patterns fell broadly into the following trajectories: *consistent career*, following a steady pattern of work in secure, skilled jobs; *unsteady career*, switching between different 'career-type' jobs; *career progression* from low skilled to more skilled; *career shrinkage*, moving in the opposite direction; *mixed jobs*, covering a mixture of non-professional work experience. Table 5.8 sets out the distribution of the 41 employed mothers who answered this question.

Box 5.3 explains the main work trajectories in more detail, showing how we can sub-divide them into more complex categories.

Four of the six mothers with 'consistent professional career' trajectories had studied as mature students. All but one were black African; the other was Irish. Table 5.9 shows the distribution of work trajectories by ethnicity.

Table 5.8: Five main work trajectories, and the distribution of the employed mothers between them

Trajectory	Number of employed mothers per trajectory
1. Consistent career	8
2. Unsteady career	2
3. Career progression	10
4. Career shrinkage	1
5. Mixed jobs	20
Total	41

Table 5.9: Work trajectories and mothers' ethnicity

Trajectory	White British and Irish	Euro, others	Black and Asian	Total
1. Consistent career				
(a) Professional	1	–	5	6
(b) Other	11	1	5	2
2. Unsteady career	1	–	1	2
3. Career progression	9	–	1	10
4. Career shrinkage	1	–	–	1
5. Mixed jobs				
(a) 'Good', fairly continuous	2	–	1	3
(b) 'Good', not continuous	1	–	2	3
(c) 'Low paid', continuous	3	–	–	3
(d) 'Low paid', steady + gap	2	–	2	4
(e) 'Low paid', unsteady	2	–	4	6
(f) Good & low paid + gaps	–	–	1	1
Total	23	1	17	41

Source: Round 2 interviews

Two of the mothers had had 'unsteady careers'. For one, this was as a result of switching careers following a period at home spent caring for her children. For the other, this had happened as a result of moving. She had been a civil servant until she moved to England and had then had to work her way back into a career from the beginning, starting with a catering job and then gaining a UK degree before moving into social care work:

"Come here, you have to start all over again." (Delilah)

None of the mothers with 'career progression' trajectories had followed a direct path to their current job. Those with degrees had gained them as mature students, rather than going straight to university from school. Some had been teenage parents and left school early. All had juggled family commitments, working their way back into the labour market after periods at home caring for their families

Box 5.3: Types of work trajectories

Work trajectory	Definition
1. Consistent career	A trajectory involving 'career' jobs in the sense that they have a reasonable amount of job security or chances of progression, and require a considerable amount of training/education. Someone with a 'consistent career' has worked in their chosen specialist field since they got there (although some have taken breaks to have children)
(a) Professional	A consistent career involving one of the 'professions' such as teaching, law, or health, and which are regulated by a professional body
(b) Other	Consistent work within a field which is not generally described as a profession, but which in other respects has followed a career path
2. Unsteady career	Work experience switching between career-type jobs with gaps in between – away from the labour market or in non-career-type jobs such as office work
3. Career progression	A trajectory which involves moving to higher-skill, higher responsibility jobs, often with better security and employee benefits. Sometimes involving significant training along the way
4. Career shrinkage	A work trajectory involving a shift from a position of significant responsibility to a job that is paid less and requires fewer qualifications. Sometimes, the mothers with 'progression' trajectories had experienced this shift when they first returned to work after a break, but they had then moved into higher paid jobs
5. Mixed jobs	Work experience that is not part of a career progression, comprising a series of non-professional jobs in the same field or in a variety of different fields
(a) 'Good', fairly continuous	Work experience involving fairly continuous 'good' jobs in that they require some skill, with the potential for training and some progression up the salary/responsibility ladder
(b) 'Good', not continuous	Work experience involving mainly 'good' jobs (as above), with 'gaps' resulting from bringing up families, being fired or being made redundant, travelling, studying, or to bring about a career change
(c) 'Low-paid', fairly continuous	Work experience in jobs that are generally not well-paid, are low-skilled, have few prospects for progression and are vulnerable to any changes in the labour market. Continuous trajectory with few, if any, periods out of the labour market
(d) 'Low-paid', steady with gap	Fairly continuous work experience apart from at least one long gap (of four years or more) because of redundancy or to bring up children
(e) 'Low-paid', unsteady	Work experience involving generally low-paid jobs, interspersed with periods of non-employment
(f) 'Good and low-paid', with gaps	The most mixed trajectory, involving both 'good' and low-paid jobs, with gaps in between

or after being made redundant. For five of these mothers, school employment had been their way back into work, with hours that suited their family commitments and sometimes personal encouragement from head teachers. Once working within a school, they had found good career development opportunities. Nine out of the 10 mothers with career progression trajectories were 'white British' or Irish, whereas only one was from a minority ethnic background.

The fifth and most common trajectory was what we call 'mixed jobs', a series of non-professional jobs, involving moves between either similar or highly varied jobs. A total of 20 of our working mothers had a work experience pattern which fitted into this broad category, so we split it down into six sub-categories to try to capture the variety of their experiences.

Those with the most precarious trajectories – a series of low-paid mixed jobs often with gaps in between – were among those most likely to be working part-time. Three of the four mothers working part-time in these jobs were black.

Two thirds of those with consistent, professional careers were currently working full-time, but so were three quarters of those with fairly continuous work experience in low-paid jobs who had taken at least one long break from paid work. Overall, current full-time and part-time workers were split fairly evenly between the different trajectories.

The following section examines each type of work trajectory in more detail. Appendix 4 shows the patterns of work trajectories for each mother in paid employment.

Looking more closely at the mothers' work patterns

Consistent or unsteady careers (work trajectories 1 and 2)

The eight mothers with consistent careers worked steadily and with few interruptions in the fields they were qualified in. Seven of the eight had recognised training and four had degrees. Only one had no formal qualifications but was trained and skilled as a tailor. The two mothers with unsteady careers both had degrees, but neither had followed a clear professional work pattern.

Career progression or career shrinkage (work trajectories 3 and 4)

Ten mothers had work progressions showing a shift from lower-skilled, less secure, poorly-paid work to positions of greater responsibility, involving training to higher skill levels and an increase in pay and conditions. Only one of these mothers had no basic qualifications; four had O-levels or CSEs, of whom two also had a specialist qualification; two had City & Guilds, of whom one also had a specialist qualification; one had A-levels; and two had degrees. All had started work in casual or low-paid service jobs; nine of the 10 had ended up working for public services, most commonly as assistants or organisers and three as teachers; the tenth had become a pharmaceutical assistant.

One mother's career had gone the other way in the trajectory we term 'career shrinkage', where she ended up as an informal carer having started off as a qualified nursery nurse.

Mixed jobs (work trajectory 5)

The 20 mothers with mixed job trajectories formed the largest group, had the most varied work patterns and the least qualifications. None of them had degrees or equivalent qualifications. Three had no qualifications at all; five had work-related basic qualifications such as NVQs, hairdressing or childcare certificates; six had O-Levels or equivalent certificates, of whom two also had City & Guilds; one had a City & Guilds plus one A-level; one had O- and A-levels; one had the NNEB nursery qualification. (We do not know what qualifications the other three had.)

Six had had a mixture of jobs with reasonably good pay and conditions; three had worked steadily in these jobs; the other three had had periods out of the labour market, for example, to go travelling or to change work direction.

Thirteen had worked in a variety of often insecure, low-paid jobs with poor conditions, three fairly continuously, ten with gaps of varying lengths (of whom half had either been sacked or made redundant at least once). We put childminding in this category because it usually attracts low-pay, weak prospects and vulnerability to change in economic conditions, even though circumstances can vary a lot. One mother's work experience included a mixture of both good and low-paid jobs.

We divided the mixed jobs between two broad headings of 'good' and 'low-paid' based on a whole bundle of job attributes including levels of pay, skills required, job security and opportunities for promotion. We had to make a judgment based on limited information about these elements of a job. The term 'good job' is not intended to imply greater usefulness or inherently better work than 'low-paid job', but to reflect a stronger combination of pay, skills, security and prospects. We did not attempt to classify jobs according to how mothers perceived them, or how we thought other people might regard their status. Later in the chapter we explore how satisfied the mothers are with what they are doing, whether they want to change anything, and what is important to them. Jobs in the 'low-paid' category were sometimes bringing great satisfaction because the nature and location of the work (for example, working with children close to home) was a higher priority to some than conditions of employment, such as pay and security.

People's current jobs broadly reflected their qualifications. However, three findings stand out.

First, quite a lot of mothers are moving into new types of public service jobs as they become more experienced and gain more qualifications. It is possible to access these jobs with only limited initial training.

Second, the women who gained degrees or equivalent qualifications (in teaching or nursing, for example) secured career jobs even though some moved in and out of work because of taking care of their children. They did not always receive a very high salary, and they sometimes worked part-time. But work conditions and prospects were reasonable and compared favourably with non-career jobs.

Third, a majority of the mothers had had a wide variety of jobs, with periods away from the labour market of varying lengths to take care of their children.

Journeys to work

We asked about people's journeys to work because this tells us about the geographical spread of the labour market for mothers. All mothers found combining work with family responsibilities a complicated juggling act. For these reasons, most worked quite nearby. The decision on how far to travel can be determined by the cost, availability and reliability of transport links; the location of jobs; and willingness to travel outside the local area, often linked to people's wishes to be near their home and to their children's schools.

How far the employed mothers travelled to work

The mothers had much shorter journeys to work than the Inner London average for women; the average journey in East-Docks was 18 minutes, around half the Inner London average of 34 minutes. In West-City, the average journey time was 23 minutes. This is close to the national average but low for London (see Table 5.10). Of the 33 women who described their journey to work, three quarters had a journey time of no more than 30 minutes and the largest group travelled for under 10 minutes. A further 10 mothers did paid work within the home involving zero travel, usually as childminders or foster carers.

Table 5.10: Average journey-to-work times of the employed mothers, compared with regional and national averages for all women (minutes)

West-City[a]	23
East-Docks[a]	18
Inner London women[b]	34
Outer London women[b]	32
Rest of South East women[b]	23
UK women[b]	21

Notes: [a] Based on information from 15 working women in both neighbourhoods. Information from three women in East-Docks was not used in calculating the average because their travel-to-work time 'varied greatly'. The 10 women working from home were not included in the calculation. [b] Labour Force Survey, Autumn 1998.

Table 5.11: Usual mode of transport to work of the mothers in the sample, compared with regional and national averages for all women (%)

	East End working mothers[a]	Inner London women[b]	Outer London women[b]	UK women[b]
Car, van, minibus, works van	20	25	52	66
Walk	30	16	11	16
Bus, coach, private bus	8	20	13	11
Railway train	–	10	11	3
Underground train, light railway, tram	5	27	12	2
Bicycle	3	2	1	2
Mixture of methods eg lift in car to work, bus home	18	–	–	–
Not recorded	18	–	–	–
Base (=100%)	40	967	1,897	26,994

Notes: [a] Round 2 interviews; [b] Labour Force Survey, Autumn 1998.

How the employed mothers travelled to work

Even though the 'transport to work' sample is small (40 mothers working outside the home), the proportion of the employed mothers travelling to work on foot is striking: 30% compared with just 16% of all Inner London and UK women (Labour Force Survey, 1998). This is clearly linked to the local nature of the work done by many of the employed mothers, and may be typical for low-income neighbourhoods. It helps illustrate how neighbourhood-focused and connected many working families with young children are, particularly mothers. The counter to this is that low-income families are often cut off from wider opportunities (Schuller et al, 2001).

Only two mothers used the Underground to get to work (one in East-Docks and one in West-City), compared to an Inner London average for women of 27% (Labour Force Survey, 1998). This is linked to the distance some families lived from the Underground, to the local nature of most of the mothers' jobs and to the high cost. The one mother in East-Docks who used the Underground said that her journey time to work had halved since the Underground was extended to East-Docks, from an hour to 30 minutes.

In the sample, those mothers walking to work had relatively short journey times; all but two had journeys of 20 minutes or less. The eight mothers getting to work by car also had journeys of 20 minutes or less, and two had journeys of only 5 minutes. The mothers using public transport had the longest journey times: three of the five mothers travelling to work by bus or Underground had usual journey times of more than 40 minutes.

For many mothers, a car was not an option because of the cost, yet public transport was often slow, expensive and inconvenient for working mothers. It is hard to know how much transport difficulties influenced where mothers worked.

It may be that the local nature of most women's jobs, particularly low-paid and part-time jobs, was the dominant influence.

Family life and paid employment: how mothers combine the two

Some employed mothers had taken just brief periods of maternity leave, made childminding arrangements, and maintained a fairly continuous presence in the labour market. Others had shifted from full-time to part-time work (and sometimes back again) to fit in with bringing up their children:

> "Eventually I want to do teaching full-time, but now is not the right time with my youngest son not at school." (Tina)

> "The hours [being a play-worker] are just perfect – it fits in with the children." (Sarah)

Some had changed jobs entirely – going to work in schools or becoming childminders for example – in order to fit in with their children's hours and holidays:

> "[I changed to childminding because I was] fed up with paying for two childminders – I couldn't afford it. Not being able to have time off in the holidays when my children were off." (Alice)

One mother had left her management job because the hours became too much, and her husband was having to do all the cooking for the family; she changed to a part-time secretarial job instead:

> "It was always World War III when I come home!" (Marilyn)

Another mother left her full-time job to become self-employed with more flexible hours, in order to put in more time to help her child:

> "Because my daughter has special needs and she wasn't getting help and she was starting to get into trouble. I was taking so many days off to go down to the council offices arguing." (Sinead)

Another mother found the homeworking that she did quite boring, but put up with it for family reasons:

> "At least you can do it and stay at home with your kids." (Carrie)

Many mothers had spent different amounts of time at home, ranging from months to more than 10 years. Sometimes these periods at home were interspersed with paid jobs.

Often, returning to paid work after a period spent at home with the family meant taking lower-paid jobs than the mothers had worked in previously, and it could be hard to adjust back into a work pattern. One mother had recently returned to work after five years at home taking care of her children. She was now enjoying the job, but had found the first few weeks really difficult:

> "Just getting back into the routine of working again. Fitting the housework in basically. I come in and don't really want to do anything." (Rachel)

Many mothers explained during the interviews how they juggled the two commitments to employer and family, illustrating how tough it could be. One mother described how she had taken on an extra commitment – a university degree – in addition to her part-time job. She completed one year of the course but, although she loved it, had realised that she could not juggle her children's needs, her job and university, and one thing had to go. One day she was washing up and trying to think of the next line of her essay when she realised that her young son was just sitting on his bed doing nothing. That was a turning point, and she gave up university:

> "They depend on you." (Annie)

For lone parents, these issues could be brought into even sharper relief. Although people sometimes had support from friends and relatives, there was not another parent there on a regular basis to share the school run, or to be there in the evening when their child got home from school, or to share other aspects of parenting apart from the practical:

> "Nothing [I've done] has been full-time work because I've decided to stay at home and be here to collect her from school etc, and be a part of her life, because I wasn't with her Dad. I thought it would be important for her to have a stable upbringing." (Flowella)

Both lone parents and mothers living as part of a couple often referred to living life in a rush. Getting children to childminders can be very difficult:

> "To pick my son up for me has been really hectic – picking and dropping from one childminder to the next." (Frances)

One mother who had recently returned to work following a brief period of maternity leave explained how hard finding good childcare was:

"It's been a nightmare – I don't understand. She is at a childminder at the moment, but it's so difficult. For the prices that people are paying – they're registered, but [I'm not impressed with] the environment.... I wish my company ... could do more for parents. Like offering us crèches – even if it meant docking our monthly wages. A lot of people have to take special leave and companies aren't sympathetic to that at all. They portray an anti-baby stance." (Shushan)

Mothers were becoming aware of the government's efforts to improve their position through the Working Families' Tax Credit. Certainly one mother, who had started working part-time in a school since the first interview, had found a leaflet about the Tax Credit very helpful:

"It gave me the encouragement and the belief that I will be able to get some help. It works out better than being on Income Support. The money is not that great – but it is better." (Andaiye)

But although the Working Families' Tax Credit includes a childcare credit towards the cost of childcare, people are only able to claim this for registered childminders. For some mothers this was off-putting, as they only wanted to leave their children with friends, relatives, or other people they knew, rather than choosing a registered childminder from a list:

"I want someone I can trust." (Cynthia)

This suggests that the government's attempts to ensure high quality 'official' childcare are working against the preferences of many mothers for a more familiar and known figure to play this important role. It is actually a different view of quality. However, the government is looking into how they can broaden the eligibility criteria for the childcare credit without compromising the standard of childcare provided (A. McKnight, meeting with the author, December 2000).

Some mothers explained why they had chosen to combine work and motherhood – financial reasons were clearly important. One lone mother was juggling three different jobs, filling up most days, evenings and weekends. She felt that she had to do this to meet the increasingly expensive needs of her children as they became older – two are now teenagers:

"You can't sit back – you have to go and look for money!" (Sasha)

But non-financial reasons could also be significant. One lone mother with four children explained how important she felt it was for her to set an example for her children by going out to work and by not claiming benefits:

"People said I was crazy to take a job 10 days after finishing [my degree]: I'm a lone parent, I could have got Income Support. But I wanted to set an example [to my children].... Because I'm working, they know I won't be happy seeing them on benefit. If I can do it – why can't you? I set an example for them to follow.... I'm working and helping them.... Sometimes we just sit down around this table and discuss our problems.... A lone parent with all this lot and a full-time job! The kids cooperated throughout my college time, otherwise I wouldn't have done it." (Hannah)

Satisfaction with current job and thoughts for the future

We asked those mothers currently in employment how satisfied they were with their current job. Over a third were very satisfied and nearly a third were fairly satisfied, although many said that they found some aspects of their job frustrating. Only 6% said they were dissatisfied.

Mothers gave different reasons for their satisfaction. For many, work fitted with family, and gave them a sense of independence:

Table 5.12: The employed mothers' satisfaction with their current job (%)

Very satisfied	38
Fairly satisfied	31
Neither satisfied nor dissatisfied	8
Slightly dissatisfied	4
Very dissatisfied	2
Not recorded	17
Total (=100%)	52

Source: Round 2 interviews

"I have time to take my kids. I have time to drop my son at school and pick him up. The money's low, but I love the clients I work with.... I don't like the idea of depending on the state. I'll be doing it for now, it's satisfying my needs." (Frances)

Some of the jobs the women are progressing into are linked to schools. Mothers enjoy working as school assistants despite the pressures and stresses it brings:

"Very satisfied. Every job gets stressful and you get fed up, but at the end of the day we can all laugh about our lives!"

Interviewer: "Do you want to leave?"

"No. Only if I win the lottery like everyone else! Depending on how much I win! I suppose we all have that little dream. No, I'm quite happy. It gets really busy sometimes, it isn't just the little job I went into when I started – it is vastly changed. Things can get on top of you sometimes, but at the end of the day we are all in the same boat. I went to that school myself when I was little and then my kids went there, so it is nice – I feel like it is my second home. You put up with all the stress." (Peggy)

Many of the women work with children and get great satisfaction from the work. They feel it is a skill they can use. One foster mother accepted the limited income because the work was so rewarding:

"I'm very satisfied doing the practical care of the children – I love doing this. I find working for social services incredibly frustrating because they are in such a mess. Lots of things go wrong and money doesn't come on time and children's cases aren't treated speedily and all sorts that cause it to be extremely frustrating. I'm happy doing fostering and I don't plan to stop for a while.… It is not paid employment – you just get an allowance for the child and we live on Income Support and Housing Benefit basically.…. The idea of making a lot of money appeals, but goodness knows how you ever do that! I've resigned myself to the fact that I won't ever have enough money to do what we'd really like to do." (Joan)

Despite the high levels of satisfaction, more than a quarter said that they wanted to leave their current job. Sometimes wanting to leave was more of a desire rather than something people were taking practical steps to achieve.

Of the 15 mothers who wanted to leave their current job, a third wanted to leave because they wanted to develop a specific career or wanted a greater challenge.

A mother working as a learning support assistant in a school wanted to train to be a teacher; others wanted a job that would stretch them more. These mothers had ambitions to progress and believed that their abilities were being underused:

"I like the job. It's just a cleaning job. Everybody is nice, but personally I think I'm capable of doing more and I feel a bit frustrated, and they can tell that because I keep applying for jobs here and there. I think I'm capable of doing something better." (Cynthia)

"I'm ready for a career change, I would like to leave. I've reached stalemate; I can't go any higher. I have done the majority of courses. I want something more interesting or challenging." (Tessa)

Nationally, one of the main reasons for women wanting to leave their current job is that their pay is unsatisfactory. In the UK 23% of women surveyed gave this as the main reason they wanted to change current jobs (Labour Force Survey, 1998) (see Table 5.13).

Table 5.13: Reason for wanting to leave current job nationally (% of those who wanted to leave)

Reason for wanting to leave	UK women
Pay unsatisfactory in present job	23
Other aspects of present job unsatisfactory	23
Present job may come to an end	13
Present job to fill in time before finding another	11
Wants longer hours than in present job	8
Journey unsatisfactory in present job	5
Wants shorter hours than in present job	3
Other reasons	14
Total	100%

Source: Labour Force Survey, Autumn 1998 (based on 1,731 respondents)

This national picture matches the mothers' views from the sample. Just over a quarter of the employed mothers who wanted to leave their current job also gave pay as their main reason:

> "When the kids are in nursery full-time, I'd like to get a job that's properly paid. A salary that I feel I can live on." (Faye)

One mother pointed out the link between low pay and long hours. She said that if she could earn a better rate of pay, she would be able to reduce the number of hours she worked:

> "They said part-time, but we're doing 45 to 50 hours a week. I don't like it – it's too much. The money is £3.70. That is why [I have to work more hours]." (Naomi)

Other mothers wanted to move from part-time to full-time work, but were seriously constrained by childcare responsibilities:

> "I want lots of changes. I want to be in a job that is going to pay me a fair wage to keep my head and my child's head above water, and I'm going to find beneficial to myself, very rewarding. I don't think I'm ever going to find the perfect job – it's going to be a mixture of all different things together."

> Interviewer: "Have you experienced any obstacles so far?"

> "Only obstacles in the sense of having a child to bring up, so it is a case of childcare and who do you trust, how do you pay etc, etc, and the longer you leave it, the less confident you feel. You have to build up your own confidence again.... I always drop her off to school and get back in time to collect her." (Flowella)

A fifth of the employed mothers who wanted to leave their job were childminders, working from home, who wanted adult company and the chance to work in the outside world. Some had found that childminding was a good option when their own children were of pre-school age, because they could look after them at the same time as doing their paid childminding. But once their own children started school, the main rationale for doing the childminding job went:

> "It's not that I dislike childminding, it's just that I've been at home now for nearly four years and I feel I'd like to go back to work. My children were very young and I wanted to see them grow up and now they are in school all day, so I don't see them in the day. I'm looking to try to get a school job – something that would give me all the holidays off." (Alice)

Some of the childminders were concerned that they would not be familiar with new ways of working or would not have sufficient skills:

> "[I want to change my job] because you're in your house all the time and you're with children all the time – you don't mix with adults. It ties you down a lot. You go out, but you're always back in your flat all the time…. But then I don't know if I can go back to office work because everything's changed." (Megan)

> "I want to get back out with older people. It's tiring around young children. I'm more [interested in the] general public…. [But] where I've not worked for so long and the job last time didn't need an application form…. Application forms now are so complicated. You've got to know someone in the company [to ask] so you don't say the wrong things." (Nicola)

Two mothers (Nicola in her early thirties and Joan in her forties) wondered whether they had suffered from age discrimination. Joan described being very upset when she tried to get full-time paid work that she felt she was more than qualified for, but had had no success:

> "It was very depressing because I hadn't applied for jobs for 16 years, but in the past I'd always got any job I went for – you went for a job, and you got it. I must have applied for about 10 or 12 jobs and got about two or three interviews. After all those years of work and experience, they didn't even want to interview me. Two interviews and was refused both [jobs]. I didn't know if it was my age, or if it was the fact that I was applying for jobs that were possibly of a lower rank than they thought I ought. Because of age and experience I should

have been applying for management jobs, and all I wanted was an
ordinary little nursery job." (Joan)

Nicola said:

> "I recently applied for a job [in a supermarket] and I didn't even get
> an interview, with six years' experience – I was completely gob-
> smacked.... I think they're looking for cheap labour – teenagers, so
> they don't pay them so much.... It's harder for my age group to get
> jobs."

These worries and experiences reveal a number of barriers faced by the employed
mothers as they attempt to change jobs: lack of confidence, childcare worries,
lack of relevant experience and qualifications, changes in work demands, being
'out of the loop', competing against younger recruits, discrimination, and not
being able to break out of the low-wage poverty trap. These issues were also
raised by some of the mothers at home who wanted to re-enter paid work. We
explore their experiences in the next chapter.

One of the most interesting and striking findings was the level of ambition
among the mothers – to do more useful and more ambitious jobs, to progress, to
put a lot into their work. Another striking finding was their strong commitment
to their children, and the limits this put on what they could achieve. Often they
had to sacrifice or limit their ambitions for the good of the children. All of the
mothers found that working created home pressures while home responsibilities
limited what they could do.

Summary and conclusions

Nearly 60% of all adults in the families are in work, but one third of the families
have no earner, and are predominantly lone-parent families. Unemployment is
much higher for people from ethnic minority groups. Far more women than
men work part-time, and more black and minority ethnic adults than white
adults also work part-time. These findings fit closely with wider studies of low-
paid work, the role and conditions of poorly qualified workers and specifically
disadvantaged groups in the labour market, such as women and people from
ethnic minority groups[1] (McKnight, 2002).

Most of the mothers with a degree or higher qualifications had gained them as
mature students. The biggest group of jobs was non-professional and unskilled,
but 10 mothers were gradually upgrading their career through more training
and through work experience.

Mothers found work a pressured juggling act, and most worked fairly locally
because of children. There seemed to be many emerging neighbourhood service
jobs that women could be trained to do, as long as childcare was also available.
Mothers preferred informal, known childcare to more formal 'qualified' help.

By analysing the work history and current work situation of the employed mothers in the two neighbourhoods, we were able to understand the pattern of work experience that they had built up. The five distinct but connected trajectories may fit the work patterns of mothers in low-income neighbourhoods more widely, since the patterns that we uncovered reflect a more general growth in service, part-time work, greater participation by women, and some recovery of jobs in inner cities (Turok and Edge, 1999).

The work trajectories range from successful professional and semi-professional careers for under a quarter to a mixed bag of low-paid and casual jobs for nearly a third. In between there are many women moving from very low-skill jobs into practical caring and support jobs in new and established services, often related to public services. Tim Brighouse, Professor of Education at the Institute of Education, London University, describes the emergence of 'paraprofessional jobs' that tap the informal skills of poorly trained residents in low-income areas, in order to support professional services such as education and health in those same areas (Brighouse, 2002). Certainly the trend that we observed among the mothers indicated the growth in such jobs.

The role of training and qualifications stands out as making a difference. Nearly all the women in professional and semi-professional jobs acquired their qualifications after starting work, and often after starting a family. Women working their way up the ladder started with the most basic qualifications but added training and new work-related qualifications along the way. Many of the mothers in work showed themselves to be keen learners, ambitious and aware of the wider changes going on and opportunities of the job market – particularly in caring services. Until 'paraprofessional' roles gain more recognition, and until those jobs increase significantly, the people filling those jobs will remain low paid and undervalued. The links to child poverty are inevitably strong (McKnight, 2002).

The mothers gave a strong impression that while money is important, three things are more directly related to satisfaction: doing a good job, being useful and being treated well; being able to combine work with childcare and being at home for the children; and managing the home. A majority of the women were in full-time jobs despite this and often had a difficult time fulfilling all these roles, particularly if they were lone parents.

Many of the women we interviewed seemed to lap up opportunity and many would go further in their careers if given the chance to train further, particularly in health, education, caring and services more generally. To do this in combination with work and family responsibilities, however, they need better childcare facilities, more support and possibly more 'hand-holding', as Helen Evans, in her study of over 100 women returning to work after having children, showed. This study was also based in Hackney (Evans, 2001). While a third of the employed women wanted to change their jobs, usually to something more challenging or better paid, the vast majority wanted to help their children more than anything. Earning money, being at home in time for their children, and getting out of the house to meet other people at work were all important and sometimes conflicting factors in the kinds of job women took up.

The three elements that would make the most difference to women's work in these neighbourhoods appeared to be: first, more training opportunities so that they could continue to progress or return to work more easily after breaks to look after children; second, better work conditions in the more casual and low-skill jobs, particularly more money to help with childcare and better childcare itself so working was less of a worry; and third, proximity, so the least possible time was spent travelling and the most with the family.

It was surprising that so many of the women in paid work worked full-time (58%), that so many had had reasonably steady patterns of work (70%), if not in well-paid jobs, that so many had undertaken training in order to get on (a third), even though many had left school with few or no qualifications.

One of the most striking findings was that although only three mothers had gone to university straight from school, a further five had gone on to get degrees later. In addition several were trying to complete degrees or had temporarily stopped studying to cope with work and the children. All the women with degrees were either progressing towards or were already in professional jobs.

There seems far more potential within poor neighbourhoods for women to contribute actively and creatively to the many service jobs and new career openings. The gaps in provision need willing and responsible hands. We will look more carefully at the scope for local families to make a bigger contribution to better neighbourhood conditions through paid work in later interviews. Given the skills shortages and the clear desire of many women to work – with family-friendly hours, affordable, manageable travel and childcare – there seems to be far more that employers could do to tap this market of willing workers. But it may require much more tailor-made training, much stronger linking mechanisms between this undervalued workforce and potential employers, and more work with schools, health visitors and nurseries to create the supports that mothers need in order to feel confident that their children will not suffer. It is this preoccupation with children that led half our mothers not to opt for paid work and in the next chapter we give their perspectives on staying at home.

Note

[1] Labour market opportunities are unevenly distributed – by education and work history, age, gender, ethnicity, childcare responsibilities, partner status, local and regional area and combinations of these characteristics (Reich, 1992; PAT 1/SEU, 2000). 'Past performance' (that is, education and work history) is a significant indicator of the *form* and a less significant indicator of the *rate* of current and future employment. Women have higher rates of overall employment but lower rates of full-time employment than men (Crompton, 1997, 1999) and are more likely to be working for lower wages (Bianchi, 1999; Warren et al, 2001). This pattern is compounded by the childcare responsibilities of mothers, especially in lower-income households, whether they are a

lone parent or not (Crompton, 1997; Auer, 2002) but especially if they are (Kiernan, 1996; Duncan and Edwards; 1999; Millar and Rowlingson, 2001). Partner status, and whether the partner is employed or not, affects people's engagement with the labour market – having a partner is linked to higher rates of employment (for both men and women), but if the partner is unemployed then rates are slightly lower than for people with employed partners. Ethnicity is a factor in labour market disadvantage for both men and women but experiences vary with gender, age and ethnic group (see, for example, JRF, 1999e; Dale et al, 2002). The local availability of employment is a final factor although it is less an issue in London, even Hackney and Newham, than in other parts of the UK (Reich, 1992; Turok and Edge, 1999; Evans, 2001).

SIX

Families and work: mothers at home

"I'd rather be at home with the baby. We are keen to have only one child and therefore you should do it properly really. And also it's quite impractical – only if you need the money – and then there doesn't seem to be much left over with childcare. And you're clock watching all the time." (Felicity)

"Say I wanted a job as a dinner lady, it would affect my benefits – you're not going to gain anything. And cleaning is no good because it's either early morning or evening. It has got to be during the daytime [because of school hours]. It's awkward – unless you go to work for someone and get paid in the hand…. I [was] doing a bit of part-time cleaning. I had to give that up because it affected my income support. I was on maintenance money where you can work and it doesn't affect you. Then I went on to Income Support and you have to tell them, otherwise it's breaking the law. I had to give it up, otherwise I'd have been working for nothing, and nobody works for nothing." (Marie)

Introduction

The mothers at work were mostly getting something out of their jobs in addition to money. But they were conscious of the constant squeeze on their time, particularly with their children. So what about the mothers who stayed at home? Did they and their children gain from the extra time it gave them, or did they lose out because of the greater shortage of money? Although we cannot measure the cash value of home time spent with the family against the cash value of a job, the mothers do explain their reasons for not working, their views of work, and their ambitions for the family without the benefit of the extra income.

At the same time, families with only one or no worker tend to be poorer than those where both parents work, or where a lone parent works as long as the work is reasonably paid. But low-paid work often does not lift families that are already poor, with low skills, out of poverty (McKnight, 2002). We try to set the views of non-working mothers in this wider context[1].

In this chapter we try to find out whether there are major differences in work experience, attitude and opportunity between mothers who work and mothers who stay at home; whether more immediate factors lead mothers to stay at home with their children; and whether low pay and disincentives to work such as benefit regimes make a difference. We compare the experiences of lone mothers with mothers living as part of a couple. We explore whether mothers wanted paid work or not, why it was important for so many of the mothers to be at home full-time to care for their children, setting the unpaid, caring and homemaking work of mothers in the context of these families' views. We asked what barriers the mothers attempting to re-enter the labour market were facing. The mothers we spoke to had children of varying ages – ranging from 0 to 18 – and we compare the views of those with pre-school-age, school-age children under 16, and 16 plus.

Just over half of the mothers we interviewed at the beginning of the research were not in paid work. Between the first and second interviews, this number fell to 39, partly as a result of eight non-employed mothers not taking part in the second round of interviews, and partly because we recorded nine moves into work (see Chapter Five). Of the mothers still at home the second time we talked to them, two fifths said that they would like to be working in a paid job. The vast majority of the other mothers were positively choosing to stay at home to care for their children. One was studying full-time. A small number were worried about the financial consequences of taking a paid job – with the effect on benefits, the potential difficulties of having to claim in-work benefits, and other costs associated with working. Of those women who did want paid work, most wanted a job with travel times and hours of work that would fit around their family commitments.

Lone mothers compared with mothers living as part of a couple

National data show that over 60% of mothers are now employed, including over 50% of mothers of pre-school-age children. But while married mothers are now much *more* likely to be employed than they were 30 years ago, lone mothers are *less* likely to be employed. Over 50% of lone mothers were employed in the early 1970s, but this had fallen to around 40% in the 1980s and 1990s (Hales et al, 2000).

Where lone mothers bear the sole responsibility for raising their children, the issue of combining paid work with caring for children becomes much starker. It is harder to manage work commitments when there is no one else to share the responsibility. Some lone mothers have other family members (such as grandparents or the children's father) who will step in and take on such tasks. Generally, however, the main responsibility rests with the lone parent.

Almost the same proportion (around three quarters) of lone mothers and mothers living as part of a couple who had a pre-school-age child were at home. This is much higher than the proportion of non-employed mothers with a pre-school-age child nationally (under 50%) (Hales et al, 2000). But where the youngest child was aged between 5 and 11, 41% of lone mothers were at home full-time, compared with just 11% of the mothers living as part of a couple. Many lone parents and those in couples pointed out the restrictions placed on them by needing to work around the school day or by the cost of childcare (see Table 6.1).

The British Social Attitudes Survey (Park et al, 2001) explored what society expects of lone mothers – whether they should go out to work or stay at home and look after their children. It found that just over a half of people felt that a lone mother with a pre-school-age child should "do as she chooses, just like everyone else". Of the remainder, more felt she should stay at home to look after her child (24%) than felt she should go out to work (17%). When people were asked about lone mothers with school-age children, 45% still felt she should do as she chose, but 44% felt she had a special duty to go out to work to support her child. Lone parents themselves (59%) felt much more strongly that they should be able to choose, rather than have to go out to work, regardless of the child's age (Hills and Lelkes, 1999).

A large majority agreed that the government should help with childcare for working lone mothers, particularly for those with children under the age of five; lone mothers themselves were particularly keen on this idea. The government is now providing childcare allowances through the Working Families' Tax Credit (Hills and Lelkes, 1999). Fewer people thought that lone mothers with school-age children should be helped with childcare outside school, even though there was still significant support for helping them (62%).

Table 6.1:The employment situation of mothers, by age of youngest child and 'couple status' (number of mothers, % at home within each age band shown in brackets)

	Age of youngest child			
	Under 5	**5-15**	**16 or over**	**Total**
Mothers in couple				
Full-time paid job[a]	1	9	3	13
Part-time paid job[a]	7	3	0	10
Studying full-time	2	–	–	2
At home	28[b] (74%)	2 (31%)	0 (0%)	30 (55%)
Total	38	14	3	55
Lone mothers				
Full-time paid job	1	10	1	12
Part-time paid job	3	5	0	8
Studying full-time	–	1	–	1
At home	13 (76%)	9 (41%)	1 (50%)	23 (52%)
Total	17	25	2	44

Notes: [a] Includes self-employment. [b] One mother whose partner is unemployed has been doing bits of cash-in-hand work since she left school at 13.

Source: Round 1 interviews with 99 mothers

Fathers and step-fathers at home

Within the 55 couples in the sample, 10 of the male partners were not working. In all but one of these 10 families, the mothers were not working either. These nine families in which neither parent (or step-parent) was in paid employment all had pre-school-age children. One of these couples had made a conscious decision to leave their paid jobs when they had children because they both wanted to look after them:

> "Why have children if you're going to have somebody else bring them up?" (Debra)

Another couple could not work because both were asylum-seekers. The father in another couple had lost his job just two weeks before the first interview because the factory employing him went bankrupt.

Of the nine mothers at home whose partners were not working either, five had had hardly any formal paid work experience or none at all. Three others had worked in low-paid jobs (farm or factory work and waitressing). The other mother (who, with her partner, had taken a conscious decision to give up paid work) had previously had career-type jobs.

The 'work-poor' couples we interviewed corresponded with a national pattern of one partner's poor employment record often being compounded by the other partner's (Gregg and Wadsworth, 1996). Nonetheless, for mothers at home with a partner (32), the large majority of partners did work (23), compared with nine who did not. In comparison, among the working mothers living in a couple, only one has an unemployed partner (see Table 6.2).

Table 6.2: Whether mothers are in paid employment or at home, by age of youngest child and employment status of partner

	Age of youngest child			
	Under 5	5-15	16 or over	Total
Mothers in paid work				
Partner has full-time job	7	12	2	21
Partner has part-time job	1	–	–	1
Partner not employed	–	–	1	1
No partner	4	15	1	20
Total	12	27	4	43
Mothers at home				
Partner has full-time job	15	1	–	16
Partner has part-time job[a]	6	1	–	7
Partner not employed	9	–	–	9
No partner	13	10	1	24
Total	43	12	1	56

Note: [a] One partner's work fluctuated substantially; he was self-employed and had regular periods of unemployment. He is included here as 'working part-time'.

Source: Round I interviews with 99 mothers

The previous work experience of the mothers currently at home

The mothers' current employment situation does not, of course, tell the whole story. The mothers at home had widely differing previous work histories. Five had never had a paid job and another four had little or no formal work experience. Others had worked continuously in a variety of different occupations. Table 6.3 describes the main types of work histories of the mothers at home we spoke to. We used the same broad work trajectories we used in the previous chapter, although only three of the trajectories actually applied to our non-working mums (see Box 5.3 for definitions). We added a new category of slender work histories to cover those with very little work experience. These slender work histories fitted three main patterns:

- no previous paid work experience, either formal or informal;
- hardly any paid work experience – less than one year;
- experience of cash-in-hand jobs such as cleaning, working in markets, but not of any formal paid job.

A much higher proportion of non-employed mothers were concentrated in the mixed jobs trajectory, particularly low-paid jobs. None of the mothers at home had experienced career progression or shrinkage, unlike the working mums. Non-employed mothers were also missing out on the chance to progress from low-skilled to better jobs simply by being out of the labour market. Therefore these trajectories are not included. Either they already had a career with qualifications, or they had worked in a mix of good or low-paid jobs, or they had little or no work experience.

This classification of work histories is an attempt to summarise some of the main kinds of experiences we encountered. It does not predict future life chances. In Appendix 4 we give a brief summary of each mother's experience and qualifications to help illustrate the range of experiences.

Table 6.3: A summary of the total number of mothers at home with each type of work history

Type of work history	Number of mothers
1. Consistent career	2
2. Unsteady career	3
3. Mixed jobs	24 of whom:
(a) 'Good', fairly continuous	6
(b) 'Good', not continuous	2
(c) Low paid, fairly continuous	9
(d) Low paid, unsteady	7
4. Slender work experience	9 of whom:
(a) No previous paid work experience	5
(b) Hardly any paid work experience	2
(c) No formal work experience, but some informal	2
Total	38[a]

Note: [a] We were not able to ask one mother at home about her work experience due to time constraints within the interview.

Source: Round 2 interviews

We have mentioned voluntary work in Appendix 4 where it seemed particularly 'job-like' (regular hours on a weekly basis, for example), and where people mentioned it as a significant part of their work experience. Many mothers held a responsible voluntary role locally, or helped out more informally in their neighbourhood, for example, with reading at school. This voluntary work is likely to equip the mothers at home with additional useful skills that they could use if they chose to re-enter the labour market in the future. Eleven of our non-employed mothers held at least one responsible voluntary role locally, such as school governor, member of a church council, volunteer classroom assistant (see Chapter Three for further discussion; see also Table 6.4).

Working full-time did not prevent some mothers from taking on extra commitments (even lone parents), but three quarters of the mothers with a demanding voluntary role were either at home full-time or were working part-time. Being at home for at least part of the week gave them a greater opportunity to get more involved in their local community. Lone parents were less able to play a voluntary role in the community, most often constrained by child-minding problems. Nevertheless, some took on significant community responsibilities.

Table 6.4: Whether mothers had a responsible voluntary role at Round 2 compared with their work situation and 'couple status'

	Working full-time	Working part-time	At home	Total
Lone	2	1	2	5
In couple	3	3	9	15
Total	5	4	11	20[a]

Note: [a] The total of 20 mothers with a responsible role, is less than the total of 22 families given in Chapter Three. This is because the roles held by two families did not directly involve the mother.

Consistent or unsteady careers

Five mothers currently at home had had either consistent careers, or unsteady careers (interspersing career-type jobs with other jobs such as office work, or switching between different kinds of career-type jobs). All five had left their jobs to either have a baby or, in one case, to look after existing children. All five are married; four to men in full-time paid work (one husband was not working).

Mixed jobs

The most frequently occurring work history was that of 'mixed jobs', a series of non-professional jobs that are not part of a traditional career progression. A total of 20 of the employed mothers, and 24 of the mothers at home, had experience of 'mixed jobs' careers.

The reasons these mothers had left their last paid job were varied. Most (11) had left their last job to raise their families, but two had left because they got married, two because they had moved to the UK, one to go to college, and one for a mixture of reasons (including falling into debt, having problems with the Child Support Agency, and having difficulties with childcare).

Of those mothers with experience of mixed jobs, six had done jobs that were 'good and fairly continuous'. But some of these women might find that after a long gap some of their skills (such as office skills) are considered to be out-of-date.

Two of the nine mothers who had worked fairly continuously in a mixture of low-paid jobs had obtained secretarial qualifications before they moved to the UK. However, in the UK, one had worked as a cleaner, the other in sweat-shops.

Apart from those with no work experience at all, the mothers in the 'mixed jobs/in low-paid, unsteady' category might have the hardest time re-entering the labour market. They were the group most likely to be studying currently. One mother had actually chosen to leave her job as a dinner lady in order to go to college and get qualifications that would enable her to get better-paid jobs in the future. Of the seven women with low-paid, unsteady work histories, five were actively seeking work, studying, or both. Appendix 5 shows the mixed job histories of the mothers at home.

Slender work histories

Five of the mothers we spoke to had never had a paid job — either formal or informal. All these mothers had gone to school in countries outside the UK and had moved to the UK as adults. Their qualifications ranged from basic schooling through to a part-qualified nurse who was forced to leave her training due to the civil war in her country. Two mothers did not have any formal work experience, but had done cash-in-hand jobs. Both had left school early, at around the age of 14. One had been doing fairly continuous cash-in-hand work ever since. The other mother's informal work had been just little 'bits and pieces'. Two others had virtually no work experience except for a short period in a factory.

Work histories, 'couple status' and ethnicity

We looked at the distribution of work histories according to whether or not the mothers were living as part of a couple. None of the lone parents had had career jobs, compared to five of the mothers living as part of a couple. Half of the lone parents had worked mainly in low-paid jobs, but more than a quarter of the mothers living as part of a couple had very slender work experience, compared to a fifth of the lone parents.

We also looked at mothers' work histories in relation to ethnic origin. The four married mothers with no previous paid work experience were either Kurdish,

Turkish, Kosovan or Albanian, and at least two of these mothers had had their career plans disrupted when they moved to the UK. Two Asian mothers had slender work histories, as did one white mother. None of the black mothers did (see Table 6.5).

The nine black mothers currently at home (of whom eight were African and one British) had all had work histories involving mixed jobs; six had worked mainly in low-paid jobs. The five mothers who had previously had professional careers were white.

In the next section of this chapter we explore whether the mothers at home wanted to return to work. Many said that they wanted to remain at home looking after their families. Among those who did want to return to work, there were varying levels of 'job readiness', and people were facing different obstacles. The variety of experiences we encountered shows that policies aimed at helping people into employment cannot be applied to everyone in the same way. We learnt from the mothers that programmes must be versatile, with a great deal of direct support, otherwise they will fail; this bears out the findings from a much more detailed study of 'women returners' (Evans, 2001).

Table 6.5: Distribution of the work histories of mothers at home, by ethnicity

Type of work history	White British and Irish and other	Turkish, Kurdish, Kosovan and Albanian	Black African and Black British	Asian	Mixed race
1. Consistent career	2				
2. Unsteady career	3				
3. Mixed jobs (sub-total)	11:	3:	9:		1:
(a) Good, fairly continuous	3		2		1
(b) Good, not continuous	1		1		
(c) Low paid, fairly continuous	4	3	2		
(d) Low paid, unsteady	3		4		
4. Slender work experience (sub-total)	1:	5:		2:	1:
(a) No previous paid work experience		4		1	
(b) Hardly any paid work experience		1		1	
(c) No formal work experience, but some informal	1				1
Total	17	8	9	2	2

Whether mothers wanted to be in paid employment

A total of 54% of the mothers at home said that they did not want to be employed. And some of those who did want a paid job did not plan to get one straight away – they were hoping to do a college course that would lead on to the type of job that they wanted.

There was a big difference between lone mothers and mothers living as part of a couple: 56% of the lone mothers said they would like to be working in a paid job, compared with 32% of mothers living as part of a couple. A total of 67% of lone mothers with a pre-school child wanted a job compared to 32% of mothers living as part of a couple (see Table 6.6).

We also looked at whether the mothers at home wanted a paid job, in relation to whether or not their partner was working. Mothers with a working partner were slightly more likely to say they did not want a paid job (69%), compared with mothers with a non-working partner (63%). Two fifths of the mothers who wanted to remain at home had a partner with a full-time job and a pre-school child.

Table 6.6: Whether mothers currently at home would like to have a paid job, by age of youngest child[a,b] and 'couple status'

| | Age of youngest child | | | | |
	Under 5	5-11	12-15	16+	Total
Mothers living in couple					
Want paid job	7	1	–	–	8
Don't want paid job	14	2	–	–	16
Not recorded	1	–	–	–	1
Sub-total	22	3	–	–	25
Lone mothers					
Want paid job	4	4	–	1	9
Don't want paid job	2	4	–	–	6
Not recorded	–	1	–	1	16
Sub-total	6	9	–	1	16
Total	28	12	–	1	41[c]

Notes: [a] Children's ages estimated from Round 1. (We did not record children's dates of birth.) [b] Answers were coded 'no' if people did not want paid employment at the time of the interview, even though they may have talked about wanting to get a job in the future. [c] We include two mothers here who were working, but only occasionally (one as a freelance hairdresser and one as a temp for a social care agency). We classify them as working in the summary statistics for the second round, and include their experience in the chapter on paid work, but we asked them the same questions about future work as we did the non-employed mothers. This applies to all the subsequent tables.

Source: Round 2 interviews

Why some of the mothers wanted to remain at home full-time

The dominant reason mothers gave for wanting to be at home was to care for their children. Table 6.7 summarises the comments made.

Table 6.7: The reasons why mothers at home did not want paid work

Reason	Age of youngest child		Total
	Pre-school	5+	
Want to care for own children	15	5	20
Would be too hard to pay full rent/ would not be much better off	2	2	4
Language barrier	1	–	1
About to move out of London	1	–	1
Total	19 comments	7 comments	26 comments

Looking after their children took priority

Of the 22 women who did not want paid employment, 20 wanted to be at home to care for their children. Of the 16 mothers with pre-school-age children, 15 gave this reason. Five of the six mothers with school-age children also gave this reason. Two of these women had children with special needs:

> "My family need me [at home more] than [they need me to] go to work." (Aliya)

> "Yes I would, but I haven't got the time. I will go back when [my daughter] goes to school." (Lesley)

> "Because I have the baby. I like to work when my baby going to start school." (Jelka)

> "At this precise moment, no. In another year, I would love to go back. I want to spend time with her while she's young. With [my other children] I never saw much of them when they were growing up, so I want to be with her. Not have someone else saying she took her first step." (Kate)

> "Because of my kids. I'd never leave my kids. I'd rather scrimp and scrape than miss out on their years. Once they're at school, I will go back to work." (Linda)

Five mothers with school-age children also felt this way:

"It's terrible to say no. I'd like to get paid ... but I'd say no still. It's terribly hard if you're working – I don't have people to leave the children with. It happens more than once a term that somebody needs to be at home here. And it would have to be part-time – I wouldn't send the children to a play centre or have them come to an empty house. I won't be looking for work until my youngest finishes primary school." (Kathleen)

"I [would] like to [have a] job, but I'm very busy with the children.... One day I hope I will get a job – when the children are grown up, I'm free." (Mina)

For some mothers there was a real pull between wanting to work, feeling they should, and not hurting their children:

"I do, everybody wants to work. But I got two children.... I can't go to work. I can't leave my children – if I leave them at home, they cry, even though they're big now. I don't know what I'm going to do." (Selda)

Often overwhelming family problems had to take priority. One lone mother with a child who has special needs described how she would never want a paid job:

"My son's needs come first. It would be too much. And having the responsibility of paying the rent myself. It would be too much for me, being realistic." (Natasha)

And another said that she wanted to prioritise sorting out her daughter's problems:

"Because I have a lot of problems with my daughter – I'm under the family and consultation centre. I'm sorry, I don't want to be working, I want to get my daughter sorted out first." (Clare)

The transition from benefits to work: fears about debt

Most political and economic debates about employment focus on incentives for low-skilled people to take low-paid employment. However, most of the working parents from the sample do not directly refer to this issue. Four women also described how it would either not be worthwhile going back to work by the time they had paid for childcare and other expenses, or that it was too daunting to take on responsibility for paying their rent when it was currently met in full through Housing Benefit. On paper, taking a job could work out marginally better than remaining on benefit. In reality, the added costs of childcare, transport, work clothes, short-cuts in shopping and preparing food such as buying more ready-made meals, leaving extra money for the children, could upset this margin. Managing on a low income meant accounting for every last penny. This issue has been examined in detail by Elaine Kempson in her study of living on a low income:

> Most people living on low incomes adjust their patterns of money management, bill-paying and shopping to a point where managing the household budget becomes almost a full-time occupation. Certainly it preoccupies the minds of most women most of the time. (Kempson, 1996, p 28)

Bob Holman's study of the same theme shows how five women budget, and underlines the domino effect on budgeting of small and short-term family changes such as moving in and out of work, on and off benefit (Holman, 1999).

Losing a single penny in the short-term, even though there might be non-financial benefits of entering employment (for example, gaining confidence, experience, and access to more opportunities), and long-term financial benefits (stepping stones to better paid jobs), could be a risk too high to take:

> There is ... a fairly widespread resistance to taking part-time, temporary and very low-paid jobs that would be inadequate to cover household bills.... People do take them if they are either skilled or white-collar workers and think it might lead onto a full-time permanent job, or they are unskilled and can see some other way of increasing their income – by working overtime or both partners in couples taking jobs. (Kempson, 1996, p 91)

One of the lone mothers we spoke to said that she felt that it would be easier to make work pay if she lived as part of a couple and both were working:

> "It works out better if there's two of you – a man and a woman." (Jackie)

The added fear of dealing with the bureaucracy of the benefits system and upsetting current arrangements which at least guaranteed your rent and council tax were covered, meant that the transition from benefits to work was often a scary prospect. Furthermore, Kempson (1996) described a general resistance to claiming in-work benefits, often because people felt that if they were working then they wanted to be independent of 'state support'. This resistance was combined with lack of knowledge about the benefits which did exist. In this sense the Working Families' Tax Credit introduced in 1999 had not yet broken through for these mothers, designed as it was to overcome the barriers of 'in-work benefits'.

Some of the mothers we spoke to felt that it did not make sense to work for hours and hours unless they were going to be significantly better off. The following discussion between Jackie and her friend who was present at the interview illustrates the difficulties people often foresaw with managing on a low wage as opposed to remaining on benefits, and the way they thought they could make the leap back into work:

Interviewer: "Would you like to be working in a paid job?"

Jackie: "Yes – if it made me better off, yes. But the way things are it's hard – the housing benefit – you'd have to make sure you'd be better off."

Friend: "A lot of people I know are working 40 hours a week to be £30, £40 better off. And you have to pay school dinners. And they only help you with childcare up to a certain age. It's not easy is it?"

Both these women saw more training and more education as important. Jackie is currently studying and hopes this will eventually lead to a good job:

Jackie: "I do want to go back to work, maybe when my daughter is in secondary school."

Friend: "The good thing about this area is that they have got a lot of learning things around here."

Jackie: "A lot of further education. The [new secondary] school took a lot of that on."

Friend: "That will help people get jobs."

But worries about a job not bringing in much more money than benefit income came up again when we asked what would be the lowest level of take-home pay they would accept. The friend said that she gets a disability premium on top of her Income Support and a carer's allowance for her daughter, which would make it even more difficult to find a job that paid the same as she currently received:

"The money I get for looking after her I don't think I could find [from a job]. I think I'd be better staying as I am and going to study for a qualification. I don't think I could go to work with my daughter the way she is anyway. She's got a learning and behaviour problem.... My cousin worked in school as a classroom assistant. If she was on the dole, she wouldn't get [much] less." (Jackie's friend)

Two mothers described how they gave up their previous jobs because they realised they would be either financially better off on benefit, or certainly no worse off. One of them was not currently employed but did want to go back to work. She had ruled out doing a cleaning job because it would not pay enough, and she actually stopped doing her previous cleaning job because she found that she was no better off than when she was on benefits.

Another mother did not want to be working at the present time because she was caring for a new baby. She had given up a job in a supermarket three years previously, before the advent of the Working Families' Tax Credit. At the time she was a lone parent. She found that as soon as she gave up work and went onto benefit, she began to have some money left each month. She said:

> Interviewer: "Why did you leave that job?"
>
> "The money side of it. It was getting harder to find someone to have the children. And then I had all these problems with the Child Support Agency. And it worked out better for me to give up work because I wasn't achieving anything, I was actually falling more into debt." (Kate)

Mothers expressed a strong belief that there was a direct link between working and being in debt, particularly with having rent arrears. This issue came up again when we talked to those mothers who *did* want to go back to work about what type of job they wanted and the level of take-home pay they were aiming for (see next section). One young lone mother, who said she wanted to go back to work, was waiting to clear her debts *before* she took the step off benefits and into work:

> "By next summer the latest – I'll be totally settled and have no debts and my little boy will be in part-time school, so I'll be happy to go back to work." (Jess)

Jess did not think she would necessarily end up better off financially when she took work, but she wanted to get a job anyway, to "give me something to do and give me a bit of independence".

Appendix 5a summarises how long the 22 mothers not wanting a job had been out of work, what kind of work they had done before, and their reasons for not wanting work at the present time.

Of the 22 mothers, 12 gave up their last job because of their children; 21 of them gave their children as the main reason for not wanting to work at the moment and 16 of them had a partner.

Why some of the mothers currently at home *did* want paid employment

> "I just wish I could get a job. I want to work. I'm trying and trying. To stay at home is boring." (Sade)

Two fifths of the mothers currently at home did want a paid job. As many people said they wanted a job for their own self-fulfilment, personal development, independence, 'to feel happier' as said they wanted a job for financial reasons, to be better off. Three people gave both reasons. Lone mothers were much more likely to give financial pressures as the main reason (6 out of 9) than mothers living as part of a couple (2 out of 8). Table 6.8 summarises all the comments made.

Financial reasons

The financial reasons people gave ranged from making ends to meet, to being able to buy a property, to being able to afford 'luxury items':

> Interviewer: "Would you like to be working in a paid job?"

> "Absolutely, definitely. I'm working so hard for it."

> Interviewer: "What are the main reasons you would like paid work?"

> "To make a better living. I can't get what I want if I live on £70, £80 a week. I've got children." (Gloria)

Table 6.8: Why the mothers and one lone father currently at home wanted paid employment (number of comments, by 'couple status')

	Mothers in couple	Lone parents	Total
To be financially better off	2	6	8
Self-fulfilment/personal development/ 'to be out doing something'	4	4	8
To benefit their children (apart from financially)	1	1	2
So don't have to receive benefits	1	–	1
Social reasons	–	1	1
Not recorded	2	1	3
Total	8 comments 8 mothers	12 comments 9 mothers 1 lone dad	20 comments 17 mothers 1 lone dad

Source: Round 2 interviews

"Just to survive, because my husband doesn't earn that much." (Rose)

"Every week you know you are going to earn something. It's not like sitting at home – nothing is coming but Income Support." (Desiree)

"I would say a bit of independence, financial, so you could afford luxury items." (Marie)

One mother described wanting to get paid work both to have more money and also because she wanted her children to respect her when they grew up. But she explained that the job had to be good enough to make it worth coming off benefits, and because she wanted her children to know she had done something more than cleaning:

"If I'm not getting paid, how am I going to live?! It is better to get a job than being on benefits. It is better to go to work. But if I only get paid £55-£60 it is better to stay at home. Because if I start working and tell the DSS, they stop paying my house rent.... I just want to do something better than cleaning and catering. If you are going back to work, you have to go to work that is going to be enough for you to pay your rent. That is a problem.... I'd like to get a better job, because when they grow up my children will ask 'Mummy, where do you work?' You understand? Doing a cleaning job – no." (Sade)

One mother specifically stated that she wanted to come off benefits:

"So I don't have to receive benefits basically." (Charley)

And one mother wanted better housing, a better lifestyle and more personal fulfilment:

"Because I know what I want for my children. I could buy a house where they will have better accommodation. I've [filled out] forms, I have done everything to move from here [council flat]. They've told me I won't move from here, even though the room is not enough. If I get my qualification and then get a good job, and then have a house for more space. I also want to go to work to afford more things and for my own personal development." (Delilah)

Non-financial reasons

The following comments illustrate how important the non-financial aspects of paid work were to many people. People often gave personal fulfilment as a reason:

> "I'm ready for it. It will be very fulfilling for me after all these studies to put it into practice. The kids are older now [aged 5 and 4]. I always believed in looking after them, but now it's time to satisfy myself." (Aminia)

Some parents find being at home boring and confining, and see work as a new horizon:

> "I want to work because I'm tired of sitting in one place. And if you do something it makes you happy. I use all my Income Support to pay the catalogue. There's joy in working." (Desiree)

Clearly work should also make you better off, given how low benefit income is.

> "Because I'd be out actually doing something, instead of doing the same thing more or less day in, day out. More money than what the social would give you." (James)

Mothers often said that being at home did not give them enough to do; they were restricted but not satisfied. One lone mother described how the non-financial benefits of going back to work would make it worthwhile even if she ended up no better off (in money terms) than when she was on benefits:

> "Mainly to get back to work. I don't think it'll make me financially better off for the hours I'll be able to do, but it will just give me something to do and give me a bit of independence really." (Jess)

Some mothers were conscious of becoming less needed at home as their children grew up, and needing something for themselves to fill the gap:

> "I get bored when I'm doing nothing, not working, and also the children are growing up – soon they won't need me. I want to have something to myself – something that is my achievement." (Hulya)

This Turkish mother, as well as wanting a job for her own fulfilment, described how learning English in preparation for getting a job would also help her children:

"And also, if beforehand I learn the language, I will be able to help my children with homework, learning." (Hulya)

Zoë said she wanted to get a paid job for social reasons – to mix with other people in the workplace:

"I'm thinking seriously about going back to work…. It sure as hell ain't for the rent and the council tax! Maybe just to get out and meet other people."

But she added:

"Left to me I wouldn't…. If I go out to work it ain't really going to be worth my while. On Income Support, although I'm short of money, at least I won't get into arrears. [A friend said] 'It's a big con going back to work'. [The friend has] got theirselves in such a state, it's hard to get out of it." (Zoë)

The type of work the mothers at home wanted

We asked the mothers what kind of paid work they would like to do, whether there was any kind of job they had already ruled out, how far they would be prepared to travel, what level of take-home pay they were aiming for, and what would be the lowest level of take-home pay they would accept. Appendix 5c summarises what the 17 mothers and one lone father who wanted paid work told us. We include information about people's previous work experience, and the time since they last worked, as this helps explain people's decision about future work. Time out of the labour market ranged from one to 11 years. This is relevant because a long period away from the labour market may make it harder to re-enter: skills may not be up-to-date, people may feel less confident and less able to 'sell themselves' to employers as time goes on, and employers may be less receptive.

Ten of the 18 jobs parents aspired to were of a significantly higher level than their previous experience reflected. Only five of the 18 parents who said they wanted a job were actively seeking work. Four were studying, and four were aiming to do work-related training courses. Length of time out of work for most of these parents, combined with a mixed, low-skill job history for many, was one of the biggest barriers, as the weak attempts to secure work underline. Only five are actively applying whereas eight are making attempts to study and upgrade skills:

"I'm trying to go on a computer course because I don't want to be a cleaner anymore. But if the crunch came to the crunch, I would do it...." (Rose)

Preferred job

Nine of the 18 people who wanted to get a paid job ideally wanted a job that was a development from their previous work experience, in the pattern of a career progression trajectory from a low-skilled, casual type of work to a more steady, more skilled, better paid and higher status role. For example, some who had previously worked as cleaners wanted to work in an office job or a job involving computers. Five specifically mentioned IT-related work even though none of them had significant experience. A mother who had worked as a carer wanted a job as a social worker. The mothers who were studying all fell into this group. People often had a clear first choice of job, but said they would be willing to do other things if they could not achieve this:

"Hopefully I'll be able to find a teacher's assistant job. If worse comes to worse, I'll work from home and do some childminding. But I'm not really looking to do that – I've been at home five years." (Jess)

When we asked people what jobs they had ruled out, in all but one case the jobs mentioned were poorer than people's first choice in terms of pay and training required to do them. Sometimes they had ruled these jobs out because they had done them before, and wanted to move up the job ladder (one mother did not want to do work that was too physical because of a back problem), and sometimes the main reason was because the pay was too low. Just one mother wanted a job with lower responsibility and said she would not consider doing the type of shop management job she had done before:

"At the end of the day, I'll do anything as long as it's a wage. I would like to do sales. Not managing because it's too demanding." (Zoë)

The jobs that most people said they would prefer fell into three main categories:

- care, childminding, classroom assistant (7 people);
- office/administration/computer work (6 people);
- sales (3 people).

Journey-to-work time and hours of work

Four of the mothers said they would want to work locally:

> "I want a job that I can take them and then pick them up from the school." (Belinda)

> "Only in the area while they're young." (Rose)

Two other mothers were willing to travel further afield (5 miles and 30 minutes respectively), but pointed out that they would need to be on a good transport route so that they could get to their children easily if they needed to. Both were lone mothers, shouldering the full responsibility for their children:

> "I don't want to travel any further than like five miles because I'm a single parent who if I have to get a job, I need to be not very far in case of emergency. I'll be the only one to be contacted. If I get a job and work very far, I don't have my own transport to get fast to an emergency." (Gloria)

> "Not very far because I've still got to think about the children – if they need me. As long as there's plenty of transport. Maybe half an hour away." (Jess)

Many of the other mothers explained that the hours they worked would need to fit in with school hours:

> "I don't mind to go far, but the problem is it has to be after 9 o'clock because of the children. They have to go to school. Two hours travel is too much … one hour is not bad … an hour at most." (Sade)

> "You need to do it within school hours. There is a scheme where you can take your children to the scheme and they take them to school for you. But otherwise [the job would need to be] 10am to 2pm. That way you don't pay no childcare, unless of course it's the holidays." (Marie)

> "I would like to do 10am to 2pm. I want it local." (Zoë)

> "Not really too far, but I wouldn't mind travelling a bit. A two-hour journey would be too much. It's really awkward because he starts school at 9.15am so if I was to start work I'd have to rearrange everything to get someone to take him to school. I'd need a job with funny times! [Would probably travel] about an hour." (Charley)

One mother who was determined to find work, and had not yet had any success from applications she had submitted, said she was prepared to travel up to two hours! Four other parents said they would travel for up to an hour:

> "Anywhere! If the train can get there and I know they have fast trains. With my situation even if it's two hours – just to get into the job market, into the system…." (Aminia)

Take-home pay

Aside from childcare considerations, the question of pay was central to the discussions we had with parents about what kind of work they hoped to get. We asked people what level of take-home pay they were aiming for, and what would be the lowest level they would accept. The target take-home pay ranged from £150 a week to £450 a week for full-time hours. The lowest level of take-home pay that people said they would accept ranged from £120 a week to £320 a week. The most frequently mentioned level of take-home pay was £200 a week. This is equivalent to an hourly rate of £5 net, or £5.80 gross, based on a 40-hour working week. Many of the semi-skilled public service, care and office jobs the mothers aspire to pay around £5 to £7 an hour.

Although this target hourly rate is significantly above the national minimum wage of £4.20 an hour gross, it is the equivalent of an annual salary of £12,100 gross. The target wage mothers quoted underlines people's modest views about their earning potential. It represents less than half the average annual full-time earnings in London of £26,047 gross, and is a long way below the South East average of £21,086 or the England average of £20,275 (National Statistics, 2001, www.statistics.gov.uk, based on April 1998 figures). It is also far below the average wages for women which are about 30% below men's average wages. Earnings are the largest part of income, so given that half of average net income is accepted as indicating poverty in this country and the European Union, this means that people are aiming to climb roughly to the point where they can begin to move out of poverty. Their aspirations are for something better than their work history suggests, but are not something wildly out of line with what is on offer. Most aim for a job they regard as useful; their success depends on the barriers to finding jobs and the training they manage to access.

People knew that they had to cover extra work-associated expenses (such as transport and childcare) in addition to other costs which would no longer be met in full through benefits (such as rent and school meals). In reality, they might continue to qualify for Housing Benefit and Council Tax Benefit, and also be eligible for the Working Families' Tax Credit which includes a childcare allowance. However, people were unsure about what they needed in order to cover all their expenses and, as we described earlier, claiming in-work benefits could be seen as both complicated and undesirable. Many were unclear about how much they might be entitled to, particularly Housing Benefit, or whether they would qualify at all.

Most of the mothers were clear that they would also want 'spending money' left over. They felt this was necessary in order to justify working hard all week, spending time away from their families, and entering into a hectic schedule of dropping children off to school or to childminders, getting to work, and collecting children at the end of the day:

> "I couldn't go any lower than £250 (clear) a week because that will need to cover everything." (Zoë)

> "I haven't really thought about it, but it would have to be enough so that I could come off benefits and be able to pay my rent and Council Tax and still have something left over, otherwise it wouldn't be worth it. It's like a trap – having to pay childcare – you can be better off staying on benefits. When I was working in a school – for 15 hours – I was receiving £80 a week, but £30 had to go on childcare. So I was left with £50 a week which is like nothing." (Charley)

> "I think that in order for me to be going back to work [full-time] I would have to be earning at least £800 a month [after tax] for it to be even a bit of help to me, considering you've got to pay your Council Tax." (Flowella)

One mother said that she would go back to work even if her income didn't turn out to be any more than when she was on benefit:

> "Maybe something like £150-£200 [per week]. I would still go back to work even if I wouldn't get more than on Income Support. But to make it work – especially for full-time – I would prefer to get in that range." (Jess)

All of the other mothers had left their previous employment (if they had worked before) well in advance of the Working Families' Tax Credit being introduced, and only one of the non-employed mothers mentioned it. She said she had heard of it but as she had not yet started work, did not know whether it would make any difference. Clearly wider knowledge about the amount of income supplement that the government is now offering for low-paid jobs within low-income families could make a significant difference to people's desire to work. Greater understanding of Housing Benefit and its role in helping those in low pay would also make a big difference to people's attitudes.

Barriers to gaining paid employment

The 17 mothers and one lone father who wanted paid employment described many barriers to getting a job, detailed in Table 6.9.

Travel was significantly *not* mentioned as a barrier, because jobs were available within reach, as the previous chapter showed, and people felt they could choose how far they would travel. This underlines the fact that in London it may not be the supply of jobs that is the problem. The most frequently mentioned barrier (by 10 people) was lack of qualifications, or the need for training for the interviewee's preferred job. Many are making significant efforts to acquire additional qualifications in order to meet their ambitions to do a better job:

Table 6.9: Barriers to getting a job for the non-employed mothers and lone father (number of comments when barrier mentioned spontaneously)

Lack of qualifications/need training for preferred job	10
Childcare cost	4
Wage levels not enough to enable coming off benefits	2
Language barrier	2
Lack of appropriate/available jobs	2
So far no success from applications/ interviews	1
No work permit (asylum-seeker)	1
Working towards specific business development idea	1
Childcare availability	1
Family commitments	1
Total	25 comments
	17 mothers and 1 father

"At the moment I'm going to the college – if I get a certificate, it will be easy to get a job. Then when I finish, I'd like to go for a [nursery] course ... they can send you to a placement and from there you can get a job if you are lucky. If you don't have the certificate, a job is not easy to get nowadays. There are too many people outside looking for jobs – it is so difficult. If they send me to a place, maybe I will be lucky and they [will] ask 'Would you like to work for us?'" (Sade)

The cost of childcare proved a real barrier for at least four interviewees:

"I tried to go back to work, but the childminder for [my four-year-old] is £75 a week, and with the other three [school-age children].... I can't afford." (Belinda)

Five people described multiple barriers, for example, lack of qualifications combined with language difficulties combined with family commitments. No one directly mentioned racial discrimination, but one black mother described having applications rejected and being unsuccessful at an interview she was called for, even though she felt her experience more than matched the job requirements:

"I was really shocked because the job was so basic. I couldn't understand it." (Aminia)

The distinction between 'wanting' to be in paid work and 'not wanting' to be because of some of these barriers was sometimes not very clear. In practice many of the mothers at home were laying the ground for a later return to work, but were quite unclear about when this would be, how they would achieve it, whether they would surmount the barriers they foresaw, and whether they would get a job good enough to lift them over the poverty line.

Summary and conclusion

The previous work pattern of mothers at home is significantly more 'patchy' than the mothers in work – 80% had done only very low-skilled or intermittent work; a few had almost never worked. This fits with wider evidence of the links between low skills, little work experience and difficulty in getting reasonably paid consistent work, and is particularly true for women (Turok and Edge, 1999; McKnight, 2002). Nearly half want work, but pay and the level of job open to them is a big barrier compared with the security of benefits. Eight were either studying or were planning to study to get better work. The main barriers for mothers were lack of qualifications and childcare. A total of 43% of all mothers were not employed at the second interview, including three quarters of those with pre-school children. But 40% of those at home want to work. In one fifth of all couples neither partner works.

Many of the mothers at home are thinking of going back to paid work and most of them expect to work in the future, like most mothers nationally. Some things stand out among their reasons for not working at the moment, and for staying at home. First and foremost is their concern for their children, coupled with worries about childcare. They simply want to do the best they can for their children and they feel that being at home and caring for them, despite financial pressures, is right. However, they did not explain to us whether being at home improved their quality of life or their children's experience. By implication home life seemed to work better for these mothers, since a paid job seemed to offer few benefits that outweighed the gains of being a full-time mother (Jarvis, 1999).

Second is the level of pay mothers believe they can access, based on past experience. If they did return to work, most would aim to earn far below the London average wage. This would be considerably more than they currently get on benefit or than they earned previously, but it would only just make it worth their while. Therefore for many it is a borderline decision that they are deferring. This is in spite of the fact that they are aspiring to do additional training and to get career-oriented jobs; and despite government measures to improve work incentives and to encourage people into work.

Third is the kind of job they want and their willingness to train for new skills. Many mothers recognise the need for qualifications based on new training and are keen to secure this. Linking what mothers at home say with mothers in work, it is clear that the biggest single group of low-income mothers have done a series of low-skill, low-status jobs in the past and are determined to improve their work position – at least to the level of half the average London wage. They hope for jobs as care assistants, school assistants and other service jobs generally dominated by women. People do not aspire to the same jobs they had when last working but to something better, carrying more recognition, more interest and more value in the eyes of their children.

A fourth element in people's choice is the problem of benefits. People often say they want independence, stimulus, company and the change of scene that comes from going out to work. But they may not be able to earn enough; they recognise the costs of work and they are afraid of the jump from the low level security and stability of benefits to the worry and pressures of a low-earning job. Some mothers did not believe they would either get sufficient in-work benefits or be able to revert easily enough to out-of-work benefits to take the risk. They were terrified of debt and in effect trapped on low incomes whichever way they turned. Most importantly, a majority of the non-working mothers had an overriding concern to stay at home to look after their children.

The situation was better if a partner was in work – less pressure to work, and more scope to benefit from a small amount of extra income. If the partner was out of work, generally mothers did not work either, reflecting the national pattern (Hills, 1995).

Nationally, most people strongly believe that mothers should not be forced into work – certainly with children aged under five at home – and should receive help with childcare. Lone parents hold these views most strongly (Hills and Lelkes, 1999). Yet the lone parents we spoke to were the group that most strongly aspired to working. For lone parents it is clearly more difficult on all fronts: income is often lower; childcare more difficult; and juggling work with home often impossible on low pay. At the same time, having more money and a broader life experience may be even more critical than for mothers with a partner.

More training and education, easier and more flexible childcare, higher wages at the bottom, and more flexible working hours would attract many mothers back into the job market. It would be surprising if employers were not aware of this potential pool of interested labour and trying to respond to the special needs of mothers willing to work. But many employers have stereotyped views of residents in low-income areas as potential workers (Rogers and Power, 2000). They may find it a lot easier to operate sub-legally – importing workers lured by London's bright lights with little option once they get there but to take what's on offer. In this way they cover many of the lowest skilled, lowest paid jobs.

The women in our East End neighbourhoods who are not working highlight the conflicts of low-paid work, and the loose and highly competitive labour markets of a booming economy. They are almost certainly right to recognise the value of training, the growing market for 'female' service jobs, and the importance of the parenting role to their children. The half who stayed at home have, for the moment, been unable to reconcile all three.

After talking to 100 families in low-income neighbourhoods about their experience of work it is much clearer why in-work benefits are so much more attractive to government than out-of-work benefits if they want people to move towards more skilled and more secure jobs. Only with more money will jobs at the bottom of the labour market look attractive in comparison with benefits, particularly for families with children, particularly so for mothers who disproportionately carry that responsibility, often alone. At the same time overcoming the uncertainties and fears of coming off benefits and facing precarious low-paid jobs is frightening for many mothers.

Clearly a mother's decision as to whether to return to work after having children depends on several factors. If she had previously done low-skilled, low-paid, short-term work, she was less likely to rate her chances of getting a reasonable low-paid job offering her some satisfaction but paying half average London wages. She was very likely to recognise her skills deficit and to want to study or train before trying to get a job. And she stressed her children's needs and her responsibility to them more than her need to work, if she was at home with them anyway. If she had a partner, in most cases he was working, taking some of the pressure off her to work. If he did not work, she did not either in almost every case. And if she was on her own she saw many obstacles, not least the fear of going into debt if she went back to work and losing the certainty of benefits. So mothers at home were willing and mostly happy to go without extra money in order to avoid what they saw as the unmanageable juggling act of trying to work for low wages, to pay for childcare and the other costs of working, as well as being there for their children.

The priorities of the non-employed mothers are more strongly focused on children, in part because they cannot see a way of making paid employment viable. Mothers at work and mothers at home have similar needs but for non-employed mothers, the skills, training and opportunity gap appears more significant.

The three missing links for mothers at home who would like to work are training, levels of pay and childcare. Closing the skills gap by tackling these barriers could simultaneously transform the economic potential of low-income areas, filling some of the vacancies in health, education and care organisations that these mothers aspire to and that beset our public services, particularly in these neighbourhoods. Mothers that choose not to work and say they do not want to work among our 100 families are in a minority. But the fact that they give high priority to looking after their children, and often, contributing voluntarily to neighbourhood organisations, should surely get recognition as a valuable contribution to society. In the next chapter we examine neighbourhood services and conditions in the eyes of the mothers.

Note

[1] Women's rates of full-time and part-time employment have both increased significantly in the past 40 years but there has not been a concomitant decrease in their hours of domestic and care work (Utting, 1996; Drew et al, 1998; Fetherolf Loutfi, 2001). The balance of such work falls to women in dual-earner couples at all income levels (Jarvis, 1999; Layte, 1999; Windebank, 2001), but is greatest among those in lower-income households (EOC, 1997; Bond and Sales, 2001). As childcare is such a significant component of all unpaid work, lone mothers carry out an even greater proportion of unpaid work – although some receive help with domestic work or childcare from relatives or friends, more so in lower-income areas. The relatives or friends who help out in this way tend to be women (Jarvis, 1999; JRF, 2001).

SEVEN

Managing neighbourhood conditions and services

"I just like [West-City]. I do feel quite safe. My children still have that freedom that they can go out. It's quite a pleasant area to live in. Little problems, but wherever you go, you end up with problems like that." (Millie)

Introduction

Hackney and Newham are among the 10 boroughs whose people have the most dissatisfaction with neighbourhood conditions and services in England (Burrows and Rhodes, 1998). We wanted to see how the sample families' feelings about their neighbourhoods compared with other neighbourhoods in London and around the country, and what impact neighbourhood services and environmental quality had on their lives. The way local services 'hit the ground' can make a significant difference to how a neighbourhood functions. Intensive, ground-level inputs are often necessary in order to hold conditions against pressures of decline (Power and Bergin, 1999). The evidence from the 100 families lends valuable detail to many wider studies of neighbourhood problems (SEU, 1998a, 2000a, 2000b, 2000c, 2001a, 2001c; Lupton, 2000a, 2000b; Rogers and Power, 2000; Mumford and Power, forthcoming). Because we were talking only to families with children, we compare our findings with findings from families in England, as well as the population more generally.

We found very high levels of dissatisfaction with local services and serious concerns about neighbourhood conditions. The much greater problems in these neighbourhoods generated many different views about family life. Some families were very enthusiastic about living within inner-city neighbourhoods, and could see all sorts of advantages to urban-based family life compared to family life in the suburbs or in the countryside. They had adjusted to inner-city neighbourhood conditions:

"People who think they can escape it are under an illusion! [A problem-free area] doesn't exist. Small towns – you could feel so trapped, no transportation. So I like it around here!" (Millie)

Some families were clear that the answer to their dissatisfaction was to move out of the inner-city neighbourhoods, and that their children's life chances would be much better in a less deprived environment:

"I want to leave – I've been too long round here. People that I used to know, they've all turned to drugs. It's not a really nice place.... I want my son to grow up ... imagine what it will be like in a few years if nothing is done." (Sophie)

Although others were dissatisfied, they were resigned to the fact that this was the way life was. Often they felt they had no choice, or had been worn down by their surroundings. Sometimes they had not had the chance to experience a different living environment.

Families often questioned whether the problems that neighbourhood conditions created – violence, restrictions on children's freedom – were specific to their neighbourhood, or represented a general and worrying trend in society:

"[West-City] hasn't changed in drugs and violence. There's still a sad thing happening here. I suppose it's everywhere in society now – it's hard not to find it – it's the times we're living in." (Sola)

Overall, the East London families were much less likely to be satisfied with their area (62%) compared with Inner London respondents (77%), or with families nationally (85%) (OPCS, 2000). When we asked the families how satisfied they were with the neighbourhoods as a place to bring up children, nearly twice the number of families were very dissatisfied, compared with how they felt about the areas

Figure 7.1: The families' satisfaction with their neighbourhood generally, compared with it as a place to bring up children

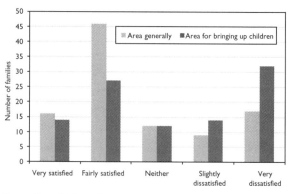

Source: Round 1 interviews

generally, as Figure 7.1 shows. Families often mentioned negative peer pressure, fears about safety, drugs and paedophiles, as well as a lack of facilities and pollution (Mumford, 2001).

Box 7.1: Sixteen measures of neighbourhood conditions from the 1999/00 Survey of English Housing

Services

Rubbish collection	Leisure	Lighting
Transport	Schools	

Problems/issues

Area appearance	Noise	Crime
Racial harassment	Dogs	Security in home
Graffiti	Unfriendliness	Litter
Vandalism and hooliganism	Neighbours	

We asked the families questions from the 1999/00 Survey of English Housing, using 16 measures of neighbourhood conditions (see Box 7.1). We used show-cards with a choice of one- or two-word responses (for example, 'serious problem'), but because the families were used to talking to us about how they saw things, involving a lot of discussion, many gave us their opinions and we recorded what they said. Their comments give more detailed insight into conditions in West-City and East-Docks.

Neighbourhood services

There was a strong contrast between the families' above-average rating for some services, and disastrous experiences of other services.

The 1994/95 Survey of English Housing found three services with which London respondents were generally more satisfied than the national average – leisure facilities, lighting and transport. The families in the East End had an even higher opinion of leisure facilities than the London average, which was far above the national average. Transport was highly rated in West-City, although not in East-Docks. However, the families were much more dissatisfied with rubbish collection, schools and lighting than the London or national average.

In order to compare the families' views with London and the rest of the country, we show levels of dissatisfaction as the main measure, based on *The geography of misery* (Burrows and Rhodes, 1998).

Figure 7.2 summarises levels of dissatisfaction with area services and facilities among the families, all London respondents, and families nationally[1]. We then look in greater detail at each of the measures and at neighbourhood quality more generally.

Figure 7.2: Dissatisfaction with neighbourhood services

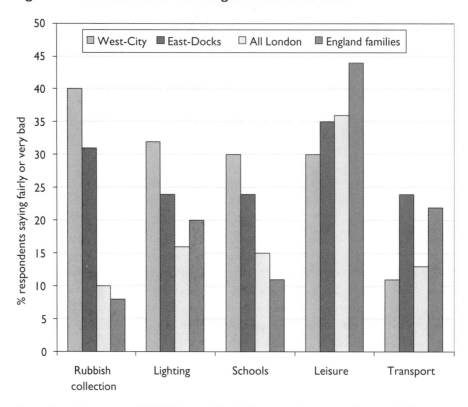

Sources: Round 2 interviews, 1994/95 Survey of English Housing in Burrows and Rhodes (1998)

Rubbish collection

Four times as many of the families in West–City, and three times as many in East–Docks, thought that rubbish collection in their area was 'fairly' or 'very bad' compared with London as a whole.

Families identified different kinds of rubbish problems: dumping in gardens, street litter, and delays in collection leading to bad smells:

> "Street-wise, you wouldn't see it as a problem. But everything – beer cans, nappies – is in my garden." (Hannah)

They also mentioned long delays in removing abandoned cars. One mother summarised the problems of managing public areas, such as streets, where no individual takes responsibility for cleaning it because lots of people have contributed to the problem. We do not know how often a road-sweeper does visit her street, but her comments help illustrate how problems build up if they are not constantly attended to:

"[My close] is not swept as much as it should be – it gets ignored. It could be my kids dropping it – you don't know who it is. You should go out and pick up after your own kids, but you don't know who it is. So it would be nice to have a road-sweeper." (Sonia)

A recurring comment in the interviews was that the rubbish collection service did its job well, but that rubbish was still a problem because people dumped rubbish without thinking (sometimes just 5 minutes after the rubbish collectors had left, according to one mother):

"Rubbish collection is good, rubbish dumping is very bad." (Sinead)

There were some examples of very well-kept blocks:

"It's good now. Very good. Every morning they clean us." (Selda)

"The caretakers are spotless! I wouldn't want to clean after the weekend, but they have it clean by Monday." (Natalie)

"[Rubbish collection is] very good. There seems to be a spate of burnt-out cars at the moment, but they are trying to deal with that." (Joyce)

This suggests that the problem is a more general one of environmental neglect, an accumulated habit of littering and dumping in public places and inadequate or infrequent street cleaning. It is also possible that refuse collection needs to be more frequent in highly built-up areas. We discuss litter later in this chapter.

Lighting

The families were more likely to be dissatisfied with lighting in their area than in London generally, particularly those living in West-City. Families nationally were also more dissatisfied with lighting than all respondents in London, but not as dissatisfied as the sample families. Of the families in West-City, 32% said that lighting was 'fairly' or 'very bad' and 24% in East-Docks, compared to 20% of families nationally and 16% of all London households. The particularly high rate of dissatisfaction in West-City may be linked to the high proportion of the families living in blocks of flats off main roads, often with insecure entrances that can be scary at night. Vandalism and poor maintenance are big problems in these entrances:

"Even the ones that we have [in this block of flats] – the boys come in and smash them. We had a letter from the council to say that they were aware of this and that they were making every effort to get them sorted – they fitted new lights. Every time the new one comes in – they just come and finish it off – break it. Half the time we don't have lights. What I'm scared of is the lights that you need to come in – the doorway into the lifts. Every time that light is broken." (Cynthia)

"It's not very well lit round here – you don't like going out of a night. It might be lit-up down [the main road] but down the side roads I don't think it's well lit-up." (Clare)

A route through the bus/tube station in East-Docks. There are few people here after dark

Schools

The families saw strong signs of schools improving in both West–City and East–Docks (see Table 7.1). Most families thought that both primary and secondary schools were getting better on a range of different fronts. The improvements identified included: new head teachers (sometimes brought in as 'trouble-shooters'); the introduction of homework; good publicity in the local press; after-school and holiday clubs; the introduction of a school uniform; improvements to the physical school building; new computers; improved academic results; expulsion of bullies; and increasing sensitivity to the needs of the Turkish/Kurdish population, including translation of documents. In East-Docks, a brand new secondary school had recently been completed and a primary school had been totally rebuilt (Mumford, 2001). Newham's Education Action Zone was also having a noticeable impact.

Table 7.1 How the parents thought their children's schools were changing overall (number of families)

| | Primary schools[a] | | Secondary schools[b] | | |
	West-City	East-Docks	West-City	East-Docks	Total
Getting better	12	21	6	6	45
Staying the same	5	2	1	1	9
Getting worse	3	1	0	2	6
Not recorded[c]	7	15	2	7	31
Total	27	39	9	16	91

Notes: [a] Includes all families who sent their children to primary schools within the boroughs of Hackney or Newham. [b] Includes families who sent their children to secondary schools in the boroughs, or to those secondary schools just over the Hackney boundary in Islington that are commonly used by families in the area. [c] Often because their child had only just started at the school and so it was too soon to say.

Source: Round 1 interviews (Mumford, 2001)

One parent said of a Hackney primary school:

> "The headmaster is more for the school, the kids and the parents. He has done a lot to turn this school around – bring it up from the bottom. He has brought funding in. He always makes time for you if you have a problem." (Liz)

However, most schools were still performing a long way below the national average, and although the families recognised improvements, they were far less satisfied with schools in these neighbourhoods than the London and national averages. Around 20% of the families, in both West-City and East-Docks, thought that schools in their area were 'fairly bad', double the London or national average. A further 11% in West-City thought schools were 'very bad', compared to 5% in London and just 3% of families nationally.

> "You either can't get into the good ones, or the bad ones are very bad." (Sarah)

> "It's very good to have as many schools as we've got, but education-wise it's poor. [My son] is leaving next year for secondary school – he's not going to know what's hit him – he's got the ability of an eight-year-old reading and writing wise." (Sonia)

Only 4% of the East-Docks families described schools in their area as '*very* bad', and many families were pleased at the progress being made at schools that they had previously been very concerned about, as a result of the Education Action Zone:

> "[Local secondary] is very good. They've had a rough run, but now the children are coming out with better marks." (Louise)

West-City parents also identified improvements:

> "The secondary school that I went to has improved. I heard that it's
> the number one in Islington. It wasn't when I was there." (Sophie)

In both areas, parents tended to be more concerned about secondary schools
than primary schools. One mother's eldest child had just finished at a local
secondary school:

> "She could have done better. That's why [my youngest child] is not
> going there. [My oldest] was on top of her class at the primary, and
> when she went to [local secondary] she just dropped." (Hannah)

This problem seems very common for the families.

Leisure

The families and London residents as a whole were much more satisfied with
leisure facilities than families nationally. The families we spoke to in West-City
had lower levels of dissatisfaction. This highlights one of the features of urban
life that can be attractive to families living in inner-city neighbourhoods – easily
accessible leisure facilities, often within walking distance. These include swimming
pools, leisure centres, gyms, cinemas and parks.

There is a popular leisure centre (including a swimming pool, sports hall and
football pitches) within West-City itself:

> "Very good ... because it's on the doorstep." (Jessica)

> "[West-City leisure centre] is quite impressive." (Felicity)

The majority of the families we spoke to in West-City used this centre – 31 of
the 41 we asked. The other 10 did not use any sports facilities at all. In addition
to West-City leisure centre, six families used swimming pools in neighbouring
areas or further afield (for example, south London). One mother went to fitness
classes elsewhere, and another used a gym in a nearby area.

Some families who lived on the outskirts of West-City expressed their
unhappiness with the recent closure of a swimming pool that had been nearer to
them. It was a pool where people could swim in lanes. They felt that:

> "Just one is not enough for this area." (Onur)

The 34 families interviewed in East-Docks used a much wider range of sports
facilities than those in West-City; no one centre catered for such a wide mix of
uses as the leisure centre in West-City. Nine said that they did not use any sports

facilities. The other 25 families mentioned 16 different sports or leisure facilities, mostly located within their neighbourhood or in a nearby area, within Newham. These included gymnastics, swimming, baseball and football in local parks, and bowling.

Some families in East-Docks were worried that one of the nearest leisure centres could only be reached by crossing a major expressway:

> "Not bad but you have to go over the [major road] to the Newham Leisure Centre which is a bit of a distance for your child to go [and it's a] busy road. Fairly good – it is just a location problem." (Barbara)

Even so, many families were pleased with the leisure facilities around East-Docks, and some had noticed new ones being developed, including a new gymnastics centre in a neighbouring area. Staff from this centre had visited a local primary school and had invited the children to go for a trial.

> "[Leisure facilities] have started to pick up really, really well." (Tessa)

> "They're popping up everywhere." (Kate)

However, some families in both neighbourhoods were worried about the cost of using leisure facilities:

> "I think [leisure facilities] are good but expensive." (Joanne)

> "The leisure centre is too expensive." (Frances)

Museum entrance is free

One mother in East-Docks explained that she pays a total of £70 a month for two of her children to do 6 hours of gym a week. She felt that prices should be lower:

> "Some of the parents are finding it a struggle – but it's something safe for their children to do." (Nora)

Transport

Only 3% of London respondents said that transport was 'very bad' compared with the national average of 9%. Among the sample families about 10% thought this. Perhaps surprisingly, given huge recent developments (connection to the Underground, new bus services), far more of the East-Docks families said that transport was 'very' or 'fairly bad' (24%) than in West-City (11%), compared with the London average (13%).

The higher level of dissatisfaction with transport in East-Docks seemed to be because of inadequate local bus services. Most people praised the new Underground station and were pleased to have access to Docklands Light Railway, which helps connect the area. But many said that they themselves were still dissatisfied with transport in the area because they needed to use local bus routes and found these unreliable or inconvenient. The Underground often does not cover the local cross-routes that are so crucial to families, and some felt that they lived too far from the new station to make easy use of it:

The new train station

"East-Docks is fairly good, but [my road] is fairly bad. There is only one bus ... and you can stand there for 30 minutes before you get a bus, which is bad isn't it?" (Sade)

"We've only got one bus near us. The other bus and the station is about 10 minutes away." (Audrey)

"Very bad for transport, especially local transport. Not [so] much the railway, with the Docklands, but the buses in particular." (Gillian)

The area is also dissected by a fast, wide, noisy, ugly, polluting trunk route which forms a huge barrier and has been a concern for local residents for more than 20 years (Smith, 2001). This road is obviously a major asset to the wider community, but very damaging to the neighbourhood:

"I still feel cut off because of where I am ... because of the [major road]." (Diane)

In both areas, people complained about the traffic, and the negative knock-on effect this had on bus timetable and journey times:

"The traffic is so annoying. It takes me longer to get to work [by bus] than people coming into London from Brighton!" (Yetunda)

"Very bad. You wait for ages [for a bus], and then it's packed." (Theresa)

One of the subways beneath the major road between south East-Docks and the shopping centre

> "Getting terrible … more traffic and congestion. There are just too many cars on the road…. A couple of times I've got the bus because the car's not going, but the buses never run to time. The driver says it's because of the traffic. It's a no-win situation." (Tessa)

Traffic also restricted cycling and made it very dangerous for children to use the roads:

> "I cycle quite a bit but not as much as I should because I don't like cycling on the roads round here." (Andrea)

Yet with all these obstacles, other families in both neighbourhoods felt that the availability of public transport was a particularly good feature of their area:

> "[It's] good for when you need to go up the West End, or places like that – two close tube stations." (Alice)

> "That's why I don't want to move – it's bang in the middle of everything. I can get a bus or a tube." (Faye)

> "I'm allowing the kids to go to the swimming pool and the pictures because the tube takes them to the door and back." (Sonia)

Many families in East-Docks were very excited that their area had at last been 'put on the map'. For some, the new transport links had significantly cut their journey-to-work times and for others they had opened up or increased ease of access to facilities outside the neighbourhood.

Chapter Ten describes in more detail families' positive reactions to the recent changes that have taken place in East-Docks.

Local environmental conditions

The neighbourhood environment reflects the way that many local services function, for example, crime and policing, housing management and security, street conditions and environmental services. We asked the families what they thought about the appearance of their area, to what extent they felt noise, dogs and litter were problems in their area, and how far environmental services were a match for the scale of problems. On the whole, the figures show that dissatisfaction with these environmental issues is higher among families than non-family households nationally, higher still among London respondents, and extremely high among the families we interviewed in East London. The environmental problem that received the most criticism London-wide, and from the families in East London, was litter, closely followed by dogs (primarily dog fouling rather than problems with stray or dangerous dogs).

The government has recognised the importance of cleaning up local environments:

> "The one public service we use all the time is the streets where we live. And in too many places, streets and public spaces have become dirty, ugly and dangerous." (Prime Minister, 2001)

The government have introduced various measures, including street wardens and Home Zones, to tackle street conditions. However, these are very patchy and do not yet exist in the study areas.

In his 2001 speech 'Improving your local environment', the Prime Minister announced that local authorities will be given extra powers and resources to address these basic environmental problems. Fines for dog fouling and dropping litter will be doubled, and local authorities will be able to reinvest these additional resources to enhance the local environment. The biggest problem lies in the quality of environmental services, the neglect of the public realm by the public bodies responsible, usually local authorities, and the general lack of civic pride, leading local authorities to greatly reduce 'street services' (Power and Bergin, 1999). It is well known that neglect generates abuse (Rogers and Power, 2000), and that disorderly physical environments are strongly linked with social malaise, fear of crime and actual disorder. Therefore this section and the views of 92 families reported in it tell a tale of public neglect and decay leading to the extremely high levels of dissatisfaction with the neighbourhood environment, shown in Figure 7.3 overleaf.

The gap between the study neighbourhoods and the rest of the country, including London as a whole, is stark. Recent figures show that nationally there has been a fall in the proportion of households reporting problems. Perceptions of problems with dogs have shown a particularly steep decline (NCSR, 2001). This underlines even more strongly the gap between conditions in the East London neighbourhoods and elsewhere.

Street litter

Mirroring the national pattern, the sample families were much more likely to think that litter was a serious problem than refuse collection. In fact, over four times as many thought that litter was a serious problem compared with rubbish. Since rubbish was three times worse in the study areas than elsewhere, litter problems were almost 'off the map'. The families' concerns exceeded London and national averages.

Figure 7.3: Dissatisfaction with aspects of neighbourhood environments

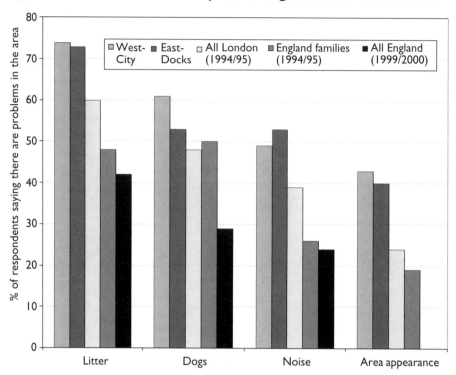

Sources: Round 2 interviews, 1994/95Survey of English Housing, in Burrows and Rhodes (1998); 1999/00 Survey of English Housing, in DTLR (2001)

Dogs

Families with children were more likely to be concerned about dogs than other households (OPCS Social Division, 1996). Nearly a quarter of the East-Docks families said that dogs were a serious problem. Two fifths of West-City families identified dogs as a serious problem – almost double the figure for East-Docks and the London average, and more than four times the national average in 1999/ 00 (9%). Families were concerned at the high risk of their children stepping or falling into dog mess on pavements, on grassy areas, and even in the lifts of blocks of flats. The particularly high level of concern in West-City appeared to be directly linked to the amount of dog mess in West-City park – the main green space in the heart of the neighbourhood – and other communal grassy areas. This was heightened because many of the West-City families live in flats and are more reliant on communal green spaces for their children's outdoor play. We explore families' use of parks further in the next chapter. The problem of dog mess was putting some families off from using the park altogether:

"I think it is serious because they … are messing the lifts up, and the parks – you can't go in the park. That West-City park is full of dog excrement. You can't go and sit down – you end up coming home with a pushchair covered in excrement." (Cynthia)

"Serious problem. On the grass and where the kids play, and on the pavement. I don't know why they don't clear it up after them." (Theresa)

"It's annoying when you've got kids. It's a lovely big green to play on and it's just full of dogs' mess." (Jessica)

Noise

Noise was a particular problem in East-Docks. A total of 29% of the families there said that noise was a serious problem, compared to 17% in West-City, 12% across London and just 6% of families nationally (OPCS Social Division, 1996). Noise problems were often directly related to neighbour problems – loud music, and being woken up by arguments, for example:

"[Noise is a serious problem.] Tenants talking loudly, music, children screaming." (Nicola)

We explore neighbour problems in more detail in Chapter Nine. Sometimes families said that the problem of noise from neighbours was not because their neighbours were behaving unreasonably, but because of very poor sound-proofing between flats, so that even ordinary household activity could be heard clearly. Traffic noise was also a frequently mentioned problem:

"I can't sleep because of all the cars. 24 hours. Music in the car shakes the whole building. I can't get used to it." (Gloria)

"You can't keep the window open when you're going to sleep. The whole house shakes when lorries go past." (Nadia)

"Traffic noise [is a serious problem]. We get a lot of traffic in this little turning. I don't think they should have all this heavy traffic coming down here. If it was posh houses down here, they'd get it stopped." (Ellie)

Noise from planes, trains and buses was mentioned by a small number of people. And a few West-City families were badly affected by noise from pubs and clubs:

> "It is a problem from the pub. My son complains because he can't get to sleep. It can get very annoying. Why do they have pubs so near the flats?" (Yetunda)

A recurring theme was that a certain level of background noise was an understandable feature of London life, or of life in a flat, and was certainly not a serious problem – you just got used to it:

> "[Noise from cars is a problem, but not a serious one.] It's normal, you live in town." (Snejana)

> "I don't take no notice – there is noise, but I'm so used to it, I take no notice." (Tina)

And a few people said that it was more likely that they were a problem to other people:

> "[Not a problem] ... because I can be fairly noisy with the music sometimes!" (Faye)

Appearance of the area

Around two fifths of the families in both neighbourhoods described the general appearance of their area as 'fairly' or 'very bad', compared to 24% of London respondents and just a fifth of families across England (OPCS Social Division, 1996). This is clearly linked to the extent of the litter and dog mess problem identified by families, and in Chapter Nine we discuss their high level of concern with vandalism, graffiti and, particularly in East-Docks, the problem of abandoned cars. These aspects of disorder have very negative impacts on the appearance of an area, as well as on people's feelings of security. Some families' dissatisfaction with the appearance of their area was also linked to the high proportion of council flats.

Comments about West-City's appearance included the following:

> "It must look awful to someone coming in – an estate like this – I call it Beirut." (Rosemary)

> "[All you see is] flats, flats, flats." (Kerim)

> "Very bad. I don't know why. Is it that this area is being neglected?

Is it the people – who put the people here? Is it because it's the East End? West London is a different area completely … they have [leisure centres and parks on] every corner…. We all live in London. Why can't we have half of what they've got?" (Delilah)

"Fairly bad. All the rubbish, loads of cars that get smashed, round the back the skips are full up." (Justine)

"The rubbish is appalling, and fly-tipping." (Kathleen)

Comments about East-Docks' appearance were similar:

"There's something about all these tall buildings and unemployment." (Aminia)

"I just think it's appalling here. It makes me angry." (Miriam)

"A lot of it seems to be looking very dirty. You've got quite a few derelict buildings. The ground surrounding the blocks could be improved." (Marie)

"[That empty pub] is a right eyesore." (Diane)

However, as Chapter Ten explains, there was also a feeling that improvements were being made on some fronts:

"Getting better, a lot more flowers in." (Linda)

"It's shaping up – renovated flats, new houses." (Sasha)

Efforts being made to improve the environment

A recurring theme in some of the interviews in both neighbourhoods (although more often West-City) was that local services were trying to upgrade the environment. People talked about efforts being made with cleaning (including the removal of graffiti), flower-planting,

The private housing management contractor continues to plant …

lighting, rubbish collection, and (in one case) noise control. The private housing management contractor in West-City was one of the key services making an effort:

"It's much cleaner now." (Yetunda)

Three families in West-City said that graffiti used to be much more of a problem than it is now:

"[Graffiti] is a problem, but it isn't serious as they have cleaned it up no end. It used to be terrible." (Joan)

Natalie commented that the "kids" kept breaking the lights, but:

"… they do try to fix it straight away."

Another West-City mother commented:

"[Lighting] is alright now. I've got a light by my door. I think they're doing it up round there." (Theresa)

In East-Docks, Annie said that the council does try to collect litter even though it is still a serious problem. Sasha said that rubbish collection is fairly good – "they are trying" – and that you even see cleaners on a Sunday.

These families recognised the difficulties facing local services and, even though the problems sometimes remained, they were very pleased to see efforts being made. They wanted to point out these efforts – it was important to them that they were recorded.

Poor conditions and low expectations

How do people know how to rate the quality of neighbourhood conditions, and what do they compare them to? Some of the comments that the families made about services, the local environment, and area problems, raised the issue of expectations – what did people see as an 'average' living environment against which to measure whether something was a serious problem or not?

"[Graffiti is a problem but not serious.] I've been to America and it's a hundred times worse!" (Sola)

The families' comments suggested that the high levels of dissatisfaction we recorded could actually have been underestimates, because they felt that to experience a certain level of problems was normal and so did not describe them as serious:

"Vandalism is a problem but not serious. It does go on. About average."
(Megan)

"Vandalism and hooliganism is not too bad, but there are a few youths
in the area that have fights with my children – so I don't like to let
them go down [to the shop]. If my son goes to the shop, they try to
take his money from him. It's not too bad, just a few of them."
(Hulya)

In an area without such levels of open criminal intimidation, the idea that a child
would experience such hostility on his way to the local shop would be shocking,
and described as a very serious problem.

Sometimes families indicated that they were comparing their local services
with other problematic services, rather than with national standards:

"[Our local primary] is very, very good. It came 10th in Hackney.
[Two other local primaries] came quite below, but were not the worst
in Hackney." (Delilah)

There was a sense in which people 'adapted' to the area difficulties around them
in order to cope – they found ways of dealing with the difficulties, or just got
used to them being there in the background. The problem of noise was one
issue that illustrated this point very clearly. Many people regarded a high level of
noise from traffic and neighbours as part and parcel of London living, particularly
flat-based living. It was less stressful to try and get used to it than to challenge it:

"You just have to compromise because everyone's living like sardines.
You could be arguing constantly if you didn't bend a little." [Rosemary,
who said noise is a problem but not serious; you get used to noise
from children, pubs, cars, and even neighbours using the bathroom
which you hear because of poor sound-proofing]

"There's a buzz in the background from the [triple-carriageway] and
the airport. It becomes a part of life." (Andrea)

And some families made the point that some issues did not seem serious when
compared to the things that were really bothering them. For example, one
family said that lighting really wasn't important – they were more worried about
education. Another commented on how dog mess was hidden as a problem to
some extent because of all the other litter about:

"[Dogs are a problem but not serious.] You do get the dog mess, but because there's so much rubbish about, you don't think of it as a serious problem. If the area was clean, it would show up more." (Justine)

Finally, people are commenting on something very personal to them – their home and immediate living environment – a central part of their lives, closely linked to their individual identity. For this reason they can feel uncomfortable being overly critical, and many people tried to balance their negative views with more positive comments. A recent study of the environmental concerns of residents in deprived neighbourhoods reported that most people found something to praise about their local area:

Perhaps most importantly, participants saw their locality as 'home'. Negative images of their 'home' were met with anger. Casual descriptions of localities as 'poor' or 'polluted' offended residents, who saw such descriptions as stigmatising their home and, by extension, themselves. (Burningham and Thrush, 2001)

Postwar council houses in East-Docks and high-rise flats

Wider services and facilities families use

We asked families about other services, such as doctors' surgeries, banks, shops, and the 'centre' of London. We wanted to know how far people travelled for different services, and the extent to which they used facilities outside their local neighbourhood.

Doctors' surgeries

The vast majority of families in both neighbourhoods went to a doctors' surgery in their local area – within a 15-minute walk of their home. Of the 42 families we asked, 40 in West-City went to a local GP; 28 of the 36 families we asked in East-Docks also used their local GP.

A wide mix of people go to local doctors' surgeries. We met some of our most vulnerable families there, together with some of our highest income families.

'Doctor loyalty' seemed to be quite strong. The two families in West-City who did not use their local GP were registered with a GP in an area where they used to live:

> "[I go to a doctor out of the area] only because I lived there when I was young and I've never changed my doctors. I like him and he is very good." (Alice)

One had changed to a more local doctor when she first moved in but had not liked him, and so had returned to her old GP near her previous address.

Similarly, three of the eight East-Docks families who didn't go to a local GP went out of the area to GPs who had been their local GP in the past:

> "Because that is the GP I've been using for 10 or 12 years – I'm used to him. I get there by bus." (Sade)

A further two families lived in a newly expanding area just south of East-Docks, where there is as yet no GP surgery. Just one family paid for a private doctor.

The sense of connection to individual GPs reinforces the view that the doctor plays a strong family role, is in a position of great trust, and is a conduit for important information about health, child-rearing, access to other services and general advice. Doctors are often needed to provide evidence for schools, housing and care services. And all families use a doctor at some time, especially if they have children.

Banks

The Social Exclusion Unit, in its report on financial services, showed how disadvantaged poorer neighbourhoods were in accessing banks (SEU, 2000c).

Neither neighbourhood contained a bank directly within its boundaries. Both had a number of cash points, but families said that these tended to be located within shops where a charge was made for each withdrawal. West-City has banks within fairly easy reach, and only two families raised access to banks as being a problem. In East-Docks, seven families directly criticised the lack of banks in their area, although there is now a cash point within the new Underground station which may help. Some remembered a time when there had been banks along one of the main roads – these had moved away some years previously:

> "There are no building societies along here anymore because they have all been done over." (Dionne)

> "That's ridiculous the bank situation. To go to a bank you've got to get on a bus. I know you need to do this if you live in the country, but you live in the city … but they all closed down." (Peggy)

> "[My bank is in another area of Newham] – a long way away. Get there on the bus. There is a cash-point closer but they charge you £2.50 to use it … I don't use it." (Gillian)

Seven of the 78 families we asked about banks said that they did not use a bank or a cash point. At this stage in the interview (towards the end) we did not usually have time to probe further, but one family said that they used the post office instead, and another added:

> "Personally I don't meet the criteria for a bank account. I would love to have one." (Marie)

A national survey – the People's Panel, run by MORI for the Cabinet Office – found that banks were used less frequently in deprived areas: 76% in deprived areas used them at least once a month, compared with 92% of residents in other areas. Correspondingly, post offices were considered more important in deprived areas than in other areas (Duffy, 2001).

The Social Exclusion Unit's Policy Action Team on access to financial services found that between 6 and 9% of individuals have neither a current account nor a savings account. Between 14.5% and 23% of people do not have a current account (PAT 14/SEU, 1999).

> People without bank accounts are disadvantaged when it comes to settling their bills, handling cheques and getting access to credit. They are also more likely to be cut off from information about other financial services products, which bank customers get from branches or by mail. (PAT 14/SEU, 1999)

Food shopping

We asked the families where they did their main food shopping. Many regularly used more than one supermarket or other food shop or source. In West-City, families mentioned two main food shopping sources per family. These were located in 13 different areas in addition to West-City itself. Nineteen of the families said they regularly used a small supermarket in West-City (Iceland), four said they bought a lot of their food at West-City market, and three regularly bought food at small local shops:

> "[Local shops] are expensive, but sometimes you have to use them."
> (Snejana)

There is a wide range of supermarkets within a few miles of West City – including Waitrose, Sainsbury, Safeway and Tesco – which families reached by driving, bus, taxi, or occasionally walking. Five families travelled slightly further than this to reach the supermarket Netto:

> "[It's the] cheapest – it's a shop from the continent." (Sola)

And three families travelled all the way to ASDA in the Isle of Dogs, who lay on a special bus from Islington to get people there and back:

> "I do travel for my shopping! ASDA are brilliant." (Niamh)

One mother regularly used three different major supermarkets as well as buying her food from a street market in a neighbouring area:

> "[The choice] is a very positive thing about being here." (Felicity)

Of course, it was much easier for those with cars. Those without sometimes got lifts or would catch the bus to the supermarket, and then pay for a taxi home when they were laden with shopping.

In East-Docks, families mentioned just under two main food shopping sources per family. These were located in eight different areas in addition to East-Docks. The most popular was an ASDA in a nearby area – about 20 minutes by bus. Seventeen families named this as their main source of food shopping. Seven families regularly used a small branch of KwikSave located in East-Docks, and four used a local Iceland. Three also regularly used local shops for their food shopping. None of the families mentioned East-Docks market as a main source of food.

Families in East-Docks travelled a bit further than those in West-City to find the major supermarkets, often to find a more economical store and to make their money go further:

"I always look for where my budget will fit in. I normally travel a bit further – 20 minutes on the bus. Other supermarkets are a bit closer."
(Gloria)

In both West-City and East-Docks, families had to travel outside their neighbourhoods to find large supermarkets with lower prices. And the local markets did not appear to meet their main food shopping needs. Local shops were useful but were too expensive.

The centre of London: the West End and the City

We were interested to find out whether the families used the centre of London much – were they able to benefit from some of the attractions at the heart of the capital? We found that, unsurprisingly, there was variation both within and between the families. For example, some parents travelled to the City for work every day, or teenage children travelled to school in one of the Central London Boroughs, whereas other members of the family never went in. Half the mothers asked use the centre once or twice a year, or not at all. And two thirds go less than every two months. We define the 'centre' broadly as the West End and the City.

Unsurprisingly, as West-City is much nearer to the 'centre', we found that West-City mothers visited the City or the West End of London much more frequently on average than did those in East-Docks. Liverpool Street is within walking distance and Ellie said "I thought this was the centre of London!".

In East-Docks, five mothers said that they never went into the centre, and a further five said that they rarely went. Only one of the West-City mothers said that she never went into the 'centre'.

There were various reasons why some of the mothers never went into the middle of London – no desire to, lack of time, dislike of travelling far from home, lack of money to spend when they got there, and the constraints of small children.

People mentioned a number of reasons why they did travel into the centre, including: for shopping (the most popular reason), often at Christmas time or in the sales, window shopping, to visit museums and art galleries, to go to the parks, to go out for a meal, to have a haircut, to attend a Court hearing, for work, and for children's schools.

The 'centre' of London is a big place, and our questioning was brief, but the data illustrate two key points. First, the neighbourhoods are different from deprived neighbourhoods in other parts of the country simply by their proximity to one of the most acclaimed centre-cities in the world, with its wealth of museums, galleries, public parks, shops and nightlife. For some mothers, these made a very positive contribution to their quality of life and that of their children.

Second, and in sharp contrast, families living in inner London can be restricted from making use of all these opportunities. Sometimes it was clear that families rarely went into the centre because they had no need to – they were not restricted, they were making a clear choice. But sometimes people faced barriers, which took different forms – they could be temporary constraints associated with having young children, or more embedded constraints linked to lack of confidence, knowledge or money:

> "I have never been in the West End! I haven't got money to go shopping there." (Gloria)

> "I get lost up there! The only time I went was to put some flowers down when Lady Di died." (Clare)

> "It used to be probably once a month. But now with the baby, I don't seem to get to a lot of places. Not that I can't, but I don't really bother." (Dionne)

While East-Docks has many of the characteristics of an inner London neighbourhood – with high levels of deprivation and an often poor overall environment – it appears quite disconnected from the centre of London. This has potential implications not only for 'quality of life' more generally, but specifically for employment links.

There are alternative 'centres' for the East-Docks families – such as Canary Wharf, the developing Stratford, and towns in nearby Essex. The new Underground linking East-Docks directly to London Bridge and Bond Street in under 30 minutes may increase the sense of connection between East-Docks and central London. The gap, however, is clearly about far more than just transport – but as that part of the gap closes, will people feel any closer to the opportunities central London affords?

The overall picture

In order to compare the views of the families on neighbourhood conditions with the views of residents in the rest of London and England, we look at the way residents rank the 16 main problems identified in the 1999/00 Survey of English Housing.

We compare what the 92 families told us about these problems and how they ranked them, with the ranking given to these same problems in other areas of London and in the country as a whole. Taking the top seven problems in the sample neighbourhoods, we find that the pattern of most serious problems varies little between these poor neighbourhoods and the rest of the country. Thus the main contrast between these neighbourhoods and others lies in the scale of the problems (as shown earlier in this chapter) rather than in the importance people attach to different problems. But rubbish, vandalism, graffiti and racial harassment are ranked higher up the scale in the sample neighbourhoods.

Table 7.2: Rank ordering of problems based on the responses of 47 families in West-City and 45 in East-Docks, compared with London and national averages

7.2 (a): Higher-ranking problems showing a similar pattern across the country

	Rank order			
Problem/issue	West-City[a]	East-Docks[a]	All London[b]	England families[b,c]
Crime	1	2	1	1
Vandalism and hooliganism	2	1	4	4
Dogs	2	6	2	2
Litter	4	4	3	4
Rubbish collection	5	9	12	12
Graffiti	5	3	7	7
Noise	7	4	6	9

7.2 (b): Lower-ranking problems

	Rank order			
Problem/issue	West-City[a]	East-Docks[a]	All London[b]	England families[b,c]
Leisure	8	9	5	3
Racial harassment	9	8	11	16
Schools	9	13	9	12
Lighting	9	13	12	7
Area appearance	12	9	8	10
Transport	12	9	12	6
Neighbours	14	7	9	10
Security in home	15	15	16	14
Unfriendliness	16	15	15	14

Notes: [a] Round 2 interviews. [b] 1994/95 Survey of English Housing, in Burrows and Rhodes (1998). [c] The figures for family respondents nationally resulted in a very similar ranking to that for all household types nationally, except that noise was slightly more of a problem for all respondents (7th compared to 9th for families).

Table 7.2(a) shows the seven highest ranking problems. This reinforces the earlier finding that it is the intensity of problems rather than the problems per se that is distinct in the most disadvantaged areas.

Table 7.2(b) shows the nine, second-order problems, generally ranked lower by residents both in the two East End neighbourhoods and in London and the rest of the country. Here there is more variation.

The most striking difference between the families' dissatisfaction in the East London neighbourhoods and across London and nationally, is in the *proportions* of people saying that a particular problem was serious or that a service was very bad. Crime received a top ranking across the board (coming second in East-Docks to vandalism and hooliganism), yet beneath this ranking lurks a startling

Table 7.3: Proportion of families in two East End neighbourhoods, in London and nationally, ranking the seven most significant problems as serious or very bad (% who say it's a serious problem or very bad service/facility)

Problem/issue	West-City[a]	East-Docks[a]	All London[b]	England families[b]
Crime	57	64	25	23
Vandalism and hooliganism	40	67	16	14
Dogs	40	24	21	22
Litter	38	29	20	14
Rubbish collection	19	11	3	3
Graffiti	19	36	11	7
Noise	17	29	12	6

Notes: [a] Round 2 interviews. [b] 1994/95 Survey of English Housing, in Burrows and Rhodes (1998).

difference. A total of 57% of the West–City families and 64% of the East-Docks families we talked to said crime was a serious problem – well over twice the proportion in London (25%) and nationally (23%). A total of 67% of East-Docks families said vandalism and hooliganism was a serious problem – more than four times the proportion in London (16%) and nationally (14%) (see Table 7.3).

We also compared the families' overall area dissatisfaction with Burrows and Rhodes' 'misery index'[2]. Burrows and Rhodes defined area dissatisfaction as 'misery' when someone identified four or more area problems as being 'serious' or 'very bad'. Table 7.4 compares the families' responses with the national picture.

Our comparison confirms a much higher level of overall area dissatisfaction among the sample families. Very few families in each neighbourhood could not identify any serious problems, compared to nearly half nationally. And almost 40% of the families in each neighbourhood were seriously 'miserable' about area conditions (that is, identified four or more serious problems) – four times the national average, of 10%.

Table 7.4: The number of issues people found to be a serious problem or classified as very bad in their area (%)

Number of issues found serious/very bad	West-City[a]	East-Docks[a]	England[b]
0	9	9	44
1	19	11	25
2	19	22	14
3	15	20	7
4 or more	38	38	10
Total	100%	100%	100%
	(47 families)	(45 families)	(19,246 households)

Notes: [a] Round 2 interviews. [b] Burrows and Rhodes (1998), based on 1994/95 Survey of English Housing. Burrows used 17 measures of satisfaction, whereas we used 16. This means that our levels of dissatisfaction are likely to be a slight underestimate.

Burrows and Rhodes identified five dominant characteristics commonly linked to high levels of dissatisfaction:

- living in London;
- living in flats (and of people living in houses, those living in terraces were more likely to be dissatisfied than those in semi-detached or detached housing);
- living in social housing (and there was a complex variation in satisfaction levels in private rented housing, with pockets of very high dissatisfaction in London and elsewhere);
- being unemployed or otherwise out of the labour market;
- not being in social class I.

Most of the families experience some of these conditions – all live in London and many experience all of these disadvantages! Housing tenure was the most influential factor in determining dissatisfaction, with renting and council housing leading to higher levels of dissatisfaction. The vast majority of the families live in social housing, or, if they are owner-occupiers, in ex-local authority accommodation within estates. Lone parents were more likely than other household types to be dissatisfied, although this did not result in very significant differences.

Based on the links Burrows and Rhodes demonstrated between socio-economic characteristics and area dissatisfaction, they then estimated levels of dissatisfaction among the populations of virtually all of the wards and districts in England. They concluded that residents of Inner London were most likely to be dissatisfied with their areas. Hackney ranked third and Newham ninth in order of dissatisfaction out of 366 districts. Only residents of Islington and Tower Hamlets were found to be more dissatisfied than in Hackney. East Dorset, at 366th, had the least dissatisfied population. Table 7.5 compares dissatisfaction among the families with dissatisfaction in the wards the neighbourhoods cover, the boroughs, and nationally.

This evidence shows that the sample neighbourhoods have higher rates of area dissatisfaction than the average for the boroughs as a whole, and nearly twice the national average. In fact, the West-City ward in the heart of the sample neighbourhood had the

Table 7.5: The proportion of people experiencing area dissatisfaction (that is, identifying four or more serious problems/issues in their area) (%)

West-City families[a]	38
East-Docks families[a]	38
West-City wards[b, c]	20-17
East-Docks wards[b, c]	19-18
Hackney[b]	17
Newham[b]	15
England[b]	10

Notes: [a] Round 2 interviews. [b] 1994/95 Survey of English Housing, in Burrows and Rhodes (1998). The borough and ward level figures are estimates. [c] The ward level data were obtained from the website attached to the report. They represent the range of results for the four wards, parts of which are included in West-City, and for the three wards which form the closest fit to East-Docks.

second most dissatisfied population of the 23 wards in Hackney, according to Burrows' estimates.

Three of the neighbourhood wards fell within the top 100 most dissatisfied wards in the country on the Burrows index, out of 8,500. Two of these are in West-City, the other is in East-Docks. The other wards fell within the top 25% of all wards. In the best ward in the country only 3.5% of the population were estimated as dissatisfied, whereas in the worst the estimate was 27.4% – eight times the rate, still far below the 37% dissatisfied among the sample families.

The fact that the wards which comprise West-City and East-Docks have among the highest levels of dissatisfaction in the country is not surprising, since we know them to be among the most deprived wards in England and Wales in terms of both 'work poverty' (deprivation based on worklessness) and the Breadline Britain deprivation index (which measures a lack of access to goods and services considered necessities in today's society) (Gordon and Pantazis, 1997). Dissatisfaction with area conditions is shown by this analysis to be strongly linked to socio-economic conditions.

However, the fact that the sample neighbourhood wards are predicted to have such high levels of 'misery' on the Burrows measure does, in part, answer the question which some of the families posed – about whether the problems in their neighbourhoods are really different from elsewhere. London fares worse than the national average. And the wards the families live in have nearly double the national average intensity of problems, according to the Burrows 'misery index'. This suggests that their actual quality of life is significantly different from other areas:

> ... the most dissatisfied groups tend to be the ones actually living in poor conditions. (DTLR, 2001)

Levels of dissatisfaction among the families were not only four times the national average, but also nearly double the predicted level of dissatisfaction for their neighbourhoods as a whole. There are a number of possible explanations for this.

We may have recruited particularly dissatisfied people. This is possible, as we did not recruit people randomly. However, one of our initial worries was that by recruiting some of the families through community groups, we might find that our sample was weighted the other way, that is, with people more likely to be happy with their neighbourhood because they were more linked in. Our finding in the first round of interviews – repeated in the second round – of optimism about the direction of neighbourhood change, underlined this concern. If anything, we would have predicted that the families' levels of dissatisfaction would be an underestimate of dissatisfaction in West-City and East-Docks[3].

It may be that even though we used the same questions, the qualitative interview setting (with a now familiar researcher) meant that people were more likely to express dissatisfaction than in a standard quantitative interview. Qualitative methods may lead to problems being overemphasised as people talk around the issues rather than giving brief responses (Duffy, 2000). One of the reasons we favour this type of research approach is that we hope over time that people will feel more able to open up and to tell us about the problems they experience, as well as the positive things in their lives. But it does mean that results from quantitative surveying are not directly comparable with our qualitative work. In practice, many of the comments made by families (discussed earlier in this chapter) suggest that people erred on the side of describing problems as less serious rather than more serious. Many mothers thought that neighbourhood problems were widespread and were not aware that their level of dissatisfaction was so much higher than average. It can, therefore, be argued that low-income households in low-income areas tolerate much lower standards.

The experience of families in disadvantaged neighbourhoods could be much harder than for other segments of the population without children, and were we able to disaggregate Burrows' results further for wards, we would be able to show this for much larger numbers of people than the sample 92 families. Certainly, the questions used to build up this particular measure of area dissatisfaction are about things that might be expected to affect households with children most – schools, public transport, leisure, the condition of the environment (given that most of the families do not have their own gardens) and aspects of crime and disorder (which families were often particularly concerned about in relation to the pressures their own children might come under and the threats they might face).

Burrows examined the national data by household type, and found higher dissatisfaction among lone parents. But this may have missed a kind of exponential effect whereby in extremely deprived areas, the difficulties of all families (not just lone parents) are greatly heightened.

Alongside extremely high levels of dissatisfaction, however, we found very wide variation in the families' responses. In both areas, 9% did not identify a single serious problem or any 'very bad' service. Just over 60% in both neighbourhoods identified fewer than four serious problems or issues. And the families in both West-City and East-Docks found their areas much more friendly than the average for London and England. None of them said it was 'not at all friendly', compared with 2% in London and England. And only 6% of West-City families and 2% in East-Docks said it was 'not very friendly' compared to 11% in London, and 7% of family respondents across England. Many of the mothers we interviewed had rich social networks and lots of facilities within walking distance, which they valued highly (as we showed in Chapter Three).

Summary and conclusions

Parents are much more worried about bringing up their children in run-down areas than they are about the areas for themselves. Generally they *are* much more dissatisfied than the national average. They encounter four times the problems with rubbish, are two-and-a-half times more worried about schools, despite seeing significant improvements, and one-and-a-half times more worried about lighting. Leisure facilities and transport, by contrast, are more popular than the national average.

Neighbourhood environments and area conditions are the most serious problems. Litter is an overwhelming problem, on twice the scale of rubbish, but litter is seen as a problem throughout the country. A total of 40% dislike the bad appearance of their area compared with 24% for London as a whole. On the other hand, many families have adapted their views on the things they consider to be serious problems in the light of their poor surroundings.

Families rely heavily on their local doctors, but other main services are often further afield. Living as they do within striking distance of the city, a world financial centre, there are no neighbourhood banks or major supermarkets and local shops are expensive. The majority of families rarely go to central London, even though for many it is only a short journey away.

On 16 standard measures of neighbourhood conditions, the sample families find many more serious problems than the rest of the population, including Hackney and Newham, as a whole. On this basis, these neighbourhoods are extremely difficult places for families and it is little wonder that nearly two fifths of them say they want to move out of the area. It reflects, in part, the condition of council estates which currently dominate these areas. Levels of satisfaction with council housing among tenants is falling fast, and much of this housing has multiple service and neighbourhood problems, as well as physical investment problems[4].

In spite of the intense concentration of problems and the unsettled communities they create, many of the families would not recognise a description of their neighbourhoods as fearful, chaotic places where quality of life is low. This is not because they are blinkered or unaware of what is going on around them – they do express high levels of dissatisfaction, as we have shown. But their experience does not match many press reports or even academic descriptions of their neighbourhood problems. Their experiences are, in fact, often conflicting, and their impressions and feelings contradictory. Problems are often serious, but these neighbourhoods are not on the brink of collapse. Our much wider study of neighbourhood decline and abandonment argues this point in more detail (Mumford and Power, 2003). On the contrary, positive things are happening in them every day and on some key measures (such as house prices, school performance and employment opportunities) the trajectory is upwards. The views of families suggest that neighbourhood services and environmental conditions are extremely significant in shaping the future for families within these areas. We look more closely at how conditions are managed in the next chapter, using open spaces and parks as our focus since families need these spaces and use them often. They are affected by almost every measure of neighbourhood conditions used in the 1999/00 Survey of English Housing. As families talked a lot about their children's need for open space, their views on public spaces offer detailed insights into how neighbourhood services actually operate.

Notes

[1] We derived the figures for families nationally by combining the figures for the two household categories 'couples with dependant children' and 'lone parents'. Data by household type was not available for London only.

[2] Throughout this chapter we use the modelled index of dissatisfaction developed by Burrows and Rhodes. This is based on reported dissatisfaction from a large national survey which is then used to predict dissatisfaction at a local level.

[3] Burrows and Rhodes' estimates could be substantial underestimates despite the detail of their method and the sample size of the Survey of English Housing. They do caution that these are modelled figures and do not capture very localised differences in attitudes towards area which are influenced by 'cultural' rather than demographic or socio-economic factors. This may well explain some of the difference in relation to the sample neighbourhoods. For example, families in East-Docks have sometimes referred to its bad reputation within Newham (particularly in the past), which contributes to a negative 'sense of place'. Also there are extremely localised estate-by-estate differences.

[4] Numerous studies have identified the problems of poor management, declining standards and low demand for council housing. These problems are not unique to council housing and can also be found in private renting and to a lesser extent owner-occupation. However, they are disproportionately concentrated in council renting (see Audit Commission reports on local authority housing 1989-2002; SEU reports 1998-2002; PAT 7/SEU, 1999; Power and Mumford, 1999; UTF, 1999; Bramley et al, 2000; Nevin et al, 2001; Mumford and Power, 2003; ODPM website: www.odpm.gov.uk; CURS website: www.curs.bham.ac.uk).

EIGHT

Parks and open spaces

"If my kids are outside, I'm looking through the window constantly, and the minute they go there I'm out through the door shouting 'Can you come inside now?' I have this fear that they're going to be taken away or something dreadful's going to happen." (Miriam)

"They [children aged 8 and 9] are not allowed outside unless I'm there because I'm on the high-rise and it would take too long for me to get to them if something happened. They should be allowed to just go out and ride their bikes, but if they do that then I should be down there with them – which is rare, because I'm always rushing to get somewhere now." (Andaiye)

"City Park is really nice. It's packed! And they've got security guards – so you know if there are paedophiles there, they can't get your children out. But it's a 40-minute walk." (Dionne)

Introduction

Parks are the lungs of urban neighbourhoods. They are invariably the major public spaces and act as social magnets for children and their parents. They are an essential safety valve in a pressurised environment. Open spaces capture neighbourhood conditions and often reflect clearly the standard of neighbourhood services. Therefore, in this chapter, we explore in depth what families think of their public environment, using this as a litmus test of how we manage cities and their neighbourhoods (Greenhalgh and Worpole, 1995; Gehl, 1996).

Particularly for families without gardens or with small gardens, living in traffic-filled streets, or unable to afford modern leisure centre activities, parks and open spaces play a crucial part in children's play, and ultimately in a families' desire to stay put or to move. They provide a place for people to meet informally and for children to mix. In this way they can contribute to the social links on which the community spirit, so important to the families, is built.

Yet the neighbourhood problems discussed in the previous chapter – such as high levels of vandalism, graffiti, dog mess, and rubbish dumping – all impact negatively on neighbourhood environments and public spaces. The problems are not necessarily intrinsic to the spaces themselves; rather the open spaces suffer most conspicuously from the wider problems of poorly run and disorderly neighbourhoods. The problems of neglect and disorder are cumulative and even highly prized spaces such as parks, which historically have received intense levels of care, start to decay. Evidence from many wider studies and policy documents lend special significance to the experience of the families (Urban Task Force, 1999; DETR, 2000).

Rough and anti-social behaviour among children and adults spills over into neighbourhood environments; stolen cars are dumped in them; gangs and large groups of youths hang out in them; litter is dropped in them; people allow their dogs to foul in them; substance abuse and other unsavoury behaviour is often sheltered within them. Even worse, they can act as pick-up points and trading centres for prostitution and drug trading, sometimes resulting in violent crime. All of this is possible because jobs have gone from within the areas. Parks are often unmanned and unguarded. Open spaces often have no regular supervision or maintenance. So parks, open spaces and the treatment they receive in many ways epitomise both the environmental and civic potential of city neighbourhoods and are one of their most abused social and community assets.

We witnessed the neglect of parks and open spaces in East London and picked up from the families how much it mattered. So we decided to look at their uses and problems more closely.

The potential benefits of parks

The vast majority of parents we spoke to felt that their children were often unable to use the open public spaces in their neighbourhoods. Children had less freedom to play outside unsupervised than they themselves did when they were growing up, because they believed that the dangers had increased. Children therefore spent less time in parks than might be expected. This was the case for parents who had always lived in the neighbourhoods, for those who had grown up in other parts of England, and for those who had grown up in other countries. Some people felt that this change had occurred everywhere – it did not only affect East London (Mumford, 2001):

> "My childhood was free. We lived in a little village and knew everyone. My children are in the house most of the time. Their social time is much more organised. I supervise them. We don't know many people and have no family here." (Nadia)

> "Everyone now it's just they go in and close their doors. Whereas before everyone's kids was outside playing." (Justine)

> "You get into debt to buy PlayStations to keep your kids off the street." (Liz)

"I'm frightened for my kids. I can't keep them trapped in this Close all their life. I want them to be able to trust in this world. But the way it's going is frightening." (Sonia)

Parks in urban areas are one of the few outdoor alternatives to playing in the street:

"It would be lovely if they could do something about it [the local park] because there is nothing else really." (Madeleine)

Seeing their children playing outside in urban parks was what families liked most about their neighbourhoods:

"It's nice to see your children out playing, instead of being stuck indoors playing computer games. I'm forever saying to my children 'It's okay to play your computer games but spread your wings – go outside and play as well'. [They play in the Close or go to the local park.] It reminds me of when I was younger. It's good to see all of them happy." (Annie)

"I like it because everything's around you – school, *park*, transport." (Kate)

"I love West–City park as it is: a fairly bare, open space." (Joanne)

"All the facilities are brilliant. All the parks." (Natalie)

Community garden, West-City

But worries about the quality and security of parks meant that they did not always fulfil these families' desires for safe, green, open spaces that their children could run around in freely:

> "The park across the road is useless. You can't keep a child in; he will need to be out, not 100% under my thumb. I want to move where he can do that." (Sushan)

> "The parks are not safe for the children to play in. We've had a couple of children almost snatched in the area before now." (Nora)

In order to set the families' views on parks in a broader context we draw on other studies of urban parks, particularly Alan Barber's analysis of Newham's parks in the mid-1990s (Barber, 1995), together with our own research into this issue. Figure 8.1 demonstrates the range of benefits that *can* accrue from parks, identified in Barber's study, as well as the benefits that we found parks specifically offered to families.

Figure 8.1: The benefits of public parks

Economical	Recreational	Environmental	Social benefits	Family benefits
Improve image	Space for sport	Wildlife habitats	Improve health	Free, shared space which all can use
Encourage investment	Venue for events	Improve micro-climates	Educational resource	Large, open spaces where children can let off steam safely
Attract visitors	Opportunities for volunteers	Reduce pollution	Promotes equality	Green, landscape very helpful to young children and mothers
Add value to property	Relief from stress	Visual contrast	Community development	Constant meeting point allows children to mix, can be used for social events

Source: expanded from Barber (1995)

Even popular, well-maintained parks cannot be a total panacea. Because of traffic, unsafe routes and lack of supervision of smaller open spaces, parents were not willing simply to let their children go to the parks. Some families commented on the effort and organisation required to take their children to the park, and this limited their use:

> "There's no garden and I don't always feel up to going to the park. And cars on the estate mean the children can't really play there – it's quite dangerous. You have to plan your whole day around going to the park – you can't just open the door and let them get on with it." (Sarah)

> "If you're a single mum, you haven't got the time to take him." (Zoe)

Use of parks is also constrained by weather conditions and daylight hours. Several families said that they used parks more in the summer, but that in the winter it was dark by the time children got home from school, and so there was a need for more organised activities indoors:

> "As a child I used to be out on my bike playing. I won't even let my kids on the balcony. Once they're home from school, they're stuck in. It's not so bad in the summer – I take them out and about, [like] to the local park." (Kate)

The fears about parks and open spaces are somewhat compensated by increasing activities in schools after hours. The schools in both areas could be an important source of organised activities, and these often had a dual role as after-school childcare provision for working parents as well as play spaces. Over a third of the families with school-age children used breakfast or after-school activities (or both).

How green are the neighbourhoods?

Our investigation of the parks, open spaces and greenery in the neighbourhoods led us to look at how they compared with other boroughs and London more generally. Hackney and Newham are highly built-up areas of London, but they have parks, garden squares, small open spaces, trees and play areas that are potentially very valuable to the families. Newham has 22 parks (two in East-Docks), just over 60 open spaces managed for amenity use (three in East-Docks), and numerous other small green sites and verges (interview with parks project officer, Newham Parks, 9 November 2000).

London as a whole is known as a 'green city' because of its large parks, its green garden squares, and its individual back gardens, all of which are found even in densely built-up inner-city neighbourhoods:

The main 'green' area north of the major road in East-Docks

> London's extensive and varied open spaces represent some of its most highly valued possessions and contribute to its world city status.... [But] open space is distributed unevenly: some parts of London clearly have little or none at all. (LPAC, 1994)

By comparison with other areas: "Newham has one of the lowest total amounts of public open space for the size of its population in Britain, and most of these green spaces serve densely-populated catchment areas" (Barber, 1995).

There are 13m² of open space per person in Newham, which is less than half the Greater London average of 28m² per person. These figures are tempered by the fact that Newham's open space is spread quite evenly through the borough (Barber, 1995), and the figure does not include smaller spaces of under 2 hectares (LPAC, 1994). Because smaller spaces fall outside of LPAC's study, it records the City of London as having no open space at all. Nor does the LPAC study count small back or front gardens. Yet smaller spaces include sitting-out areas, and paths alongside canals for example, which can be "particularly valuable in high density areas"

Table 8.1: Area of publicly accessible open spaces (parks)[a]

	Publicly accessible open spaces (parks) (hectares)	Total accessible area as % of area of borough
Islington (least)	44	3
Newham	252	7
Hackney	289	15
Camden	377	17
Richmond upon Thames (most)	1,817	33
London total	14,617	13

Note: [a] This is based on a 'hierarchy of parks' ranging from regional parks, via metropolitan and district to local parks.

Source: LPAC (1995)

(LPAC, 1994). In New York these small spaces have turned into 'green streets' and 'pocket parks', with strong encouragement of community involvement and family use (Rogers and Power, 2000).

East-Docks appears greener than West-City to the casual observer because of the greater number of houses with private gardens, and the presence of grass verges not counted in Table 8.1, but Hackney as a whole has a higher proportion of public open space than Newham. Parts of Hackney (such as Hackney Downs) have much larger expanses of open space than West-City. Table 8.1 shows the difference between the boroughs.

At neighbourhood level, there is an impression of unkempt, built-up and 'unloved' environments. In both areas, families commented on the lack of greenery in their area; the bleakness of the environment; the lack of attractive public spaces to walk through and for children to play in; the built-up character of the area, unbroken by trees. This created a sense of real deprivation:

> "Inside, some of the flats are beautiful, but outside is grey." (Sinead)

> "There's one thing that's really preying on my mind. There's a school across the road, but it doesn't have playing fields, just concrete. I grew up across the road from [a really large park] – there's nothing like that round here." (Felicity)

> "I wouldn't really want to walk about round here – it's not a nice outlook and it ain't a nice walk. If I go over my friend's in Kent, I feel quite nice being there. You can walk across the road to a duck pond, a nice little pub with a garden. It does make a big difference." (Lesley)

> Interviewer: "What would most help your family?"

> "An area that's more open – it's very compact round here – an area where they can run around and enjoy themselves." (Nicola)

The lack of green open spaces was driving some families' desire to move away altogether:

> "When you take them out of London and you see them running around, and big open spaces, you think 'Am I really depriving them by not giving them this more often?'." (Jane)

> "I would move more rural to have more space, more greenery, rather than look out of the window and see rows and rows of houses." (Andrea)

Families' criticism of their neighbourhood environments concerned not only the amount of open space, but also a desire for more trees. Newham is the most treeless area of London, apart from the City; it has half the London average. Hackney has just below the London average.

> "More trees – I'd like to see more trees. And sometimes you see a car park and you think 'If only they'd built a bit of a brick wall round that and put a few bushes there, that would have looked 10 times better than just a car park'. Just a few trees and bushes." (Peggy)

The comparison with the neighbouring borough of Islington is fascinating. Islington has the least open space per resident of any inner London borough. To help compensate, it adopted a proactive tree-planting policy in the 1970s and 1980s, involving residents in sponsoring trees outside their own doors. Now its density of trees far exceeds the London average (see Table 8.2). One reason for the tree-planting campaign was the acute lack of open space, which is highlighted in Table 8.2.

Green spaces can reinforce and add to community resources, generating more contact and more links, identified in Chapter Four as important in building social cohesion. Many families referred to the advantages of urban living because of the shared spaces and amenities:

> "I've been happy growing up here. I don't really like Essex because it's quite quiet and there aren't many shops and things. But here it's quite busy. I like the town, I wouldn't like to live in the countryside." (Grace)

Table 8.2: Density of trees in London (summer 1992)

	Individual trees per hectare
City of London (least dense in London)	7.9
Newham	14.5
Hackney	25.9
Islington	34.6
Kensington & Chelsea (most dense in Inner London)	35.4
Sutton (most dense in London)	42.9
All London	27.6

Source: London Tree Survey in LPAC (1995). There was no close correlation between individual tree cover and Inner-Outer location. A sampling method of survey plots was used which may have led to error at the borough level, so caution must be taken with these figures.

> "I like this area because of familiarity. I'm used to it. You make your own little village wherever you are – it might be a mile, it might be 50 yards." (Peggy)

Communal open space seems to play a big part in the families' sense of identity with their neighbourhood, and in their quality of life. For these reasons, we explore carefully the use people make of these green spaces.

Families' use of and views about parks

The vast majority of the families (84%) used local parks even though they might be critical of their shortcomings. We define 'local' as a park within approximately 10 minutes walk of home. This is in line with national figures, showing that the vast majority (70%) of people walk to parks, and 68% take less than five minutes to get to their local park (Greenhalgh and Worpole, 1995). A Newham survey of women found that 87% go to the park on foot, suggesting very local usage, but almost half the respondents had also visited a park outside Newham (Barber, 1995). Among the sample families too, nearly half used a park that was not their local park. These families were prepared to travel further afield to get the environment they sought for their children:

> "We decided yesterday we would go to a park and ended up going to Ilford because it's the nicest park around. We went by car yesterday, but otherwise it's quite a trek for the littl'un." (Rachel)

Nearly all the families use parks and most use local parks at least sometimes. A third more families in East-Docks than West-City only used their 'local' park. Hackney families are near to Victoria Park, a major open space that acts as a magnet for the area and yet it is not strictly a local park. Table 8.3 shows which parks families use.

Families identified many changes they would like to see. The New Deal for Communities has prioritised the main local park in West-City for a total makeover as a result of resident opinion:

> "We just use West-City Park to cut through to the doctors. It's a bit big and boring and flat. I saw in the doctors' surgery there are plans for regenerating it. I shall be very interested – it's a good space. At the moment it's just not worth a special trip." (Felicity)

Table 8.3: Families' use of parks (number of families)

	West-City	East-Docks	Total
'Local' parks only	18	27	45
Local plus other parks in or out of borough	24	8	32
Other parks in or out of borough, but not local	4	4	8
Do not use any park	1	2	3
Not recorded	0	4	4
Total	47	45	92

Table 8.4 summarises the families' views of parks in response to an open question 'Would you like to see any changes to the way the parks are currently run?' These comments relate to any park the family used. A cry for more supervision was top of the list in East-Docks; this was mentioned directly by fewer families in West-City because both the main parks there have an element of supervision already. Overall, in both areas, the supervision, management and maintenance of the parks, alongside more equipment and activities, came top of the list.

Supervision and maintenance

In all, 71 of the families' comments concerned supervision and maintenance – including the need to clean up dogs' mess (26), a desire for on-site staff including bringing back the old park-keepers (16), the need to tackle the rough behaviour of older children (8), the need to repair or replace old-style play equipment (8), and a desire for supervised toilets (3).

Table 8.4: Parks and open spaces: changes the families wanted (number of families)

	West-City	East-Docks	Total
Supervision and maintenance			
Clean-up dogs' mess, create dog-free areas	15	11	26
Supervision, bring back the old park-keepers	4	12	16
Repair/replace old play equipment	0	8	8
Tackle rough behaviour of older children	4	4	8
Introduce organised activities	0	4	4
Introduce supervised toilets	0	3	3
Better cleaning	2	1	3
Remove public drinkers and drug users	2	0	2
Lock parks at night	1	0	1
	28	**43**	**71**
Add extra features/equipment			
More play equipment	18	9	27
More variety, purpose, make park more exciting	9	5	14
Gear more to younger children	2	2	4
Plant more trees	2	1	3
Introduce benches	0	2	2
Water features eg swimming pool, pond	2	0	2
Coffee place/drinking tap	2	0	2
Build a small, secure playground nearby	1	1	2
	36	**20**	**56**
Happy with the parks as they are, no changes needed	8	7	15
Total comments	72	70	142
(some families made more than one)			

Staff presence

The reintroduction of staff based on site was a clear priority for the East-Docks families:

> "You need parkie back for a start!" (Dionne)

> "A bit like the old days – get your park keeper! I know they have a parks constabulary, but it's not the same." (Madeleine)

> "Maybe a park watchman [would help] because it's like nobody's around." (Miriam)

> "Years ago, they had park keepers. Now they go all round different parks, rather than being just for one park. They should go back to that. So at least someone's in the park if there's trouble. You get a lot of prowlers in the parks, and people driving round by the parks as well. The thing is half the parks are empty now because the parents are too scared to let them go." (Jackie)

Eight families (four in each neighbourhood) were concerned about the rough behaviour of older children in the parks, including swearing. This is linked to the need for good supervision and more varied provision of facilities:

> "[We need] more supervision and locking the parks up of an evening. So that if older ones are smashing things they can be told not to." (Linda)

> "I took my five-year-old daughter to the adventure playground one day, but older children were there and doing a lot of swearing and cursing. I thought I'm not ready for her to be in that environment yet." (Faye)

> "That park is on the housing estate where you get a lot of the teenagers that are causing problems. So with the younger ones you have got to be careful. They've got no consideration." (Kate)

One of the biggest problems is older children occupying space designed for younger children:

> "You get older children sitting on things and younger children don't get the chance to play [on them]. I think that's bad. There again, you need something for the youth." (Sophie)

A very popular park with the East-Docks families was a large park situated to the north of the neighbourhood run by the City of London. We call it City Park. The park has permanent staff on duty, which makes a big difference. They offer security, direct supervision of play areas, emergency help and back-up, if needed.

> "I'm happy because I've not seen or heard of any danger that has happened in the park. Staff are always there [including] a first aider. There's always a security guard around." (Gloria)

> "We also go out further to other parks, including City Park. They're quite nice parks because you've got people that go around. In the play area you've got people that sit there all day so they keep their eye on it, so no one's actually misusing anything." (Kate)

City parks are neither cheap nor easy to run. Hackney Parks Department highlighted an ongoing lack of investment in parks as one of the key problems it faces; parks are not a political priority at local level even though the government is now promoting reinvestment. The confidence and morale of Hackney park staff has been further eroded recently because of the financial crisis besetting the council (B. Makkar, notes of meeting with Hackney Parks Department, 2001). Sadly, the Urban Green Spaces Task Force report *Green spaces better places* fails to recognise either the full revenue needs of parks or the absolute requirement that they be tended permanently and on a full-time basis by committed and experienced staff (DTLR, 2002).

The removal of permanent park keepers happened across much of the country from the 1980s onwards, due to the cost-cutting associated with Compulsory Competitive Tendering (CCT). On-site staff were usually replaced by mobile contractors and security services. To save money on the contract, councils therefore reduced the amount of time staff spent in parks. Staff had built-in incentives to speed in and out, to carry out the very basic tasks (such as cutting the grass) as quickly as possible. Parks facilities and ornamental features requiring high maintenance were removed to further cut costs. Mobile services can actually have the effect of signalling danger rather than providing reassurance because park staff tend not to be there in a positive, proactive way, but as a response to incidents. And park users rarely see them because each visit is cut to the shortest possible time and is invariably motorised – in a van or on a mowing machine.

Staff become less familiar with the terrain and no longer have a strong local identity. Families and children no longer recognise them as the staff change and move constantly. The low level, familiar presence with continual attention to detail is replaced by a more fragmented, clipped and narrowly targeted service (Greenhalgh and Worpole, 1995).

Park keepers are not there specifically to provide security, but people feel safer because they are around, and they know them. The park keepers have a local base and a link to the outside. Once on-site staffing levels are reduced, fewer people use the parks, the likelihood of attacks on staff increases, and supervision is then further withdrawn. This has happened in several London boroughs. If adult staff occasionally suffer actual assaults and are withdrawn from the parks, it is no wonder that parents are concerned for their children.

Wider societal changes have also had an impact – the increasing intensity of anti-social acts and adults increasingly unlikely to challenge the behaviour of other people's children because they fear retaliation by them or their parents. These wider changes are combined with exceptionally high levels of disorder in both the neighbourhoods, which we discuss in the next chapter. As a result, public spaces and the services that manage them come under intense pressure:

> "Thirty years ago social behaviour was very different and an adult within the park may have been enough to deter problems. Today this would not be the case, especially within impoverished urban areas." (correspondence with authors, Newham Parks, 27 June 2001)

When we spoke to the families, Newham's parks constabulary service was providing mobile supervision to its parks and open spaces. At that time, a parks officer reported that the general feeling among the community was that they were not living up to expectations. People tended not to see them, and they were often not there when trouble was actually taking place. This mirrors the experience of estates that replaced resident caretakers with mobile caretakers and the police reducing its street presence (Power, 1987; Power and Tunstall, 1997).

However, during 2001 Newham changed and enhanced the parks constabulary service in response to community concerns that officers were not high profile enough. There are now 25 officers (an increase from 15) who spend 100% of their time during park opening hours in Newham's parks, and are attached to specific parks:

> "Officers are assigned specific parks so as to build better relationships with park users. They have a specific role of interacting with the community and will attend focus groups and community meetings as required." (correspondence with authors, Newham Parks, 27 June 2001)

This matches the views of the families we spoke to. It also fits with critical views of the government select committee reviewing parks and open spaces (DTLR, 2002).

The parks constabulary in Newham is now responsible for the closing of parks every day. Other local authorities are also introducing parks police to help contain problems (Middleton, 2002):

"This firmly puts officers in the parks at a time when traditionally there have been higher levels of anti-social behaviour." (correspondence with authors, Newham Parks, 27 June 2001)

The parks service emphasised that there was a need for a *permanent presence* to be restored to the parks, but argued that this should not simply be one park keeper; rather, they envisaged a whole range of different activities with staff attached. The intention is to make people feel safer, to attract and entertain more children, to generate more life and, if possible, revenue, by creating managed facilities within parks:

"Leased facilities, such as cafes and after school centres can generate much needed income for the park as well as provide increased user levels and a form of permanent presence which will deter aspects of anti-social behaviour." (correspondence with authors, Newham Parks, 27 June 2001)

The council is hoping that these facilities can be set up and run by community groups. The increased level of activity and the local involvement should then have a positive knock-on effect on feelings of safety in the park as a whole, as long as community groups are strong enough and sufficiently supported to be able to manage such facilities in wide-open spaces. Parks will still need core supervision and security in order to do this safely and effectively, given the problems that parents reported. One incident or attack could be enough to close a park playgroup down. The developing constabulary service is also likely to have a key role to play:

"As the level of officers grows they are becoming an effective system in preventing serious problems of anti-social behaviour within parks." (correspondence with authors, Newham Parks, 27 June 2001)

Dogs

Dog mess is a real problem not only in the parks and in other public open spaces, but also on the pavements. But in these inner urban areas, dog owners have few alternative places to take their dogs. If they do not clear up after their dogs in the limited spaces that do exist, the problem quickly becomes concentrated. Dog mess in parks was a big problem in both neighbourhoods. A small number of families also commented that their children were afraid of dogs, and this restricted their enjoyment of parks:

"It's the dogs – my little girl is afraid of dogs. They don't do anything, but there are so many dogs there she doesn't move freely." (Andaiye)

"We're a nation of dog-lovers but children-haters." (Rosemary)

It was dog mess specifically that caused the most serious concern:

"There's nothing in West-City park! It's a dogs' toilet basically." (Joan)

"The only thing I don't like is the dogs' mess. It's really not nice for the kids, because they're always rolling about on the grass." (Jessica)

"You go out on a nice summer day and you've got dogs poop around you, and it's not fair." (Clare)

The extent of dog mess sometimes put families off from using the park at all:

"Dogs have made West-City park unusable." (Debra)

"It's very rare that I will use the parks round here. For reasons like – things have been vandalised or dogs have fouled around the place." (Flowella)

"I could let them play down there [green outside block] but there's dogs' muck and glass." (Linda)

Newham Parks Service had very limited success with attempts to enforce 'poop scoop schemes', but then there was no on-site presence to supervise the schemes:

"It costs loads of money, and people still let their dogs go anywhere. Half the bins got vandalised." (interview with parks project officer, Newham Parks, 9 November 2000)

This may change with the new parks constabulary. Newham has plans to install dog-free areas such as picnic areas, children's play areas and sports areas.
Families in both areas praised the few parks that had dog-free areas (these were all outside the immediate neighbourhoods), and wanted them introduced in their local parks:

"Maybe they should make a separate park for dogs!" (Dominique's child)

The dual problems of lack of supervision and dog mess did seem to hold families with young children back from using open space as much as they wanted.

Organised activities, play equipment and variety

One of the ways of making parks more attractive, better used and therefore safer is to provide more for people to do in them. Four families in East-Docks wanted organised activities within the parks, and one remembered a time when this used to happen:

> "It is quite a shame that there isn't a lot more going on for them. You used to have a lot of things going on in the parks at one time years ago. There was these park people employed in the parks. There'd be a lady there who would work during the holidays and she would do games, drawing, painting.... Perhaps parks could be opened up again or something." (Peggy)

There are some activities in the parks already, including a supervised adventure playground in West-City and 'Arc in the Park' near East-Docks, whose 'play team' offer an adventure playground, garden project and off-site trips. These make a big difference as they offer indirect supervision as well as actual organised activity, which informally brokers the use of the park for families. In a densely used environment the shared common spaces come under intense pressure, and any activity that draws groups in helps to reduce the potential for wider trouble. Over a long time, play schemes and adventure playgrounds have shown this (National Playing Fields Association, 1995).

Twenty-seven families felt that the present play equipment was inadequate and did not cater for the full range of children's ages. This was a big priority in Hackney because of its bare local park. And eight families in East-Docks were concerned at the poor state of existing equipment:

> "[We need] more swings and maintenance. The swings have got in a dreadful state over that big park." (Natasha)

> "The swings and things for younger kids need to be fixed. A lot round here are broken or have graffiti on." (Constance)

Newham is actively investigating possibilities for extra investment. It recognises that: "play equipment is old, dated and in need of replacement. It is still probably the biggest attraction of the parks for people" (interview with parks project officer, Newham Parks, 9 November 2000). The New Deal for Communities has committed funds for improving equipment in the area just north of East-Docks, and for a total revamp of West-City park. A recreation ground in the heart of East-Docks is due to be completely redeveloped, with a children's play area and football provision.

Fourteen families specifically mentioned the bareness of local parks; they wanted more variety within them. Some parks were not attractive, lively or child-friendly.

One park was so bare that a family referred to it as the 'wasteland'. Bleak open spaces feel uncared for:

> "There is nothing basically! No benches even to sit on! There is only one slide." (Sasha)

> "[Our local park] is really big – but there's nothing there to play with. They could do better to make that really good for the kids – especially as we're living in council flats with no balcony, no nothing." (Frances)

> "When they were little, I used to take them to the park. As they grew up (now nursery and primary age) they need more – there's just one swing. They get bored of it. They stay home now." (Aminia)

> "There is a local park, but there is nothing in the park." (Sade)

> "West-City Park is a bit full of dogs' muck and not much else. I would like to see a playground, a sandpit – and one that's supervised." (Jane)

> "West-City Park has got nothing in it, so it's not worth it. We do go over the green sometimes in the summer, but the kids get bored with it." (Lesley)

Since city parks are often quite small and enclosed by buildings, careful design and meticulous upkeep can make a major difference to how many different age groups and activities can co-exist.

Learning lessons from popular parks

One sixth of the families expressed satisfaction with the parks as they were; they did not identify any changes needed:

> "They're always nice and tidy and clean. Everything seems to be well-maintained." (Nadia, using parks south of East-Docks)

> "I think it's alright really. There's quite a lot round here." (Megan)

The three parks almost universally praised were 'City Park' in Newham, 'Thyme Park' neighbouring West-City, and Victoria Park (real name) in Tower Hamlets. Victoria Park was used not only by 13 West-City families (who are reasonably near it) but also by four East-Docks families. At weekends nearly 10% of Victoria Park's visitors are Newham residents (Barber, 1995). These parks stand out because

Table 8.5: Positive characteristics of three popular parks: 'City Park', 'Thyme Park' and Victoria Park

	Variety[a]	Big	Swimming or paddling pool	Supervision	Well-used	Clean	Toilets	First aid	Pond	Dog-free areas	Trees
City	✔	✔	✔	✔	✔		✔	✔			✔
Thyme	✔	✔	✔	✔	✔	✔	✔			✔	
Victoria	✔	✔	✔	✔		✔			✔		

Note: [a]For example both open and secluded spaces, play equipment to suit younger and older children, a mix of activities.

of the consistently positive comments families made about them. The most prominent were the size and level of constant supervision, the variety of spaces and activities within them, water, paddling and swimming pools. Table 8.5 shows the positive characteristics families identified in City, Thyme and Victoria Parks.

The three most popular parks were not the *most* used because they were not situated directly in the areas. West-City Park and 'East-Docks Central' were the most used by the sample families (27 and 14), although both these parks received very few positive comments. While these are much the most local, they are far from the best parks. This illustrates the importance of open space close to home. In addition, 13 West-City families used small playgrounds within the estates. If people did not have a playground on their own estate, they would sometimes use those on other estates.

Summary and conclusion

Parks and open spaces are an extremely valuable communal resource to the families in these neighbourhoods, often providing the only outdoor play space for children. Even when families identify serious shortcomings with their local parks, most (84%) still use them. Most families wanted more supervision, maintenance, activity and equipment in their local parks, to attract more use, prevent trouble and create greater community benefit. The quality of parks, and the amount of greenery in the local environment, help shape families' feelings about the area. Parks, and the environment more generally, play an important part in families' sense of place and connection with their neighbourhood, and can reinforce the advantages or disadvantages of urban living. Because of their public character and usage, they require a level of ongoing care that reflects the quality of local services. In areas where neighbourhood services are inadequate, the local environment will suffer. This chapter reinforces the findings of Chapter Seven, demonstrating that the current level of care is inadequate for the task.

Yet neighbourhood disorder impinges on parks. Parks and other public spaces become a focus for anti-social behaviour and criminal activity, particularly in the absence of effective supervision. This inevitably encroaches on families' desire to use them, setting off a downward spiral of withdrawal, loss of control, abuse and further withdrawal. The families' strong desire for more supervision underlines the importance of a sense of order and protection in the arrangement and use of open spaces in urban neighbourhoods.

Parks can work extremely well in inner urban areas – and three parks were particularly popular with the families, all within East London. There is clearly no definitive set of characteristics that makes parks work. But the main features of these popular parks closely match the families' suggestions for changes to the other parks they use, and the findings of other studies: "interesting things to see and do, where everything is clean and well cared for and there is visible stewardship" (Barber, 1995).

Popularity breeds popularity – the more people use a park, the more attractive it becomes. Some characteristics of parks are clearly fixed and unchangeable, such as the sheer size of the park. Some elements take 20 years to change, such as tree planting and mature plant growth. Other elements have significant costs associated with them, such as the management of a swimming pool. But meeting families' wishes for supervision, cleanliness, and variety should be achievable. And with long-term commitment, care and dedication it should be possible to plant and protect more trees today for tomorrow's children in many small spaces around these neighbourhoods. But even tree planting only works with supervision and community involvement, bringing us back to how distressed neighbourhoods should be run. The conditions and problems of parks only reinforce the need for high quality, on-the-spot neighbourhood services.

Encouraging initiatives are underway, such as the developing constabulary service in Newham, the redevelopment of the recreation ground in the heart of East-Docks, and the New Deal for Communities funding for West-City Park. There are also simple and affordable models of compensating for lack of open space, such as Islington's 'tree for a tree' scheme and the way the three 'star' parks the families use are run. However, as long as high levels of neighbourhood disorder continue, public open spaces will be underused and the management and maintenance of small local parks will continue to be an uphill battle for hard-pressed public services within these neighbourhoods. The idea that local community groups can themselves make urban public spaces work is disproved by the evidence we collected. It needs strong public leadership and organisation to provide a framework within which communities can participate without fear (site visit by author, New York City Green Spaces, 2000).

In the next chapter we look at how serious the problem of disorder is, and whether there are ways to contain and control it. We believe that parks and open spaces have a critical role in creating or undermining community safety. By caring for open spaces, encouraging children, teenagers and adults to use them, employing teams of locally known people to run, clean and maintain them, opening them up to community activity and initiatives, they provide alternative magnets for energy (Centre for Architecture and the Built Environment, 2002). By creating 'green lungs', turning grey streets into tree-lined and safe pedestrian pathways, by turning every corner and verge into a privileged green space that young families can enjoy, people will walk and children will run through the spaces that were previously bleak and dirty – 'unused and therefore abused'.

Cities all over the world struggle with how to provide free, relaxed, informal yet supervised public spaces. London neighbourhoods have their fair share of parks and open spaces, but more than their fair share of abuse, which cuts into their value. It is to this problem we turn next.

NINE

Disorder in the neighbourhoods: families' experiences of crime, gangs, neighbour problems, vandalism, graffiti, drugs and 'rough' behaviour

"Mainly it's teenagers haven't got nothing to do – it's fun to steal it, crash it, burn it." (Carrie)

Introduction

When we first talked to the families, we found that crime, drugs, insecurity and fear were the main reasons for the overwhelming feeling of the majority that their children had restricted childhoods. In West-City, these problems were a strong reason for some families wanting to move out of the area altogether. A few in East-Docks gave crime and disorder as their main reason for wanting to move out, but many other families expressed general concern about their sense of security. Their children's freedom was often curtailed by fear. We wanted to find out how grounded that fear was in reality.

We asked the families directly about crime, neighbour problems, vandalism, graffiti, drugs and insecurity the second time we visited them, in order to understand better their actual experiences, and whether their fears were based on more than a general feeling of insecurity. Our findings show that at the extreme end of neighbourhood problems, many families are living through a tangible breakdown in social control that is largely external to their own family lives. This split between how families saw their own lives and how they saw this particular aspect of their neighbourhoods was particularly undermining to their confidence in the future. In this chapter we relay the families' experiences, focusing on the devastating impact on morale, stability and social relations of constant insecurity.

Crime

A very high proportion of the families felt that crime was a serious problem in their area (61%), more than four times the average for families nationally (14%), and far more than in similarly deprived areas across the country (36%) (Whitehead and Smith, 1998; DTLR, 2001).

Table 9.1: Whether crime is a problem in the area (%)

	West-City[a]	East-Docks[a]	7 SRB areas[b]	London[c]	England families[c,d]
Serious problem	57	64	36	17	14
Problem but not serious	28	11	–	46	46
Not a problem	13	22	–	37	40
Don't know	2	2	–	–	–
Not recorded	–	–	–	–	–
Total (= 100%)	47 families	45 families	–	2,779,000	5,643,000

Notes: [a] Round 2 interviews. [b] MORI survey of seven deprived areas nationally for the DETR in 1996/97 (Whitehead and Smith, 1998). [c] 1999/00 Survey of English Housing; [d] England families comprise lone parents and couples with dependent children. The data was not available for London families only, so we show the figures for all London respondents.

Nationally, concern about crime fell during the 1990s; 22% of all respondents thought that crime was a serious problem in 1992, compared with just 12% in 1999/00 (DTLR, 2001). Actual crime in England and Wales also fell, by a third during 1995-2000, according to the latest British Crime Survey (Travis, 2001). These national reductions suggest an even starker gap between the 'average' experience and the crime problem in the sample neighbourhoods.

The main types of crime the families identified as a problem were mugging, car crime (vandalism, theft from, theft of), and stealing from both houses and shops (see Table 9.2). Families in West-City saw mugging as the main problem (50% of families mentioned this). In East-Docks, car crime was mentioned most frequently, with 20 comments about the problem of car vandalism and theft from cars, and a further 18 comments about the problems of car theft, joy-riding and car dumping. We explore car crime in more detail below.

The families mainly talked about crimes against the person or against property, rather than other forms of law-breaking such as traffic offences or fraud. Only

Table 9.2: Type of crime that is a problem in the area (number of families among those who thought crime was a problem)

	West-City	East-Docks	Total
Cars – vandalism/theft from	13	20	33
Cars – theft of/dumped cars/joy-riding	7	18	25
Mugging	23	9	32
Other violent crime against the person eg murder, shooting, stabbing, fights	9	3	12
Stealing from homes, shops	14	13	27
Drugs (mentioned separately from drug-related crime such as some muggings)	4	7	11
Other including alcoholism, petty crime, vandalism, benefit fraud	11	8	19
Total comments (many families identified more than one type of crime)	81	78	159

one mother specifically raised benefit fraud as an example of the type of crime that was a problem in the neighbourhood. And, on the whole, people talked about crime in the external environment rather than within the home, visible crime rather than less visible crime such as domestic violence, and crime carried out by strangers. One mother did describe the ongoing domestic violence she was experiencing. Another talked about the domestic violence a neighbour was experiencing, and one said that 'domestics' (meaning fights within families that could spill out into the streets) were a problem in the neighbourhood.

The families' personal experience of crime

Personal experience of crime undermined people's confidence in their environment; 39% of the families we spoke to had experienced a crime within the last 12 months:

> "I think I know who did it. It just makes you a bit more wary."
> (Rachel)

> "I just don't feel safe here anymore. [The assault] has really made me
> feel very determined to move out of here." (Marie)

The 36 families who had personally been victims of crime in the past 12 months had experienced 47 incidents between them. These incidents ranged from petty theft out of gardens to serious assaults. Car crime was the most frequently experienced (with 17 incidents of vandalism or theft from cars, and a further five incidents of stolen vehicles). Particularly worrying were attacks on children; five children had been mugged, threatened or assaulted, two at knife-point. The types of crime experienced are detailed in Table 9.3.

A further eight families in West-City and six families in East-Docks talked about their recent close experience of crime, such as witnessing a crime, for example. And eight of the families who had personally experienced crime had also had wider experience of it. In all, these 22 families had witnessed or directly come across 31 separate incidents, shown in Table 9.4. This is likely to be an underestimate as we did not ask people directly about this wider experience of crime; we simply recorded it when they raised it during the interview. In addition, many families talked about problems with abandoned and burnt-out cars, but not necessarily in relation to their experience of crime.

Table 9.3: Types of crime directly experienced by the families in the past 12 months

	West-City	East-Docks	Total
Car vandalised	4	5	9
Theft from car	4	4	8
Theft of car/van/motorbike	2	3	5
House burgled/broken into	4	I	5
Child mugged or assaulted and/or threatened with knife	3	2	5
Racial harassment	I	2	3
Theft of push-bike	I	I	2
Petty theft from garden	I	I	2
Adult family member assaulted	–	I	I
Other harassment	–	I	I
Domestic violence	I	–	I
Other (eg theft from bag, road rage)	2	3	5
Total	18 families	18 families	36 families
	23 incidents	24 incidents	47 incidents

Table 9.4: Families' wider experience of crime

	Total
In the past 12 months:	
Witnessed stabbing or other serious assault	4
Witnessed car on fire/car vandalism/stolen cars	4
Witnessed break-in to home/ shop/other theft	3
Witnessed mugging	2
Witnessed threatening behaviour	I
Neighbour's house broken into	3
Neighbour mugged	2
Elderly neighbour 'conned'	I
Relative murdered	I
Nearby relative broken into	I
Body found on estate	I
Heard gun shot	I
Mentioned crime within last 3 years (including racial harassment, mugging, car crime, break-in)[a]	7
	22 families
	31 incidents

Note: [a] Seven families mentioned earlier experiences spontaneously.

What this means in practice is that 50 of the 92 families, almost the same proportions in each neighbourhood, had either directly experienced or been closely involved in incidents of crime in their area. There was not an exact match between experience of and concern about crime, but two thirds of those who said that crime was a serious problem in their area had had direct or wider experience of it. Correspondingly, three quarters of those who said crime was not a problem had not had any experience of it either. The families' very high level of concern about crime was based to a large extent on actual experience or on neighbourhood events they could not escape knowing about.

In all, at least 54% of families knew directly about, witnessed or suffered as victims of crime in the previous three years. This does not include signs people saw of more general disorder, such as vandalism to public property, smashed up cars or rubbish dumping, which are linked to higher crime risks for residents (Mirrlees-Black and Allen, 1998). Thus the gap between crime experienced and concern felt is small, since 61% felt that crime was a serious problem.

The British Crime Survey has consistently shown that, although people tend to overestimate the crime problem, fear of crime is strongly related to actual levels of crime. Concerns are greater in higher risk areas and among those who have been victims of crime, and falling levels of crime are generally matched by falling levels of concern (Mirrlees-Black and Allen, 1998).

Reporting crime to the police

We asked those families who had experienced a crime within the last 12 months whether they had reported it to the police. Half of those in East-Docks, and just two fifths in West City, had reported all the crimes they had experienced to the police. A further 17% in each area had reported some of the crimes they experienced, but not others. A significant minority – one third of families who had experienced a crime in West-City, and one fifth in East-Docks – had not reported any crimes.

In West-City fewer families consistently reported crime than reported it 'only sometimes' or 'never'. In East-Docks, more families reported crime than did not. Even so, nearly 40% 'only sometimes' or 'never' did. The under-reporting of crime across the country is widely acknowledged:

> Repeated 'sweeps' of the British Crime Survey … have established beyond doubt that the official totals reflect only the tip of an iceberg of crimes known to victims, the majority of which go unreported and unrecorded. (Maguire, 1994)

Initial findings from the 2001 British Crime Survey suggest that around four times as many crimes were committed in 2000 as were actually reported to the police (Travis, 2001).

We asked the families who did contact the police how they found the response from the police. When we classified the results from 'very good' to 'very poor', we found that three times as many families had found the police response positive or 'okay' as found it 'poor'.

Sixteen crimes were not reported: this represents a third of the total incidents experienced by the 36 families in the past 12 months. Of the crimes not reported, most concerned car vandalism or theft from cars. Unreported crimes do, on the whole, involve "much lower levels of financial loss, damage, and injury than those reported to the police" (Maguire, 1994).

We asked the families why they had not contacted the police. The main reason given was that the police would not be able to do anything about it, so there was no point. The following comments illustrate the feelings of those who did not see the point in reporting the crimes they had experienced:

> "[The police] won't even walk on the streets, let alone look for a mobile phone … they're going to laugh." (Rosemary)

Another mother did not want to bother the police with a trivial theft from her garden:

> "I'm sure the police have got better things to do!" (Joyce)

One mother preferred to deal with her child's muggers herself, although she did not find them. We do not know what 'dealing with them' would have involved, but use of personal force was implied. This mother was certainly extremely angry:

> "I looked for my child's muggers – I would have dealt with it myself. I would have dealt with it my own way." (Liz)

Putting the families' experience into context

It is important to set the families' experience in a wider context. The high level of crime reported by the families reflects the serious difference between these areas and elsewhere. The boroughs in which the two neighbourhoods are situated both have significantly higher recorded crime rates than the Metropolitan average, and the England average. In London, the average rate of violence against the person and sexual offences is *double* the England average and the average rate of robbery in London is *triple* the England average. The recorded rates of these crimes in both Hackney and Newham are higher still. For example, Hackney's

**Table 9.5: Index of recorded crimes per 1,000 population[a]
(July 1997-June 1998)**

	Criminal damage	Violence against person	Sexual offences	Robbery	Burglary, dwelling	Burglary, other	Drugs supply	Vehicle crime
Hackney	144	173	155	226	162	105	200	165
Newham	128	128	100	171	141	114	100	148
MPD[b]	100	100	100	100	100	100	100	100
England and Wales	94	54	55	35	105	148	80	104

Notes: [a] Per 1,000 households for residential burglary. [b] Average crime rates for the whole of the Metropolitan Police District were set at 100. Each borough's figures are then expressed in relation to this index.

Source: London Borough of Newham and the Metropolitan Police, 1998/99 in Mumford (2001)

recorded rate of robbery is more than double the London average, and more than six times the England average. Newham's rate of robbery is nearly five times the England average. Hackney's crime rate is much higher than Newham's for all categories of offence apart from burglary of premises other than dwellings (see Table 9.5).

A local crime survey conducted in West-City in 1998 suggested that the reported crime rate was even higher in the sample neighbourhood than in the rest of Hackney. It calculated 256 crimes per 1,000 people in West-City compared to 179 for Hackney as a whole, 124 for the Metropolitan Police District and 97 nationally (Lupton, 2000a, 2000b; West-City New Deal Trust, 2000a; see Figure 9.1).

The local police inspector in West-City identified the main problems as vehicle crime, young people troubling elderly people, and fear of crime (R. Lupton, interview with police inspector, West-City Police Station, 17 May 1999). The very high crime rate is linked to a high level of vehicle offences (R. Lupton, discussion with author, 4 June 2001), and to drug-related crime in one specific ward (West-City New Deal Trust, 2000a).

Overall, the reported crime rate for East-Docks is about the same as for the rest of Newham. However, local officers identified the area as having an established illegal economy, a problem with stolen cars, and a number of well-known criminal families living there. They believe that no more than about 12 persistent young offenders are responsible for much of the local crime (Lupton, 2000a, 2000b).

Maguire (1994) compared the results of the British Crime Survey (which aims to identify both reported and unreported crime) with local surveys of people's experience of crime. The first British Crime Survey report in 1983 calculated the average risk of an individual experiencing certain types of crime. It found that 'a statistically average person' over the age of 16 across the country could expect a robbery once every five centuries, and a burglary in the home once every 40 years. This "is a situation light years away from ..." the results of the first Islington crime survey in 1986, which "indicated that a third of all households had been touched by burglary, robbery, or sexual assault within the previous 12 months" (Maguire, 1994). This level is akin to that reported by the families in Hackney and Newham.

Figure 9.1: Crimes per 100,000 people: West-City compared with borough, London and national averages (1998)

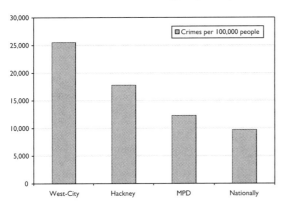

Source: Lupton (2000); West-City New Deal Trust (2000)

It is important to keep in mind the huge gap in the experience of crime between high crime neighbourhoods, such as the sample, and the rest of the country, when thinking about family life in these areas.

The West-City New Deal Trust conducted a survey of 10% of all the households in West-City in 1999, which bears out the reports from the sample families (see Table 9.3). It found that 27% of households had experienced at least one of the following crimes or anti-social acts in the previous 12 months:

- personally threatened or frightened
- mugged or robbed
- racially harassed or racially abused
- deliberately hit or assaulted
- something nasty pushed through the letter box.

In other words, violent, aggressive attacks on people's right to peaceful enjoyment of their home and living environment was a fairly continuous experience (West-City New Deal Trust, 1999). Since most families know at least several neighbours, word of these multiple incidents criss-crosses social networks, fuelling the insecurity the families reported.

Yet clearly not every resident of West-City and East-Docks has had personal or even indirect experience of crime. As we showed in Chapter Seven, nearly a tenth of the families we spoke to in both areas did not identify a single serious problem in their area. A total of 13% of the West-City families and 22% of the East-Docks families we spoke to said that crime was not a problem at all in their area. Analysis of 'police call data' in America found that:

> ... there was considerable variation in the victimization rate (as measured by call data) of specific micro-locations even within high crime rate areas – that is, even high-crime areas have their relatively safe specific locations.... (Bottoms, 1994)

This ties in closely with our findings.

Roughness between children and fights between parents

There is a continuum between the problems of actual crime, the incidence of lower level disorder and neglect of the physical environment in high crime areas. American studies have long maintained this connection (Kelling et al, 1996), but British studies have found it harder to prove (Hope and Foster, 1991). Nevertheless, the success of US action against incivilities creating a positive deterrent to actual crime made this a particularly important subject for our studies. We were struck in our discussion with families by the very wide range of bad behaviour they reported.

Fifteen mothers expressed concern about rough behaviour between children:

> "Out on the streets you can hear the verbalism of the children ... atrocious." (Nicola)

Much more worryingly, there were signs of intimidation over crime:

> "[One time] there was a younger one amongst [this group of boys]. I think he was asked to go and do something that he didn't want to do.... He was running away, and this big one just grabbed him by the shirt and said 'You are not going nowhere – you stop with us'.... 'You grass on us and I will beat the hell out of you'." (Cynthia)

Half of the comments about roughness related to experiences in parks and playgrounds, reinforcing the problems underlined in the previous chapter. Parents were concerned about swearing, fighting, and the loud, threatening behaviour of older children:

> "There's too much roughness in the park." (Shushan)

Sola had been deeply shocked by an incident that had left someone fighting for their life in intensive care. She described how two children had had an argument. One was black and one white, and she felt that race played a part in what happened next. One of the mothers intervened, hitting the child who was not hers. Then the mothers fought each other (a broken bottle was used). Other members of each family got involved, and one of the black family members was stabbed. The girl who had been stabbed was on a life support machine at the time of the interview:

> "It doesn't need to escalate like that. Children play.... It doesn't matter what nationality you are – we're all one nation. It's ignorance – people that haven't travelled." (Sola)

Two other people described how parents sometimes got involved in disagreements between children, escalating the conflict well beyond a 'childish squabble':

> "I took my daughter to the park, and all there was was stabbings between adults over kids." (Liz)

But Sola concluded "I would never intervene in children's fighting", which obviously could in itself allow bad behaviour to escalate. It seemed hard to find a balance between trying to control children's behaviour and the scale of reaction that might follow:

"It makes you think, is it a nice world to bring children into? I feel very fearful for my grandchildren." (Sola)

Parents could end up feeling that their children were exposed from both ends – bad behaviour among children and aggressive responses among parents. We return to this point below.

Gangs

We did not ask direct questions about gangs in the interviews, but 14 mothers – nine in West-City and five in East-Docks – specifically mentioned gangs. The type of gang they were referring to varied. Three mothers in West-City described what they called gangs of about 20 to 30 young people who they saw regularly:

"Gangs hanging around – about 20 kids – older kids, in their twenties." (Megan)

The assumption was that they were up to no good and parents and children were generally afraid of them. One mother said that it was her son who was aware of the gangs in the area – she had not seen them:

"[My teenage son] is very aware of gangs. I think the kids are very aware that there are gangs and groups – they're more wary [than me]. I haven't seen any." (Sinead)

Another mother described a 'pack' of boys aged 14 to 15. One thought that organised gangs were using young drug users hanging around the area to carry out muggings.

There was a racial dimension to this fear as some white mothers referred specifically to black youth:

"There's a gang of blacks – 20 or 30 of them – hanging on the corner at night, waiting for someone to mug." (Linda)

Two other mothers linked gangs to racial divisions. One said gangs of black youths were mugging elderly white women, and one said that it was gangs of white youths versus black youths. Another mother was worried that her family was going to come into conflict with a local gang of mainly black young men who they thought had mugged a family friend. Her family was mixed race and it was therefore not as simple as 'white on black'.

One mother reported that intimidation and fear of getting involved was a big issue. The gangs she thought were mugging elderly women were protected by their own violence:

"No one would grass 'em because they'd be too scared. They're gangs. They've got knives – they stab each other – they wouldn't think twice about stabbing somebody else." (Liz)

The mother who talked about a young boy being threatened if he didn't do what the group wanted him to do, echoed some of these descriptions of 'gang culture':

"He didn't want to be with them, but he couldn't leave because he might have got beaten up or something." (Cynthia)

In East-Docks, two mothers talked about organised gangs – one which targeted the local shops and one which got teenagers to spy on local activity and then came in with vans to steal equipment which the teenagers had reported back to them. Another said that there were specific local gangs which she saw all the time. One said that gangs hang around the flats.

People used the word 'gang' to mean different things. One mother in East-Docks, describing groups of children involved in vandalism, stressed that she did not think these were 'gangs':

"The children doing [the vandalism] are getting younger, getting away with it. It goes on to become a culture. *I don't mean gangs.*" (Diane)

She was referring to a culture of environmental abuse, devaluing property and public spaces through damage and a desire to destroy them. This was a more pervasive problem than teenage gangs, involving a general acquiescence in the unstoppability of many such acts. Like many problems of disorder, it was also cumulative. The more it happened, the less people felt able to stop it, and the more it tended to happen. There seems to be a culture of vandalism, starting among children and simply carrying on.

In the survey of 10% of all West-City households carried out by the New Deal Trust, between 37% and 50% of respondents (depending which of the four smaller areas they lived in) said that gangs of youths were a big problem. The experiences parents described to us, combined with these survey results, suggest that in West-City there is more than one large group of young people (mainly teenage boys and young men in their early twenties) who are undermining people's sense of security and actually threatening children's safety in some cases.

The problem of children's rough behaviour, and the level of violence and intimidation they often witness, inevitably spills over into teenage behaviour. For boys in particular, it can feel very unsafe *not* to be part of the street culture of youth gangs once gangs have gained some hold over street conditions, unless the boy's family can create an alternative environment away from the streets. This pressure on boys once control of public spaces has shifted from the community and public authorities to gangs on the edge of or outside the law is something some of the parents live in fear of, and the wider society largely runs away from.

Neighbour problems

'Neighbours from hell' have received massive media prominence. A few extraordinary cases of the constant harassment of neighbours by violent, anti-social, disruptive households has shaped our understanding of social breakdown. Lower level conflict between neighbours is part of a continuum between small incivilities and arguments and higher level conflict and abuse which can come to dominate the atmosphere of certain neighbourhoods (Power and Mumford, 1999). Because so many families live in such close proximity, it is easy for one disruptive family to have a disproportionate impact.

It is also the case that a small number of such families can compound the impact of disorder and create the conditions for gangs to emerge. The sheer level of intimidation that disruptive families and their out-of-control children are able to exercise by simply flouting the law can gather its own momentum. This then pushes far out of line the experiences of ordinary residents in those neighbourhoods compared with more normal areas. One major causal factor is council housing, because of the obligation on local authorities to house potentially homeless families. Abusive, out-of-control families are extremely likely to be under constant threat of homelessness due to their anti-social behaviour. In an area dominated by council housing this tends to be a circular problem, with a revolving door of problematic families moving around unpopular estates or blocks.

Figure 9.2: Whether neighbours are a problem in the area (%)

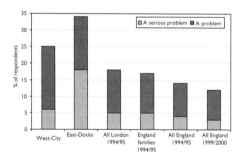

Sources: Round 2 interviews, 1994/95 Survey of English Housing, in Burrows and Rhodes (1998); 1999/00 Survey of English Housing, in DTLR (2001)

We asked the families whether they had experienced problems with neighbours in their area. Many more of the families we interviewed in West-City and East-Docks said that neighbours were a problem (25% and 34% respectively) than the London average (18%) or families nationally (17%). And the families in East-Docks were at least three times more likely to say that neighbours were a *serious* problem than families in West-City, London and nationally.

The comments that families made indicated that neighbour problems were wide-ranging, including noise, drug dealing, arguments with other neighbours, and other anti-social behaviour such as leaving rubbish lying about:

> "There was a big fight the other night [between two neighbours]. It's just escalated ... for the past year ... and it finally got completely out of hand and the police were called. And noise from neighbours is a problem.... Last summer, I had a noisy neighbour all summer and it became a serious problem because it affected me personally and it drove me absolutely crazy. But because it stopped it seems like it isn't serious anymore." (Joan)

Eviction could sometimes solve the problem for the families affected as in this case, where the neighbours were drug users but were evicted:

> "At the time they were here, I felt very insecure, but now it's not so bad." (Jess)

People felt that there were many lower order neighbour nuisance problems that they could do little about:

> "If I want to sit in my garden and I've got someone bashing out music really loud, that's a serious problem to me. It's harassment, an invasion." (Diane)

> "It doesn't affect me personally, but you get the conflict and you're in the middle of it ... they shout about it in the early hours." (Rachel)

> "Some of them are [a serious problem]. Throwing stuff out the windows, leaving rubbish on the stairs, fouling the lift up." (Marie)

People's lack of control over their immediate environment and the inability to stop nuisance behaviour or get anyone else to stop it is one of the biggest problems, as we saw in the previous chapter on parks. It generates a sense of powerlessness that makes people want to escape, despite the good things. The problematic experience of neighbours in both areas existed alongside a high level of friendliness and a sense of community within the neighbourhoods (see Chapter Three). It underlines just how fragile these positive elements are.

Vandalism

We asked the families whether they thought vandalism and hooliganism were problems in the area. Two thirds in East-Docks and two fifths in West-City felt they were a serious problem.

According to the families, problems of crime and vandalism were much greater in these neighbourhoods than in other deprived areas, where 30% of residents said they were serious problems (Whitehead and Smith, 1998). Families in East-Docks were even more likely to feel that vandalism was a serious problem (67%)

**Figure 9.3: Whether vandalism/
hooliganism is a problem in the
area (%)**

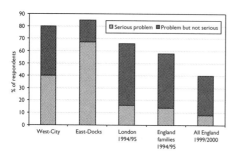

Sources: Round 2 interviews; 1994/95 Survey of
English Housing, in Burrows and Rhodes (1998);
1999/00 Survey of English Housing, in DTLR
(2001)

than crime (64%). By contrast, in West-City significantly more families felt crime was a serious problem (57%) than vandalism (40%). There was clearly an overlap between what constituted 'vandalism' and what constituted 'crime'. For example, ripping car windscreen wipers off is simultaneously an act of vandalism and an act of criminal damage and theft. Much vandalism in fact constitutes criminal damage. In addition to vandalism to cars, people mentioned children smashing bus stops and telephone boxes, and occasionally setting bins or garages on fire:

> "The kids are always busting the bus stops, telephone boxes, and setting bins alight. Certain parts is worse than others." (Jackie's friend)

Vandalism to cars is a particular blight on the environment and a strong signal of disorder. Families feel very upset by vandalism because of the signal it gives of decay, neglect and latent violence. But abandoned damaged cars are a particular blight because they often sit on the street for days or weeks, inviting ever more abuse, dumping of rubbish and arson (DTLR/DEFRA, 2002):

> "[Dumped cars] are [among] the things that make the area look rough." (Diane)

> "It really gets me down when I see stolen cars smashed to pieces. That's when I really want to move away." (Annie)

We counted damaged cars in 20 streets (chosen randomly) in each neighbourhood. We found nearly four times more damaged cars in East-Docks (43) than in West-City (11) (Mumford, 2001). Most families in East-Docks (69%) talked about the problem of car vandalism or abandoned cars at some stage in the interviews; 47% of West-City families talked about it.

We did not ask direct questions about car crime. Families mentioned it in response to questions about whether vandalism and crime were problems in the area, the type of crime they thought was a problem, whether they themselves had experienced a crime in the last 12 months, how the area was changing, and how good they thought the general appearance of their area was. Nearly a quarter of the families in both neighbourhoods had directly experienced some form of car crime in the past year – their own car had been stolen, vandalised, or broken into. The following are typical of the comments made:

> "I've seen a few changes for the worse. This is ongoing – it always happens – but it seems to have happened rather a lot more in the last few months. Cars have been pinched and left abandoned, and they are there for weeks before the Council picks them up. It is awful and it looks terrible." (Peggy)

> "The biggest crime at the moment is stealing cars, dumping them down this road, and then they come back and set light to them. Very, very regular." (Barbara)

> "I've noticed a lot of … stolen cars that have been dumped. On my way to school, I see a different dumped car almost every day." (Charley)

Newham has recently introduced a pilot scheme which aims to wheel clamp untaxed, 'nuisance vehicles' and remove them after 24 hours. If this scheme, and a similar pilot in Lewisham, is successful, the government plans to implement it nationally (Prime Minister, 2001).

Interestingly, abandoned cars were emblematic of neighbourhood decay in the famous American study by Wilson and Kelling in the 1970s that established the 'broken windows theory' (1982). This showed that neighbourhoods which took no action against smaller-scale vandalism – 'broken windows' – ended up with large-scale crime.

Graffiti

Far fewer families in each neighbourhood thought that graffiti was a serious problem, compared with crime and vandalism. Even so, graffiti seems a much more serious problem in the sample neighbourhoods than national levels would suggest, particularly in East-Docks, where 36% said it was a serious problem, nine times the national average (4%). A total of 57% in West-City and 60% in East-Docks thought it was a problem or a 'serious problem'.

Overall, one fifth of respondents nationally think that graffiti is a problem compared with nearly three fifths of the sample families. People worry about graffiti because it strongly signals a disorderly environment. It suggests a lack of care or supervision, and underlines the lack of ownership or control of many spaces in urban neighbourhoods. It reflects a negative attitude towards the environment and a desire to make a mark on it by those who feel most alienated by it. Graffiti in itself is probably the most harmless of disorderly behaviours, but as a sign of how poorly supervised or controlled a neighbourhood is, it has a symbolic importance out of all proportion to the actual harm it does. The fact that it is expensive and difficult to remove reinforces its value to graffiti 'artists' and its damage to the overall sense of control. In line with the 'broken windows theory', graffiti begets graffiti. It can become abusive, insulting and racist, thereby provoking community divisions, creating fear and making people stereotype all young people, who are assumed to be the perpetrators. In this way graffiti can generate much wider feelings of animosity. The combination of vandalism, graffiti, rough behaviour and public neglect generates a sense of 'anything goes' that signals the withdrawal of people, particularly families and older people from public spaces, and the takeover of these areas by semi-illicit or illicit activity. Thus crime is clearly fed by the atmosphere of neglect.

Drugs

The problem of drugs is probably at the extreme end of the scale, a huge worry for most of the parents. It is directly linked to crime, and sometimes violence. We give it greater prominence because of the disproportionate attention parents gave to the subject.

The scale of the problem of drugs in each neighbourhood

The majority of families in both areas – three quarters (77%) in West-City and over half (53%) in East-Docks – felt that drugs were a problem in their area. Only 11% in West-City and 24% in East-Docks did not think so (others did not know). The particularly high level of concern in West-City is consistent with the exceptionally high level of recorded drug supply offences in Hackney – double the Metropolitan average. Research for the East-Docks Single Regeneration Budget Partnership found that drug abuse was frequently mentioned as a concern, but less so than crime and anti-social behaviour among children and young people (Wilson, 2001). Newham's rate is the same as the Metropolitan average, which is 20% higher than the national average (see Figure 9.4).

An independent, Home Office funded study in some of the neighbourhoods in the Centre for Analysis of Social Exclusion's 12 Areas Study has explored the operation of local drug markets. East-Docks was part of this study,

Figure 9.4: Index of recorded drug supply offences (July 1997-June 1998)

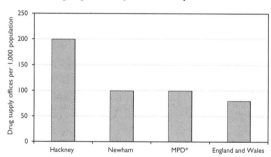

Note: [a] Average crime rates for the whole of the Metropolitan Police District were set at 100. Each borough's figures are then expressed in relation to this index.

Source: London Borough of Newham and the Metropolitan Police, 1998/99 in Mumford (2001)

so we have more information about the drug market there than in West-City (Lupton et al, 2002).

The study found East-Docks to have a high level of availability for all drugs, in common with other areas of Newham. Heroin, cocaine, crack and cannabis are all easy to obtain. The heroin/crack market is primarily local, used by local residents rather than outside buyers, unlike some other areas in Newham. Some dealers are also thought to live in the area. The police report that this local drug activity causes less problems than in other parts of the borough, and drug-related crime is not extensive (Wilson, 2001).

Sometimes the families' worries were based on hearsay, television coverage and newspaper articles, but often they stemmed from their own experiences of near where they lived – people behaving unpredictably, committing opportunistic crime, demanding money, openly dealing or using drugs within their sight. Thirteen families also talked about direct experiences of drug misuse among friends, acquaintances or family members.

The main problems drugs caused for families across both neighbourhoods related to their impact on children and young people. In West-City, crime was the most frequently mentioned drug-related problem. Table 9.6 overleaf shows all the problems that the families identified.

We now turn to look at the most dominant problems drugs cause.

Bad influence on children and young people living in the neighbourhood

Twenty families expressed concern about the negative influence of local drug use and drug dealing on children living in the area, and the temptations and pressures their children would face as they grew older:

> "I think drugs are rife. The problem is the influence. My children are out there when it's happening." (Annie)

> "You don't see much. [But] when you talk to some parents and they're admitting they're smoking this and that, you think 'Where are they getting it from?' It's got to be somewhere local. Ultimately that goes on to the kids – they find it a more acceptable thing. It does worry you. You think of the children in these families – they're not getting a very good message there. Then it becomes a peer thing as well." (Rachel)

> "I think children are in danger of drugs – that is what worries me sometimes because we've even got a couple of parents who are on drugs and, if they're on it, what hope is there sometimes for some children? That worries me. Surely children would make you want to lead some sort of better life? I don't say everyone is doing it – they aren't. There are a lot of decent people in the area, but there is a

minority – you see silly little things, and you think it isn't very nice."
(Peggy)

Parents have also heard about drug pressures in schools:

"You hear a lot. This is another thing that's worrying me about
secondary schools. You hear that there are people selling drugs to the
children and nicking things from them (eg mobile phones) to get
money for their own things." (Lesley)

"I'll be quite worried when my children are teenagers because they
could be quite easily misled." (Sarah)

**Table 9.6: Why drugs (and alcohol[a]) cause a problem (number of
comments, made by families who believed drugs to be a problem in the
area)**

	West-City	East-Docks	Total
They are a bad influence on children and young people/children and young people are vulnerable/children shouldn't have to see it going on	9	11	20
Drug-related crime	12	4	16
They wreck the lives of individuals using them, and have a terrible impact on the families of those individuals	7	2	9
Cause general uneasiness/fear/distrust	6	3	9
Visible drug litter/the public way drugs are used	7	2	9
Users can behave unpredictably violently/abusively	5	3	8
Parents on drugs cannot cope	–	2	2
Not nice to see drunk men[a]	–	2	2
Under-age drinking is a concern[a]	1	2	3
Lots of coming and going late at night causes disturbance	1	1	2
Give the area a bad name	1	–	1
Leads to vandalism	–	1	1
Not a direct problem to our family/no particular problem recorded, but it is a problem in the area	8	2	10
Total	57 comments 36 families	35 comments 24 families	92 comments 60 families

Note: [a] We did not ask people specifically about alcohol – our question referred to 'drugs' – but of
course alcohol is a drug, albeit a legal one, and these five families expressed concern about public
drinking and under-age drinking. It is possible that more people would have raised concerns about
alcohol had we asked them about this directly.

Some parents were able to have open conversations with their children about drugs:

> "I'm just really glad they talk to me about it. I always try to leave the line of communication open." (Annie)

> "They're so well-educated on it, I don't think they'd even dare to go into it." (Louise)

Children living with parents who were drug users faced special problems:

> "I know a few parents who are on drugs. They try and cope, but you can't cope when you are on that stuff." (Barbara)

> "It's a very big problem in my block. The person who is using them, I'm talking from my own experience, I find the person who uses it has an effect on everyone. It affects their children's lives, their family. And because it is affecting their children's lives, their children then go on and affect other people's lives. If the child doesn't get the right amount of attention at home, they will come out of the home and do certain things that are not the right thing to do. And then go on to tease and taunt other people. They know they aren't going to get corrected because no one is interested in what they've got to say. It is sad really. They know they can swear or smash something and no one is going to take a blind bit of notice of them within their home. It doesn't matter if someone knocks on the door and complains; the parent is not going to respond in the way they should do." (Flowella)

Young people often behave disruptively in order to get a response from adults around them, and from their peers. Even a negative response is better than no response at all. Children then gain recognition among their peers through notoriety, and their behaviour often becomes more extreme in order to continue to evoke a response. Much of the 'rough' and abusive behaviour parents reported, and the way they described youth gangs in the neighbourhoods, reflected this pattern. It can lead to the eventual breakdown of order (Power and Tunstall, 1997).

Drug-related crime

Families made a direct link between crime – mainly street crime and burglaries – and drug use:

> "Lately there's been a few stabbings, people being mugged. And I think it's due to a lot of the drug problem that's going about." (Alice)

> "They go out first and they're experimenting and then they get hooked
> ... and you're breaking into shops, people's homes, robbing people
> on the streets ... to feed the habit." (Louise)

Twelve families in West-City raised concerns about drug-related crime, compared to just four in East-Docks. The study of the East-Docks drug market found that the increased availability of drugs did not appear to have led to a corresponding increase in crime in this neighbourhood. Although the non-working drug users funded their drug use through criminal activity, they seemed to travel out of the area to commit the crime, or to target commercial rather than residential properties. The fact that the drug market's main users are local to the area also means that drug-related crime by outsiders happens less than may be expected (Wilson, 2001).

Wrecked lives

Some people spoke vividly of how drugs had shattered the lives of people they knew, how it had changed their personalities altogether:

> "On an emotional note, you know so many people you grew up
> with, and their lives are just wrecked. Some are dead." (Rosemary)

> "I think [drugs] trap people completely, physically, emotionally,
> spiritually, relationally, socially. Everything, I think, can be ruined."
> (Joanne)

> "They're just destroying people's lives – it's changed the person
> completely. I still say 'hello' to them, but that's as far as it goes now."
> (Sophie)

General uneasiness, insecurity, distrust

Drugs felt to many families like a veiled threat – something they could not quite get hold of or sort out. Nine families described the underlying insecurity and distrust that such fear could engender, their frequent inability to challenge people they saw openly using drugs. This had an impact on the overall quality of life they experienced in their neighbourhood:

> "You're scared to venture out, especially in the evenings or early in
> the mornings, because you just don't know. I might not know anyone
> on drugs, but it has an effect on us as a community." (Miriam)

"Sometimes you feel like you want to say something, but you're frightened." (Diane)

The most important knock-on effect of drugs may be people's loss of confidence in their community:

"It makes you suspicious of everyone." (Marilyn)

"[You see] people on the street in broad daylight completely off their faces. They're unpredictable. It makes you wary of people – you're not as trusting of people as you might be." (Debra)

There is a strong association in people's minds between drugs and crime and intimidation:

"I don't feel safe walking round the shop. I won't walk out after 8pm." (Liz)

A major problem with drugs activity in an area is its illegality. It therefore creates an underground and illicit atmosphere in the spaces it occupies, mainly the poorly supervised and maintained public spaces which are then abandoned or avoided by families – in turn making illegality and crime easier. The problems of parks, other public spaces and crime fit together within this circular process.

Behaviour

Eight families were concerned about the unpredictable, violent or abusive behaviour that they associated with drug use, and had sometimes experienced personally. This was particularly worrying when they had children with them. One family described an incident involving a gun. Others talked about reckless and dangerous behaviour:

"[Recently] someone came out with a gun. My cousin managed to calm him down. He was stoned out of his head. It makes you think … knives are frightening, but guns are final." (Tina)

"When they're drugged up to the eyeballs and start being stupid, or even violent, throwing things. And you can't reason with them. It doesn't happen often, but it does rear itself every now and again." (Joyce)

"For a start off, they don't care. The drugs take over and they'll just mug you for a fix. They don't give a damn about anyone else. Their attitude. They're not thinking." (Justine)

> "They're violent on the come-down off their drugs. There's a lot of evilness out there." (Liz)

Sometimes parents could not protect their children from what they met on the street:

> "It puts us in danger because you don't know what they're taking and what it's going to do to them. And having to explain to the kids what they're doing there." (Kate)

Families generally felt harassed by drug misuse and were frequently bothered by people asking for money or cigarettes:

> "You see people that you know's out of their nut. They ask you for 10p or a fag, which is quite intimidating when you've got children with you, because you just want them to be away from you." (Jessica)

Drug debris

Seven families in West-City described the problem of drug-related litter, particularly syringes, but occasionally discarded tin foil or 'crack bottles':

> "They go round leaving their needles on the steps where the children are going up and down. A friend's child had a needle in his pocket. If they've really got to do all this – do it in their home, don't bring it out on the street." (Zoe)

Only one family in East-Docks said they saw syringes. The problem has lessened in recent years through needle exchanges and a more concerted effort to clean up drug debris. But it may mask an increase in heroin use via other methods, such as smoking (Wilson, 2001).

Drinking as a worry, including under-age drinking

Five families talked about the problems of public drinking in similar terms to drug misuse – its negative impact on public spaces and the general sense of unease that it generates:

> "When you go out and see two or three men drunk, that makes me feel very bad – so early in the morning you're not supposed to see people sitting around drinking." (Constance)

The problem of drugs and drink sometimes overlapped:

> "You see one of them and they look like they've had stuff and they get abusive and they start fighting. And you've got the drinkers who sit outside the supermarket and they abuse the customers that go in and out of the shop. You shouldn't be subjected to that I don't think, not on the street, not when you are just going to do a bit of shopping." (Gillian)

Under-age drinking was a worry to parents who fear for their own children when they have to become part of their peer group, and are beyond parental control:

> "What worries me is that these are very young kids. I've seen them grow up, I saw them in primary school. But now I wouldn't even dare say hello to them because they don't even want to know you anymore. You see them holding a bottle of beer. I've got a son coming up 12 now, and I get worried. There is no garden here for him to play out in, so he would want to start going out there. I will probably have to move out of here before he gets to that age." (Cynthia)

Alcohol, like illegal drugs, causes serious neighbourhood problems – noise, fights, loss of control. Among children it leads to over-sleeping and an inability to concentrate or to take responsibility. However, illegal drugs have now probably overtaken drink as the biggest parental worry.

What seems particularly disturbing to parents is that these things happen in public places, which means that they can neither escape from them nor shield their children from them except by staying indoors. It means that they and their children are hemmed in by problems within their own community.

Bad reputation

One family described the major 'whole-area' problem that drugs caused: the negative impact on the area's reputation:

> "[It doesn't cause a problem] to my family directly. But they don't seem to give the area a good name. It has overshadowed every other good thing that comes out of the area. One man comes to deal here, and where he lives could be seen as a very, very clean area. Yet he comes here to deal – and now the name of this area is tarnished." (Delilah)

Better-off neighbourhoods appear to experience these problems far less, yet the drug market survey showed that many drug users from better-off areas come to find drugs in poor areas. The fear of the streets and open spaces in high crime areas facilitates this process and generates a vacuum that can then be filled by drug dealers and drug users.

Most families find it very difficult to live in high crime, high drug abuse areas. Making families with children feel they cannot use public spaces is a major cause of more general disorder as it reduces informal supervision and control (Power and Tunstall, 1997).

Not a direct problem

A small number of families described how drug use in the area did not really bother them:

> "They don't give us any aggravation – they go out of the area. In West-City I have always felt safe because I know the junkies by name. I know all the muggers." (Natalie)

> "It's at night and you're inside." (Megan)

> "I think it's around, but it doesn't affect me. Maybe if I lived in the flats I'd see it more." (Sinead)

One mum said that she felt drugs were not more of a problem in West-City than in other areas:

> "I think they're a problem everywhere – not more here than anywhere else. I used to live in [South London] and it was such a beautiful street, but next-door they were drug-dealing." (Linda)

The families' direct experience of drugs in the neighbourhoods

We wanted to find out how much of the concern families felt about drugs was based on direct experience of drug use rather than hearsay and negative publicity. The families revealed a high level of quite direct experience; only 10 of the 60 families who felt drugs were a problem said that their experience of the problem was just 'what they heard' or that they 'just know it's going on'.

Most people talked about 'drugs' generally, rather than specifying particular types of substance, so we do not know, except by inference, how many were referring to hard drugs. In all, only six people in West-City and four in East-Docks named specific drugs. Others differentiated between smoking or injecting, but did not name the specific substance:

"They exchange it by the lift – they smoke, they sniff … I can't specify the type of drug." (Eve)

A few people commented on their naivety about drugs. Sometimes even those describing the drug misuse problem of family members did not specify the type of drug. We did not probe for this information, as we did not want to make people feel uncomfortable.

In West-City, four people mentioned crack. Two of these talked about crack houses, one mentioned crack bottles, and one said that crack was one of the main drugs taken in the area. One mother referred to ecstasy and another to cannabis. One of the mothers, who specified crack, also said that heroin and cocaine were prevalent. She resented the fact that the drugs issue had forced

Table 9.7: Families' experience of drugs in their area (number of comments, made by families who believed drugs to be a problem in the area)

	West-City	East-Docks	Total
Interviewee knows someone who uses or deals drugs (outside their own family)	4	5	13
Interviewee or other family member currently has or used to have a drug or alcohol problem themselves	3	1	–
Have seen/experienced strange behaviour, vandalism or criminal activity believed to be drug-related	9	3	12
Have seen groups of users/suspected users	7	5	12
'Just what you hear'/'know it's going on'/read in newspaper/no direct experience but worried	6	4	10
Have seen syringes/foil lying about, smelt drugs eg in lift	7	1	8
Have been asked for money/cigarettes on the street	6	–	6
Children talk about it	–	2	2
See dealing on the street	1	1	2
Saw needles in the past	1	–	1
Neighbour warned about dealing in the block	–	1	1
Prostitutes moved onto the estate – linked to dealers	1	–	1
See street drinkers/friend was abused by street drinkers	–	2	2
Not recorded	2	–	2
Total	45 comments	25 comments	30 comments
	37 families	24 families	61 families[a]

Note: [a] Includes one mother who didn't think drugs were a particular problem in her part of the neighbourhood but whose ex-partner (and the father of her children) used drugs.

itself on her because of where she lived. She felt bad that she had to confront this evidence:

> "A-class drugs: crack, heroin, coke [are the main problem here]. They probably take a mixture of things – uppers and downers – whatever they can get to relieve not having the other one. Methadone tends to just make them greedy. Isn't it awful to know these things?" (Rosemary)

In East-Docks, three people talked about marijuana/cannabis, and two specified cocaine. One of the mothers who said that cocaine was the main problem said that speed and ecstasy were also around. Table 9.7 summarises the families' experiences of drugs in their area.

Of the 13 families who personally knew friends, other parents, neighbours, old acquaintances, or had family members who were using or had used drugs, nearly all were concerned about these individuals' drug use. Most personal experience was of a serious nature:

> "I had that drug problem in my daughter and her friends. Thank God everything seems to be alright now. Maybe not 100%, but it's a lot better. It's so serious in this area. I had to send my daughter out of the area for a while because she was in the wrong company." (Sola)

In one case a mother had had to take over the care of her nephew:

> "If you have a member of your family who's an addict, it affects you as a person. There's loads of issues. Like my nephew – both his parents are drug addicts – that's how I ended up with him. Their personalities change." (Faye)

People inevitably change their attitudes when they know a drug addict. It destroys relationships:

> "Some people that you know are on drugs and they come into your home, and you don't trust them. We've really tried to pull them away from it. But it's their decision at the end of the day whether they want that help or not." (Louise)

A very small number of families talked about drug use being the individual's choice; their only concern was if they did it publicly and left drug-litter behind:

> "I know people that smoke the weed – but that's their business at the end of the day." (Zoe)

Twelve families said they had seen or directly experienced odd behaviour or criminal activity that they believed was drug-related. And 12 families said that they saw groups of people hanging around who they knew or believed to be users:

> "I know there are lots of them. They hang around all over. Sometimes they will be in the lift, holding the lift. Especially in the evening, in the dark. I am very scared to go out in the evening because of them." (Adeola)

We cannot be sure whether these actually were drug users, but it is unlikely that the families' level of concern had no grounding. Eight families said that they encountered direct evidence of drugs: dumped syringes and foil, and lingering smells (often in lifts). Two people were particularly concerned about dealing on the streets:

> "There's no discretion used. They hang round the schools. They do it on the street now." (Joyce)

> "On [that] road you see people quite openly dealing from dusk onwards." (Felicity)

One mother had overheard children discussing a parent who was a dealer:

> "I heard a child the other day saying 'you can go to so and so's mum to get drugs' and you think 'Christ, these are babies'." (Nora)

Parental concern

Parents mostly wanted more help, rather than punishment, for any users, and preventative activities in the neighbourhoods. Most of the families did not want to blame drug users and dealers for all the evils of the world, as a knee-jerk reaction towards an easily stereotyped group. Rather, they were expressing concern about the impact of individuals' behaviour on their safety and that of their children, on the atmosphere of the neighbourhood as a whole, and on the area's wider reputation. Most of all, they were concerned about their own children being exposed to drugs and coming under pressure to take them. A few parents described how this had already happened:

> "They need to sort something, especially for the young people. If you lose them to the drugs and crime, it's hopeless. There's no help available – they turn to drugs. My daughter told me one time that

she wanted to die. Thank God for a mother like me, she says, or she wouldn't be here today." (Sola)

Parents often expressed sympathy for the reasons why people had developed drug habits, and wished that more could be provided for young people to give them alternatives and to steer them away from drugs:

"There's so many hurting." (Sola)

Although it is hard to provide direct evidence that the availability of local drugs (as opposed to the prevalence of drugs in society generally) encourages drug use among young people, it seems likely that drug availability combined with vulnerability, and a tendency for young people to gather in groups on streets, puts young people at greater risk of coming into contact with drugs (Wilson, 2001).

How secure people feel in their own home

One of the knock-on effects of crime, vandalism and drug abuse was the level of insecurity they generated. There is a big difference between how secure people feel inside their own homes, particularly with the security measures they have taken, and how secure they feel walking around their neighbourhoods or even in the entrance to their block of flats. Certainly the families' responses to our questions about crime and drugs suggest a much higher level of worry and insecurity outside the home than inside it. But the wider worry carried over into the home.

We found much greater feelings of insecurity among the families than among Londoners generally, or the population as a whole (Burrows and Rhodes, 1998; see Figure 9.5). A much higher proportion of the families – 19% in West-City and 13% in East-Docks – said that they felt 'not very secure' in their own house compared with the London average of just 5%, and the average for families nationally of 6%. On the other hand, only a very small proportion of the families we spoke to, or in London, said they felt 'not at all secure' in their own home – 4% in West-City, 2% of families nationally, 1% in London. None reported feeling this way in East-Docks.

Figure 9.5: Feelings of insecurity inside people's own homes

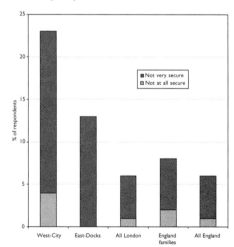

Sources: Round 2 interviews, 1994/95 Survey of English Housing, in Burrows and Rhodes (1998)

One mother expressed her "not very secure" feelings as:

> "I make sure I come home early so no-one will do anything to me. I just take each day at a time. I haven't had anyone physically assaulting me, but then you don't know." (Frances)

Some of the East End families who felt secure in their own home said that this was because of special steps they had taken, such as fixing metal gates across their front doors. It was easier to secure your home which you could defend, than the streets which you could not:

> "I feel OK now, I've got a gate. It was put in a year ago." (Theresa)

> "I feel secure, very secure, because I've got that gate and the entry-phone." (Gillian)

And some parents would fight to defend their hard won sense of security:

> "Quite secure – because I have got a big truncheon, and a partner. And I would beat the living daylights out of anyone who came in." (Linda)

Given all the neighbourhood problems we have described, we would have expected a much higher proportion of London respondents and families in the sample neighbourhoods to feel insecure. The fact that many do not is almost certainly explained by density and the proximity of neighbours who are known and trusted. So the argument goes full circle from high crime, high disorder, worry about street conditions and their impact on children, back to that sense of community and the importance of trust that we talked about in the opening Part 1. In spite of high crime and disorder, within people's immediate ambit, they generate a sense of security though basic neighbourliness. This matches wider findings that new households can find higher density attractive if it is coupled with security, supervision and care (JRF, 2000e; *Sunday Times* 'Property Supplement', August 2001).

As Sonia said:

> "[I feel very secure] because I've got neighbours – we watch each other."

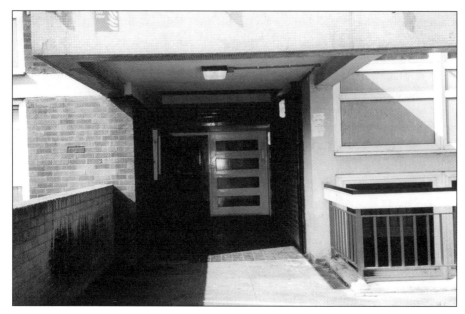

Insecure concealed entrance to tower block, West-City

Summary and conclusions

In the neighbourhoods 61% of the families felt that crime was a serious problem, four times the national average. Nearly 40% had experienced crime directly in the last 12 months. Most worryingly, five children had been attacked, two at knife point. The police response to actual crime was more often good than bad, but parents complained about lack of street policing and often did not report crime because they felt that the police could do nothing.

Many parents were worried about peer pressure and local gangs occupying public spaces. Nearly one third of families experienced neighbour problems. Some blamed the way that lettings were made in council housing. Often too few checks are made and there is little on-site enforcement to control abuse, as we argued in Chapter Eight. A high proportion of flats multiplies the impact of bad behaviour and the poor reputation of some estates means that they are often let to more desperate and therefore more troubled households (Power, 1999; Mumford and Power, 2002).

Drugs, particularly in Hackney, were a serious problem, setting a troubling example to children and young people, impacting on families through unpredictable behaviour, secondary school problems and a generally 'shady' atmosphere in some places. Over half of the families directly witnessed these things.

All in all, the families related to us many direct experiences of crime, disorder, vandalism, anti-social behaviour and drug abuse. Some incidents were extremely violent, others more trivial. But adding together the many different experiences of neighbourhood disorder painted a picture of a worrying absence of control of street conditions and public spaces, a tolerance of abuse and fear of intervening to stop it, and a wider breakdown in neighbourhood conditions. This was compounded by the presence within the neighbourhoods of people willing to run the gauntlet of the law, people for whom the law did not appear to apply.

Parents' deep anxiety about drugs, about their children's exposure to rough behaviour, about the general visibility of disorder in the neighbourhoods, seemed to be borne out by the actual incidents and examples they gave. It ran counter to their idea of community and deeply threatened it. But it also partly explained why community spirit was so much more important to families in these areas than in areas with lower crime and less disorder. It helps explain why so many wanted to move away from where they lived.

The 'broken windows theory', where neglect and decay generate a spiral of crime and disorder, certainly fits with how the 100 families describe conditions of abuse in their neighbourhoods (Kelling, 1996). According to the well-known American study, high crime, high abuse in neighbourhoods can be explained by the inability of the community and of public bodies to stamp on and put right the small abuses such as vandalism, graffiti, disrepair, and litter. This then generates more general 'incivilities' which can spin out of control and become pervasive signals for a tolerance of crime. We know from the British Crime Survey that there are strong links between physical disorder, actual levels of crime and the fear and insecurity they engender. We also know that physical and social disorder are far more common in poorer inner-city neighbourhoods (Home Office, 2000). So unless we change the way we manage neighbourhoods, the amount of street care and basic maintenance we put in, thereby creating the constant supervision that inner-city neighbourhoods require, we are unlikely to reverse the high levels of crime and disorder that our families so anxiously have to live with. For the kind of problems they told us about could not be dealt with by individual families or community groups unaided. Managing the collective conditions of urban neighbourhoods is a task that requires overarching authority, coordination and ground-level inputs (Power and Bergin, 1999).

In the final chapters we look at how the neighbourhoods are changing, how the extra efforts of regeneration programmes affect conditions, and what the families feel they do to neighbourhood conditions. Many reports examine these impacts. Here, however, we capture the direct experiences of people living through them. Is the disorder that so concerns these families being tackled? Do interventions actually avert the risk of breakdown?

TEN

Changing places: the families and their neighbourhoods

"A couple of improvements – the park [within the estate] has been done – the refurbishment of that. It's much safer. It's nicer for the kids to have somewhere to play that's safe. I've noticed a few improvements in the area – little things like intercoms – nothing specifically to this block – but improvements in the area." (Charley)

"You can *feel* there are changes coming up [in West-City], but you can't see the effect at the moment. Hopefully in the next 2 or 3 years you can see the effect of what they're planning to do." (Delilah)

Introduction

The 100 sample families care a lot about where they live. They see their children's lives buffeted by challenging conditions. The government, too, says that it cares about neighbourhood conditions. It is trying to make urban streets more 'liveable', safer, and more environmentally appealing. At the same time, efforts are going into schools, health, public services and the regeneration of poorer areas[1]. The two sample neighbourhoods are prime targets for many of these efforts, with new funding to help parents and young children, schools and employers. So how the families react to all these changes will give us some idea of how things are working, whether the extra effort is really making any difference. We first asked the families in 1999, not long after the New Labour government was elected, how they saw the changes in their neighbourhoods, and we asked them again a year later. Their views and feelings changed quite a lot over the year. In this chapter we analyse what the families said, to try and understand why. In follow-up interviews, we will be able to examine change over a much longer period, covering also the contrasts between the Northern families and the 100 East End families we report on here.

Table 10.1: Proportion of the East End families saying that their area was getting better in the first round, compared with views nationally (%)

	West-City families[a]	East-Docks families[a]	Families in seven SRB areas, before regeneration started[b,d]	Families nationally[c,d]
Area is getting better	52	44	16	10

Notes: [a]Interviews. [b]MORI survey for the DETR (1996/97). [c]1995/96 Survey of English Housing; [d]The MORI and SEH figures represent how families with dependent children felt their area had changed in the previous two years. A further 8% of families nationally had lived in the area less than two years and so were not asked this question.

Source: Mumford (2001)

How the families felt their neighbourhoods were changing

When we first visited the families, their positive views of area improvement were striking, compared with views of area improvement nationally (see Table 10.1). When we asked the families the second time we visited whether overall their area was getting better, staying the same, or getting worse, we found their responses were tempered much more strongly with worries that security in the neighbourhoods was decreasing and disorder increasing.

Box 10.1 summarises what families told us about the changes in their area when we first talked to them in 1999.

By 2000, far fewer people were saying that their area was getting better overall – half the proportion in West-City. Between three and six times more families were saying that their neighbourhood was getting better in some ways, but worse in others. The more open questions we asked about neighbourhood change in the second interview allowed this nuance to show clearly. But 18 of the 31 families who now felt more negative about their neighbourhood had had recent direct or very close experience of crime (for example, witnessing a crime, or a close relative being a victim of crime), and a further seven families had noticed increased vandalism, 'gangs' hanging around or other evidence of disorder. Thus, 25 of the 31 families with more negative views were influenced directly by real experiences.

Many families had only recently moved into the area, so this meant that on our first visit they were less informed; by the second round they were 'plugged in'. However, the proportion of families saying that their neighbourhood was getting better or getting better in some ways but worse in others, actually increased slightly, from 58% to 62% in West-City, and from 52% to 56% in East-Docks. In other words, they could see some positive movement in their neighbourhood's fortunes despite continuing problems (see Table 10.2).

Box 10.1: Ways in which the study areas are changing

West-City families' comments in 1999

- Physical improvements to housing
- Better services and community facilities including: new community college providing a big 'uplift'; school improvements; revamped museum; new library; new community centre; new doctors' surgery; more playgroups; a better cleaning service in one block of flats
- Changing ethnic composition – talked about positively, negatively and neutrally (see Chapter Four for discussion)
- Rocketing cost of property and money pouring into the area, which is becoming increasingly trendy. Filming in the area, seeing famous people around. Some positive comments, but also questions about whether gentrification will benefit local people, and concerns about noise and other nuisance from nightclubs:

"West-City is becoming trendy. There's more money coming into the area. It's encouraging that people are getting their own businesses in West-City. I don't like the fact that people are trying to open up discos, but I think the area is progressing." (Andaiye)

- Loss of local libraries
- Increase in noise and traffic
- Area more 'overcrowded'
- Crime and drugs getting worse

East-Docks families' comments in 1999

- Physical improvements to housing, schools, the market
- New schools (and improvements in school standards), a new community centre, new train station, the nearby Dome, an exhibition centre, university campus and a pedestrian bridge:

"East-Docks is looking up – it's shaping up – it's changing its image." (Oni)

- New job opportunities as a result of these developments
- Improved community facilities including a new youth project and increased adult education facilities
- Extra money coming in through regeneration schemes and commerce with new shops and businesses. But some had mixed feelings about private housing developments or felt that the Millennium Dome had been a waste of money
- Changing ethnic composition – talked about positively, negatively and neutrally
- Crime and drugs getting worse
- Loss of community spirit, children lacking respect for adults

Table 10.2: The families' views of the direction of neighbourhood change: the first and second interviews compared (%)

Neighbourhood change	West-City (%)		East-Docks (%)	
	Round 1	Round 2	Round 1	Round 2
Better	52	26	44	27
Better in some ways/worse in others	6	36	8	29
Same	26	23	24	27
Worse	10	15	20	18
Not recorded	6	–	4	–
(Base = 100%)	50	47	50	45

Almost the same proportion of families think that the areas are getting worse or staying the same at both interviews. The much more mixed opinions about changes that one third of the families hold underline the really mixed situation on the ground. Some things seem to be getting better, particularly physical and environmental conditions, but social problems, particularly disorder and anti-social behaviour, seem to be getting worse. We look at the two neighbourhoods more closely below[2].

West-City

Key improvements identified by families in West-City

Families in West-City commented on a wide variety of improvements, with 72 positive comments. Physical improvements stood out, but families also identified positive changes in social conditions, the local economy and the management of local services. Figure 10.1 summarises the improvements people talked about. These were spontaneous comments made in the course of each interview.

Figure 10.1: Summary of neighbourhood improvements identified by families in West-City

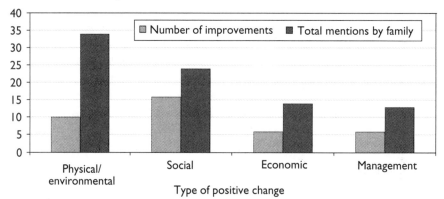

Note: Some comments were counted twice if they related to changes in more than one category, for example, new building on derelict land was counted as both a physical and an economic improvement.

Source: Round 2 interviews

Some improvements had already happened or were underway during the first round of interviews. Certainly the New Deal for Communities (NDC) had really got off the ground, with a series of 'Quick Win' projects, such as the installation of intercoms.

Physical improvements were the most significant – 10 separate physical improvements received a total of 34 comments. Table 10.3 details these physical changes.

Table 10.3: Physical and environmental improvements identified by the families in West-City

Positive physical and environmental changes	Number of families identifying each change
Refurbishment and improvements to blocks of flats, and renovation of private housing (apart from door-entry systems)	14
Installation of secure door-entry systems and intercoms	6
New building on derelict land, including a former factory site	3
Physical improvements to schools eg school security (NDC money improved one school playground)	3
Improved appearance/environment	2
Better lighting	2
Doctors' surgery – building improved	1
Local museum refurbished, with new galleries	1
Park within one estate refurbished	1
New housing association building	1
Total	34

Homes being built for housing asscoiation shared ownership, West-City

The positive change identified by the greatest number of families (14) was the refurbishment of council blocks of flats and renovation of private housing. The installation of secure door entry systems with intercoms was also popular (mentioned by six families):

> "Things is getting like a kick-start … the renovation of the whole area. It's getting better." (Millie)

> "A lot of these derelict houses are being done up." (Sinead)

> "It seems as if a lot has been done on the environment. I think the New Deal is it? … you can see that most of the blocks are being done. Parking – now the residents have to pay but it's better that way [before it was really difficult to find a space]. So many buildings are being renovated." (Andaiye)

Three families mentioned positive changes to school buildings, school security and playgrounds, which we classified under physical improvements:

> "I feel that the school is really improving – more money going in. Physically the school has improved. That has to uplift you! [New roof, improved swimming pool, waxed floors.]" (Kathleen)

The families identified 16 separate social improvements (see Table 10.4). Often each positive social change was quite localised, such as the funding arrangements of a local playgroup, computer classes, a reduction in noise, and the removal of drug dealers from two specific estates.

Three families talked about local schools getting better, including improvements in school–parent links, and in performance. A local primary school had been reaching out to parents, trying to encourage them to come in to the schools:

> "We have been having small things to show improvements, for example the new swimming pool, the new numeracy project (60-80 people came) … need to tap into those things. Having curriculum evenings is a really positive part of it. [A lot of people came to the maths evening] – probably because they're insecure with it and want to help their children. The school will be getting some artists in residence – in return for studio space they will do some teaching." (Kathleen)

Six separate positive economic changes received 14 comments (see Table 10.5). There was a sense of money coming into the area – through the investment of NDC (which people often mentioned directly in connection with the improvements to council blocks), through high-income households moving in,

Table 10.4: Social improvements noticed by the families in West-City

Positive social change	Number of families identifying each change
Improvements to school performance and links with parents eg numeracy project, offering English classes to parents	3
Drug-dealers ejected from two estates, and one mother said she no longer sees syringes	3
The area is 'up and coming'	3
Less car vandalism	2
People with money moving in	2
Prominent theatre project	1
New Deal's West-City Festival	1
Local playgroup got a grant and is now free of charge	1
The new college has increased provision for young people	1
Strip clubs have closed	1
There are 'more things to do'	1
A community project organised really good summer activities for children on estates	1
More facilities eg computer classes	1
Less noise	1
Traffic lights installed	1
Regular meetings informing residents of regeneration plans eg park redevelopment	1
Total	24

Table 10.5: Economic improvements identified by the families in West-City

Positive economic change	Number of families identifying each change
New building on derelict land, including the site of a former factory	3
New shops have opened, including a clothes shop	3
House price rises	3
People with money moving in	2
Money is being invested in the area	2
Market doing well	1
Total	14

house price rises, or through the new development of residential and commercial property on previously derelict land.

People saw social change leading to economic change, which they thought would help:

> "Decent people are moving in, ones with money." (Natalie)

"We are near the Centre – this area maybe is going to be [developed]. When we bought this flat – £60,000 or £70,000. Our neighbours sold their flat for £110,000 – that means this area is going up I think." (Narin)

"In some ways, this little area is getting better – houses are selling astronomically." (Kathleen)

House prices far exceed national standards, and are far higher than the Greater London average, despite the area's deprivation. The area's proximity to the City, the encroachment of City services into the southern part of the area, and its convenience for young City workers, all help to push up prices. By 2001 the average London price was £221,000 (Lupton, forthcoming).

Six separate improvements in the management of local services received 13 mentions (see Table 10.6). Three families felt that cleaning and rubbish collection services had improved. They specifically mentioned the good work of the private housing management contractor that has responsibility for all council housing in the neighbourhood. Improvements in school performance and school–parent links reflect positive changes in the management of local schools. School changes are often related to better management as well as making a positive contribution to social conditions. We therefore include them in both categories:

"Maybe it's because I'm [working] in the school now – but I'm finding the schools are getting much, much better." (Andaiye)

Table 10.6: Management improvements identified by the families in West-City

Positive management changes	Number of families identifying each change
Improvements to school performance and links with parents eg numeracy project, offering English classes to parents	3
Improved cleaning and rubbish collection (private housing management contractor specifically mentioned)	3
Improved appearance/environment	2
Less car vandalism	2
Better parking arrangements eg resident permits	2
Regular meetings informing residents of regeneration plans eg park redevelopment	1
Total	13

Ways in which families thought West-City and the surroundings were getting worse

Fewer people identified negative changes than identified positive changes; overall, there were 56 comments about worsening conditions compared to 72 comments about improvements. The great majority of negative views derived from problems relating to some form of social disorder or rough, tough behaviour; 39 of the 56 negative comments concerned these issues:

> "The crime has got worse since the last time we spoke. It's quite worrying that side of things. I can see that things are improving, but not on the crime side of things…. In the space since the last time we spoke, I witnessed two [different] stabbings from standing outside my front door. Two incidents right close to each other." (Charley)

Table 10.7 shows the scale of this problem.
   Families worried a lot about crime:

> "Crime has gone up. Every night you hear one thing or another, bag snatchings and…. How you know a place is not doing well – it's not just one person – a lot of the neighbours around are not happy." (Sushan)

Table 10.7: Crime and bad behaviour identified by families in West-City as contributing to worsening conditions

Negative change	Number of families identifying each change
Crime rate increasing – muggings, stabbings, gangs	14
More drug dealing, visible use (one family specifically mentioned crack houses)	6
Neighbour problems	3
Bored teenagers hanging around the streets	3
Dirtier streets, rubbish dumping, overall appearance declining	3
Rudeness and roughness of children, children fighting	2
Noise nuisance from new bars, concern about the developing night-time economy	2
Car crime – stolen and burnt-out cars	2
Public drinking	1
More graffiti and vandalism	1
Seeing prostitutes	1
'Rough' people coming in	1
Total	39

Table 10.8: Summary of service decline identified by families in West-City

Negative service change	Number of families identifying each change
Dirtier streets, rubbish dumping, overall appearance declining	3
Local library closed	2
Lack of discipline at school	1
Intercom has been put in but not yet connected – but rent has already been increased	1
The repairs service has got worse	1
Housing benefit delays	1
Cleaning of the playground has got worse	1
Nurseries are being closed	1
A summer play scheme for children with special needs didn't go ahead for the first time in over a decade	1
Total	12

"The crime's gone up, well it seems to have ... you hear of a lot more people being mugged late at night.... The area isn't very nice. Well, it is coming up a bit, but you have still got a lot of crime on the streets, but I think you've got that everywhere. You do hear a lot." (Alice)

"You still see teenage children – if only we could have something for them to do, instead of loitering around. Unfortunately cars are still being broken into." (Andaiye)

Several services had declined or shut down since our first visits, and families were fed up about this. A local library had been closed, a play scheme had folded, and nurseries had shut. Nine negative changes in local service provision and management received 12 specific mentions.

Three people said that cleaning services were getting worse:

"The streets are even dirtier than they've ever been. They're going to private cleaning in Hackney – I don't think it can make it worse. You get worn down by the system – constantly calling. [It takes 4-6 weeks to move a dumped car.] Sometimes you feel you're fighting a lost cause which is why I think some people don't bother." (Kathleen)

"The council doesn't look after, clean. All streets there is rubbish. [Discarded] meat is getting germs. I phoned them and said it's really bad – flies come in – not healthy for our child. After a couple of weeks, they clean up." (Narin)

Megan was upset that although a new secure door-entry system with an intercom had been installed, it had not yet been connected, despite the fact that her rent had already been increased to cover the cost of it. She also felt that the repairs service was getting worse – the response had got quicker, but the repair problems were not being properly tackled:

> "They come out quick within a couple of days but then they don't do the job good enough – they're off out again. The central heating was leaking – they came round – the next day it was pouring everywhere. The lifts breakdown every Monday. They come out, do them – but by the end of the day they're gone again." (Megan)

Kathleen was very concerned about the poor administration of Housing Benefit in the borough. She described her involvement in a voluntary project that is fighting bankruptcy as a result of the backlog of Housing Benefit payments:

> "Housing Benefit has been in a total and utter state of chaos in Hackney and Islington."

Worsening physical and environmental conditions received far fewer mentions than negative social changes – only eight, in fact. They included dirtier streets, car crime, graffiti and vandalism.

The families' generally positive view of changes in the physical fabric of the neighbourhoods was particularly striking. However, clearly very difficult social conditions risk swamping this progress. As well as the 39 comments about social disorder, there were six comments about the additional pressures of car parking, gentrification and density. Three people expressed their concern at a worsening parking situation. One mother linked the greater pressure on car parking with the influx of more and better-off people with more cars and less space per person, while her own conditions actually declined:

> "There are new buildings built and completed. But it has not benefited us, it is the other way: more people and less places to park cars. Maybe it is a good thing that new buildings are built and completed, but the building we live in was not restored." (Hulya)

Worries that in the long term the area would be overtaken by more wealthy people were reinforced by the valuations of council property. One family had been very concerned about the steep increase in 'Right to Buy' valuations on their estate, which was putting the purchase of a council flat way out of the reach of most tenants:

> "Affordability is a key thing ... but all these areas are being gentrified. Where's the sustainability if everyone's forced out?" (Alan)

Right to Buy valuations rose by 96.5% between April 1999 and March 2000 to an average of £106,000 (West City New Deal Trust, 2000). This contrasted with reports from local estate agents of a 30-40% rise in private property prices since the beginning of 1999 (West-City New Deal Trust, 2000b).

A local tenant, with the support of his estate committee and the New Deal Trust, successfully challenged the valuation of his flat. His one-bedroom flat had been valued at £127,000 but, following an appeal to the District Valuer, it was revalued at £82,500 before discounts, a reduction of 35% (West-City New Deal Trust, 2000c). A member of the West-City Residents Panel said:

> "This decision sets a marker down not just for [this block] but for the whole [area]. It puts a stop to the expanding gentrification of West-City and gives hope that our community can thrive...." (name witheld)

However, there is continuing controversy over the windfall profits of price escalation in high demand areas resulting from follow-on sales of Right to Buy flats, particularly in London. It is probably one of the most galling experiences for some of the families living in poor conditions (Murray and Evans, 2002).

East-Docks

Key improvements identified by families in East-Docks

Families identified many improvements in East-Docks, making 110 comments about positive changes. Better public transport was top of their list. Figure 10.2 summarises the positive changes.

Physical improvements received the most mentions (66), followed closely by social improvements (60), then economic improvements (54). Management changes were mentioned 20 times. We summarise the improvements in East-Docks under the same headings as for West-City.

Figure 10.2: Summary of neighbourhood improvements identified by families in East-Docks

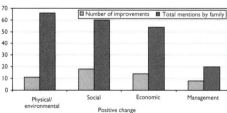

Note: Some comments were counted twice if they related to changes in more than one category eg public transport was counted as a physical, social and economic improvement.

Source: Round 2 interviews

Positive changes in public transport were the most frequently mentioned, and represent improvements in the neighbourhood's physical fabric, social conditions and economic environment. The new Underground, bus and train stations are having a marked impact. It takes under 25 minutes to get from East-Docks into central London on the new Underground or Docklands Light Railway. Sixteen of the families we spoke to praised this development:

"The new station is really brilliant! Actually it has helped people. The whole place is changing! And even outside, the people they are talking about it." (Sasha)

"The tube is amazing – that they put East-Docks on the map!" (Natasha)

A local professional anticipated that the new transport links would bring significant social and economic benefits to local people in the medium to long term:

"The inadequacy of the transport links over the years has led to many of the other problems that we see today. The rapid and dramatic improvement has yet to work its way through, but I think it will ultimately result in more people seeking and getting employment elsewhere, in consequentially greater wealth and in a greater sense of satisfaction in the area." (Director, local community project, quoted in Mumford, 2001)

Another key change – both physical and social – has been the opening of two new schools (a secondary school in East-Docks, and a primary school just south of East-Docks), and the complete rebuilding of an existing primary school in East-Docks, which also houses a local church:

Table 10.9: Physical and environmental improvements identified by families in East-Docks

Positive physical and environmental changes	Number of families identifying each change
Public transport – new station with tube connection, extra bus services (from 1999)	16
New secondary school built (opened autumn 1999), new primary recently opened nearby, another primary school totally rebuilt	10
Large exhibition centre nearing completion (some thought it would create jobs for locals)	9
Continued renovation of local authority housing	9
Improved environment and overall appearance	6
New building, 'developing'	5
A new hotel (and some thought it may bring jobs)	4
Leisure facilities getting better, new sports centre being built, new gym centre nearby	3
Better lighting	2
'Regeneration money'	1
Improved shops eg new shutters	1
Total	66

"The impact of the new [secondary] school opening has been very good. [There has been a lot of pressure to get in – a lot of people who live slightly further away have had to go to appeal to get in].... It proves the point that parents want the best for their kids and fight for them. It is quite nice, because sometimes it seems that they don't." (Joyce)

Nine families talked about the continuing renovation, modernisation and redecoration of council housing. These improvements are being funded through the Single Regeneration Budget:

"Regarding the modernisation, the infrastructure – it's looking beautiful and I really appreciate that." (Frances)

"They've changed our windows, the appearance of the whole area for the better.... Environmentally, everything has changed for the better." (Hannah)

"When my mum came and visited she said the area was so much better, you wouldn't think this was a rundown, deprived area, it's amazing what's here.... The cosmetics of the area are looking a lot better.... You can walk around and see how much nicer it looks." (Joyce)

SRB-funded improvements to low-rise flats/masionettes

Two landmark changes have the potential to bring local job opportunities: the opening of a large exhibition centre and a new hotel. Some families were optimistic that local people would get the new jobs; others were concerned that they would be left out.

In addition to the positive changes in public transport and the building of new schools, social changes included: improvements in school performance with two local schools coming out of special measures; positive community activities, for example, a children's 'Party in the Park'; the continued expansion of services and activities at a community-led project situated in a former church; the building of a new centre whose provision will include an after-school group; and a greater social and cultural mix.

Eighteen separate social improvements received 60 mentions, detailed in Table 10.10.

We interviewed at least three mothers who had attended a parenting course at one of the local primary schools, run by a local family support project, which had been ongoing for more than a year. All had found this a very positive experience. (We have not used names here to preserve anonymity.)

Table 10.10: Social improvements identified by families in East-Docks

Positive social changes	Number of families identifying each change
Public transport – new station with tube connection, extra bus services (from 1999)	16
New secondary school built (opened autumn 1999), new primary recently opened nearby, another primary school totally rebuilt	10
Improved school performance, including two local schools coming out of special measures	4
Better involvement of local people in decision making	4
The nearby Millennium Dome	4
Leisure facilities getting better, new sports centre being built, new gym centre nearby	3
East-Docks is 'on the map', 'up and coming'	3
Greater class and/or cultural mix	2
Local church transformed into a community centre, activities still expanding	2
More after-school and summer holiday clubs	2
Efforts by the police, government and local authority to combat racism and racial harassment	2
Reduction in crime, vandalism and graffiti	2
New centre being built on edge of park – will house after-school club	1
New university nearby	1
Drug dealing reduced	1
Parenting course continued at local school	1
Party in the Park for children	
Car park being built (following campaign by residents)	1
Total	60

"It would be brilliant if all schools provided them. If your child is having problems, it's nice to be able to come into a group, not to be judged, talk it through. It's just hard to get people to come along.... A lot of the children at [this school] are down as having problems, but when you get to know them, they're so lovely."

They described how the group had evolved over time to include evening and weekend social activities, as well as daytime courses, with the mothers going out together on a regular basis. The organisers of the group had funded a holiday to the coast for them all, and planned a summer play scheme. At least one of the mothers had gone on to do a personal development course:

"I go to a parents' group with the school – we've been on outings, there was a play scheme for the kids this summer, and we've been doing adult ones – money is provided for us to go out to the pictures and to have a meal. It has been really good meeting people – really interesting."

The parenting group involved people from different ethnic backgrounds, and seemed to be an important way in which people who otherwise might not have formed relationships were brought together. For one white mother, her only black friends had been made through the group. And one of the mothers said that the parenting group was the place she got any information that she needed: "otherwise I wouldn't find out about anything".

Furthermore, four families reported better involvement of local people in decision making, including through the Education Action Zone, through regeneration, the local authority's community forums, and a local community centre:

"The area seems to be changing all the time – little changes. I've noticed a difference in some of the people I see about. There seems to be more of a mix of people – culturally, and people with middle-class accents. It's good to have different people around, all inputting in different ways into the community.... And I think there is an improvement in the environment.... And I have read in the paper about the council making an effort, for example community forums – where people can go and have a say and the council will listen." (Andrea)

Positive economic changes identified by the families are shown in Table 10.11. They included: members of the black community opening new shops and salons; more business investment; more jobs; an increase in private house prices; and better information about jobs and training:

Table 10.11: Economic improvements identified by families in East-Docks

Positive economic changes	Number of families identifying each change
Public transport – new station with tube connection, extra bus services (from 1999)	16
Large exhibition centre nearing completion (some thought it would create jobs for locals)	9
New building, 'developing'	5
A new hotel (and some thought it may bring jobs)	4
The nearby Millennium Dome	4
East-Docks is 'on the map', 'up and coming'	3
Greater class and/or cultural mix	2
Black people opening food shops and salons	2
More jobs	2
More business investment/new businesses	2
Increase in private house prices	2
'Regeneration money'	1
Improved shops eg new shutters	1
Information on jobs and training	1
Total	54

"House prices have shot up around here.... Houses round here are now going for more than £100,000. A year or so ago, you couldn't give them away. You'll always still have an area that is rough – but generally it's improving.... I don't think you'll ever be completely comfortable in this area – or in London – [but] it's got a lot of potential – looking forward to the future." (Madeleine)

"I think it is getting better definitely. A lot of things are going up, a lot of things are changing.... A lot of developing and making things nicer. Obviously there is a lot more work. They are doing the [exhibition centre] and everything. A lot of money is going into the area." (Barbara)

Management improvements that the families noticed included better cleaning, rubbish collection and maintenance. Two families felt that the police, government and local authorities were increasing their efforts to combat racism and racial harassment. Table 10.12 shows these changes.

There was a real sense that East-Docks was 'up and coming' and the phrase 'on the map' recurred in both rounds of interviews with the families, backing what young people had told us in a local secondary school:

"East-Docks is on the map – especially with the Dome.... So many people are coming in because of the new houses...." (Sasha)

Table 10.12: Management improvements identified by families in East-Docks

Positive management changes	Number of families identifying change
Improved environment and overall appearance	6
Improved school performance, including two local schools coming out of special measures	4
Greater involvement of local people in decision making	4
Efforts by the police, government and local authority to combat racism and racial harassment	2
Subway is cleaner	1
Action taken to stop vandalism to one block	1
Better rubbish collection	1
Better maintenance	1
Total	12

"It's a strange thing, because you'll be watching telly and they'll have News reports and you've got people in different countries talking about this Dome. And you realise that it's a big thing. But you think, well when I go to sleep of a night I can see it out my window. And these people are like 'Wow! This is a new thing, symbol of the millennium'. And you're like 'well it's on my doorstep!' It's weird.... I don't think you realise how lucky you are. When you look in the paper and you read about ... other big places in different countries. And [we think] 'Oh I'd love to go there, that'd be really nice'. And people must think that about us! They've got it on their doorstep, and we've got this on ours. And they're opening so many other things around here.... As well as the exhibition centre, they're going to be opening hotels, restaurants, cafes, lots of different things. It's hard to explain, but with all these new things around us, people know where East-Docks is. It's like putting Newham on the map." (15-year-old girl in secondary school discussion)

"There's some big changes. There was a really old looking train station – now we've got a brand new train station. We've got the Dome over there – which to us it feels like we are part of the Dome. People say it's part of Greenwich, but we say it's part of Newham as well.... When we hear about a big story in the newspaper [regarding the Dome] – we're really pleased – that's ours! We feel more related to it.... We've got a new exhibition centre that's opening in the year 2004. There was an exhibition by Tomorrow's World TV programme up in the NEC. And you think, I've got to go to Birmingham to have a look. But then you realise the possibility of [the new exhibition centre] which is only five minutes away from here. You can go there, you can go in and have a look.... Our local MP when he came round, he said 'We're going to put East-Docks, we're going to put Newham on the map'. And I think that's exactly what's being done with all the new projects." (15-year-old boy in secondary school discussion)

Ways in which families thought East-Docks and the surrounding areas were getting worse

Families in East-Docks also identified many ways in which their neighbourhood was getting worse, or in which very worrying problems remained. Improvements got roughly twice as many mentions as worsening aspects, however: 110 compared to 57.

Figure 10.3: Summary of worsening neighbourhood problems identified by families in East-Docks

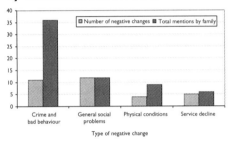

Note: Some comments appear under more than one column, for example, run-down shops are both physical and economic problems.

There was less of a consensus among people about worsening problems than there was about improvements; most of the worsening aspects were only mentioned by one or two families. However, as in West-City, there was one prominent theme to emerge from the range of comments – crime (including murder), insecurity, 'social breakdown', as one mother described it. Of the 57 comments about negative changes, 36 concerned crime and anti-social behaviour. Figure 10.3 summarises the negative changes.

Table 10.13 overleaf shows all the worsening crime and bad behaviour problems identified by the families.

Families felt under acute pressure from the visible signs of social breakdown:

"I reckon it's getting worse. I want to get off this estate – it's deteriorated – there's more families coming on that are more of a problem.... We live below a family – you can hear them beating the children." (Nicola)

Someone had recently been shot dead in a nearby pub, evoking this comment from another mother:

"Some different changes which I wasn't really expecting. There has been a lot of shooting people round here. These things are scary, very scary.... According to the local news, so far it's not very good in the past six to eight months. In [area near East-Docks] they steal cars,

Table 10.13: Worsening crime and bad behaviour identified by families in East-Docks

Negative changes	Number of families identifying change
Car crime, including damage, theft, joy-riding, dumping and burning	9
Murder and attempted murder, including a recent pub shooting	4
Children hanging around on the street, lack of youth provision	4
Rubbish dumping, litter, poor area appearance	4
Drug use and dealing	3
Mugging	3
Other crime (theft and assault)	2
More alcoholics/public drinking	2
Prostitutes pushed nearer the estate by CCTV on nearby High Street	2
Damage	2
Rows in the street	1
Total	36

burst them into flames. Those things are very scary to me, having kids around." (Gloria)

Wider social problems were mentioned by one family each, as shown in Table 10.14.

Many of these issues are interlinked, for example, insecurity is linked with the worsening crime rate described above and also with 'new faces'. In turn, comments about new people moving in are linked to points people were making about pressures on the rehousing system, and about the changing ethnic composition of the neighbourhood. However, these are distinct points and so we list them separately in Table 10.14.

Table 10.14: General social problems identified by families in East-Docks

Negative changes	Number of families identifying change
Insecurity	1
More 'problem families' moving in	1
Strangers/new faces	1
Immigrants getting priority	1
Reduction in the white population	1
Depression among the refugee population	1
Tension	1
Gypsies	1
Beggars	1
No improvement in the degree of racism	1
Local people don't 'fit' into the new jobs because of a lack of training	1
Too many people being 'squeezed in'/couldn't get rehoused	1
Total	12

People were worried about refugees and the pressures that greater numbers were creating:

> "[There] seems to be a lot of [apathy] at the moment. I'm not racial – but I think a lot of refugees, they must be down when they come in and I think that adds a little bit to the [apathy] of the place. People who live here think that they are being shut out a bit, and of course refugees must come into the country very depressed, so you just get that feeling that there isn't a lot of happiness there on both sides."
> (Peggy)

Tension and racism were also troubling some residents:

> "[Racism hasn't improved.] To change people it takes time ... it's educating them. Recently they scratched a car I had just bought."
> (Frances)

Families made nine references to physical neighbourhood conditions such as an untidy environment, vandalism and loss of green space to make way for car parking. Worsening service provision and management received only six mentions in East-Docks, which was not nearly as bad as Hackney.

Improving physical and economic conditions alongside worsening social problems

We tried to summarise all the families' views, both positive and negative, under the main headings they identified. In both neighbourhoods, it was clear that physical conditions were improving at the same time as problems of social disorder were becoming more acute. Table 10.15 illustrates this gap.

Physical improvements are the most noticeable. Families also see improvements in the areas' local economies and in service provision. But the impact of all these improvements is severely muted unless social conditions and behaviour also

Table 10.15: Summary of the kinds of positive and negative changes the families identified (number of mentions)

	Changes in West-City		Changes in East-Docks	
	Positive	Negative	Positive	Negative
Physical/environmental	34	8	66	9
Crime/behaviour/social	24	39	60	48
Economic	14	–	54	3
Management/service provision	13	12	12	6
Total	85	59	192	66

Note: This summary is based on all the comments families made, both negative and positive.

improve. Problems of social disorder were persisting or even worsening despite these advances:

> "Buildings might be getting better, but they need to do something about the crime. Even if you mind your own business, you can get attacked by people for silly little things." (Sola)

The positive economic changes identified by the families included house price rises, new building, new shops opening, and a sense of money coming into their area both through private wealth (higher-income individuals moving in and business investment) and public investment (the regeneration programmes, for example). A key challenge in the regeneration of East-Docks will be to enable local people to be linked into new employment opportunities arising in the heart of the neighbourhood. None of the families in West-City mentioned new job opportunities.

We found little obvious resentment of the new wealth in the neighbourhoods, apart from two families in West-City who expressed their concerns:

> "In the short term, if the upper-class came in they'd have to make the area better because they'd be more forceful. But in the long term, perhaps all the working-class people would have to move out because it would be unsuitable. They would be priced out of the area or something." (Ellie)

The impact of the new wealth on the everyday lives of families was limited to better shops and services, better buildings and a sense of greater wealth. Some families who had already bought homes were very pleased to see the value of their homes increase. Many families, however, did not feel they would directly benefit. Some were amused that people were willing to pay such high prices to live in their neighbourhood.

Families identified a range of positive changes in local management and service provision, but identified few successes in tackling social disorder. There were just seven comments in West-City and six in East-Docks about reducing disorder, including the removal of drug dealers from two estates in West-City, a reduction in vandalism in both neighbourhoods, and efforts to combat racial harassment in East-Docks. This contrasts with 39 comments in West-City and 36 in East-Docks about worsening social disorder problems.

The families we spoke to in East-Docks mentioned positive improvements over twice as often as those in West-City. The high profile, visible changes in East-Docks (such as the Millennium Dome, exhibition centre, new station and Underground link, new schools as well as the refurbishment of council housing) do seem to be contributing to a generally optimistic feeling about the neighbourhood. And regeneration investment in East-Docks via the Single Regeneration Budget has been ongoing since 1996, whereas the NDC in West-

City submitted its delivery plan in 2000 and it has been subject to many delays. However, negative changes received similar prominence in each neighbourhood. The problems of social disorder appear to be deeply entrenched.

Generally people feel that their lives and the lives of their neighbours are under great social pressure. They are coping with immediate problems that most people never have to face.

Talking about change

Some people could see their neighbourhood getting better in some ways, but felt that, overall, the direction of change was downwards; some felt the opposite and some felt that overall the neighbourhood was remaining the same.

Parents often commented that conditions could fluctuate. Area conditions are not static, and do not necessarily follow a simple trajectory implied by our question of 'better', 'same' or 'worse'. One mother described how drug dealing fluctuated on her estate as the drug dealers went into or came out of prison. Some families had experienced the negative impact of improvements in another part of the area, for example, better surveillance on one high street had, argued two mothers, just pushed the prostitutes operating there down the side streets and onto their estate:

> "We got prostitutes [here] the minute they put up CCTV on [high street in area near East-Docks]. When you've got children in the playground and they're standing there…. It doesn't seem right." (Clare)

One mother described how the installation of an intercom had increased problems because drug dealers in the block left it open for their clients, or their clients disturbed her late at night by ringing on her bell:

> "The people coming in and out. Sometimes midnight, 2am. And they keep on pressing your bell. Some time ago, I had to switch mine off." (Hannah)

There was also a feeling that positive change was *about* to happen – that the right measures might be coming into place, but it was too soon to see the impacts of these:

> "The council say they've got a lot more money now to do up the flats [in West-City]. That's changed. They're going to do the windows, general painting, the building." (Sophie)

We observed a *real* shift in people's experiences. Optimism about area improvements in 1999 was often prompted by the visible physical changes underway (renovation, new building) and publicity about new money (government regeneration and private money reflected in house price rises, for example). Much of this optimism remains and indeed, has increased slightly (shown by the greater number of families identifying at least some improvements in their neighbourhood). But many families also described their direct experience of acute problems, and their feelings fluctuated, becoming more mixed over time as they began to wonder whether their children would enjoy the benefits in time.

People's attitudes towards their neighbourhoods

What influences people's thoughts about the direction of neighbourhood change? Visible changes in the living environment clearly influenced the families' answers – either changes for the better or worse in the physical fabric or social conditions of their neighbourhoods. So too did the media, for example, local newspapers, television, and regeneration newsletters. And we found that, unsurprisingly, personal experiences in the neighbourhood changed people's perceptions of their living environment. A positive experience such as getting a job in a local school, or a negative one such as being mugged, feeds directly into people's life decisions. It also influences the perceptions of those they talk to, creating a mixed picture of things getting better and worse at the same time.

People's feelings about their living environment are also clearly influenced by the stage they are at and the things they really value. For example, Jessica and her family in West-City had decided that they wanted to move out, not because of any particular change in the neighbourhood but because they had started to really want a garden. This was becoming a priority. Jessica had said in the first interview that the neighbourhood was getting worse because she often heard people talking about crimes that had been committed locally:

> "[It's getting worse.] From the amount of people that say 'Oh my car got done' and robberies and burglaries and old people getting broken into."

In the second interview, she felt that this problem had not continued to get worse, that the neighbourhood had stayed more-or-less the same. But she now wanted to move because her lifestyle preferences had changed:

> "My feelings have changed a bit…. I didn't want to move before, but now I'd like to get out of here. No particular reason – I just feel I would like to have a garden, more than anything."

Emily, a young mother in West-City, felt that the neighbourhood had remained the same, but she remarked on how her feelings towards it had changed. At the first interview (when she had only been living there for a few months), she had been determined to move out as quickly as possible. She had felt sure she would achieve this soon, and had not put carpets down in the flat for this reason:

> "I'm not happy with the area at all. I just hate it. This is a temporary place. The most they can put you in is for two years. With my dad on the case, we should be out of here soon – once they clear the Housing Benefit backlog we'll start the letters."

By the second interview, nine months later, Emily seemed to have come to terms with the fact she would probably be living in the flat until her two-year tenancy came to an end. She had put down carpets, and described how she was feeling better about living in West-City:

> "I'm not as bitter as I was. I feel more comfortable with the area – making do with it. And I know a couple of the neighbours now. In the last few months I know their names!"

In the first round of interviews, we found that people's opinions about the direction of neighbourhood change were linked, to some extent, with the length of time they had been living there. No one who had been living in their neighbourhood for under two years thought that the area was getting worse. And people who had been living in the neighbourhoods for more than 21 years and/or their whole lives were much less likely to think their area was getting better. Those who had lived in the neighbourhood for 11-20 years were most likely to think the area was getting better (Mumford, 2001).

In the second round of interviews, one mother commented on how she was now beginning to notice the crime around her for the first time. At the first interview, nine months previously, when she had been living in the area for less than two months, she had said that there was nothing she disliked about the area. Now she had grave concerns about the level of crime, although she did not think this was necessarily anything new to the area, and said that she thought it was staying the same:

> "Before we [were] new, that's why we're noticing crime now.... Three murders in the last three to four months: gunshot to head. I [am] really scared." (Mina)

Table 10.16 compares people's views of neighbourhood change at the second interview with their length of residence in the area. For the parents who have lived in the neighbourhood for two years or more, the majority feel that the neighbourhoods are getting better, or at least getting better in some ways.

Table 10.16: Views of neighbourhood change of 92 families at the second interview, compared with length of residence in the neighbourhood

View of area change (% within time in neighbourhood)	Time in neighbourhood (years)			
	Under 2	2-10	11-20	21-30/ whole life
Getting better	–	26	39	24
Better in some ways, worse in others	17	26	50	34
Staying the same	83	31	6	17
Getting worse	–	18	6	24
Total (%)	100	100	100	100

Those who had lived in the neighbourhood for 21–30 years, or their whole life, were still the group most likely to feel that their area was getting worse. Exactly the same proportion of this group (24%) said in both the first and second rounds of interviews that their neighbourhood was getting better. At the second round, however, a lower proportion of this group said that the area was getting worse (24% compared to 32% in the first round), and more said it was getting better in some ways and worse in others (34% compared to 16% in the first round). This suggests that even longer-term residents were beginning to feel the impact of neighbourhood improvements, but that at the same time much shorter-term residents were becoming increasingly aware of area problems.

We tried to identify what had been particularly key in changing a family's views of their neighbourhood by considering everything the family had said. We did this both for 'positive' shifts and for 'negative' shifts, that is, for people who by the second interview felt the direction of change had reversed. We were able to pick out what had been particularly influential on a family's thinking, although this may not fully reflect the complexities of neighbourhood experience discussed above.

Positive shifts in people's attitudes towards their neighbourhood

The reasons for feeling more positive unsurprisingly often mirrored the improvements in each neighbourhood discussed earlier. For each of the people who were feeling more positive about their neighbourhood, we found a factor that seemed to be closely linked to this positive shift. These factors fell broadly into three main categories: visible changes in public services, visible changes in private investment (or private/public partnership), including nationally prominent developments, and much more personal factors such as moving house. Box 10.2 lists these factors.

Of course, many things informed people's views of their neighbourhood – it was never just one factor. And feeling that the neighbourhood was now getting better did not automatically mean that someone would not want to move out.

Box 10.2: Factors helping individual families feel more positive about their neighbourhood

Improvements in public service delivery, availability and communication
Public transport improvements
Existing school improved
New school built
More after-school clubs
Blocks of flats refurbished
Better appearance of neighbourhood environment
Reduction in drug problem
Regular meetings held to keep people informed of the area's development

Increasing private or private/public investment
House price rises
The Millennium Dome being nearby
New exhibition centre being built

Personal experiences

Interviewee gained job in a local youth centre and now feels much more positive about how young people are engaging with services on offer
Interviewee moved house and is much happier in the part of the neighbourhood she is now living in
Involvement in parenting group

Negative shift in people's attitudes towards their neighbourhood

A 'negative shift' meant that people went from feeling that the neighbourhood was getting better or staying the same overall, to a feeling that it was getting worse, or was now getting better in some ways, but worse in others. We found a very clear pattern when we explored what was most closely linked to this shift in attitude – crime stood out very strongly. Ten families who now felt that the neighbourhood was getting worse had had recent personal experience of crime or harassment. A further nine families had had recent, nearby experience of crime – for example, their friends or neighbours had been victims of crime, they themselves had been witnesses to crime, or a serious incident had occurred in a nearby street. And a further seven families had observed increased vandalism, gangs hanging around or other evidence of disorder. In all, for 25 of the 31 families who now felt more negative about their neighbourhood, crime, disorder and fear played a major role. Other factors were more personal, such as losing a job, family troubles, a child dropping out of college, or noticing things more because of being at home.

The following testimonies from individual mothers illustrate the impact of crime and disorder on the feelings of some of the families we spoke to.

Annie

Annie described how her feelings about East-Docks had changed since the first interview because she was seeing a lot of new faces around the place, and because there had been a few muggings nearby. She felt particularly shocked about the mugging of an elderly man, who was much respected in the community. Although the appearance of the area was still improving, the 'community' was weakening.

In June 1999, she had said that East-Docks was getting better because of the regeneration money going into it – new buildings, improved appearance: "If something *looks nice*, it makes you smile, doesn't it? Yes, I think it's on the up."

At that time, her husband had wanted to move, but she wanted to stay as she enjoyed having her family living nearby:

> "My husband wants to move away from here because he totally hates the area, and he just says it's getting worse. I say 'What about my mum and everything?' He always says we can drive down, but it's not the same. Sometimes I might not go to my mum's, but knowing she's there, or my sister's round the corner, makes all the difference.... There's positive things here, and I think even if something is negative, you can still make things good for yourself. There are people here who care, and people who are working to make the community better."

By May 2000, Annie wanted to move away from the area herself. She felt the appearance of the area was still getting better, but "East-Docks is not just the buildings, it's the people. I don't feel as at home here as I was nearly a year ago. There's so many new faces around".

She commented on the 'steady influx of refugees', which was contributing to the increase in 'strangers'. She explained that she did not feel negatively towards individual refugees, and that she always tells people that if there was a war in England, she would like to be able to take her children to another country and be welcomed there. "I say 'live and let live'." But there were just so many 'strangers', East-Docks was feeling too 'open'.

Annie felt that there was security in a close-knit community, in knowing people's faces. But now there were a lot of young men who looked 'shady'. The mugging of the elderly man nearby was particularly shocking: "It's so frightening. Before he could have walked down the street, and there would have been so many eyes looking at him.... When [mugging] doesn't happen at all, and then it happens, it just seems massive."

Miriam

Miriam had been very optimistic about the direction East-Docks was moving in at the first interview, in October 1999. At that time she said:

> "I've seen a lot of improvement in East-Docks. And that is why I believe in East-Docks. I don't want to lose that dream that in a couple of years' time it's going to be the place that people wouldn't think twice about coming here to live. And that our schools will have not just average education, but *above* average. I don't see why we can't do it."

The family had already been the victims of crime – their car had been broken into several times. And they were concerned about the groups of kids vandalising empty properties nearby. But Miriam believed the neighbourhood was on the brink of a positive turn-around:

> "I'm very excited about East-Docks. I think if we get the message over, and people start investing and local people start being more outspoken … then things could start looking up. But you have to have that drive … you have to have something to keep you going."

Nine months later, in July 2000, Miriam was feeling increasingly concerned about problems in the area. She had experienced increasing car crime problems, and the council had provided her with no information about the fate of the boarded-up properties near her home:

> "Since I last saw you, there has been theft, car break-in, people doing all sorts of things. I have heard about drugs from reliable sources.... There are lots of stolen cars parked here – I see them smashing them up.... Increase in car theft – lots of cars being dumped, joy-riding. Every week they go joy-riding. We've had one or two murders. But that doesn't mean I'm not optimistic. If we give up now, what future do the kids have?"

She had also transferred her job from a central London hospital to a local one, and so was being confronted with the difficulties of her area on a daily basis:

> "I will be honest – I am extremely concerned about Newham.... Now I'm seeing the problems in front of me every day. People's lives that have messed up. How are we as a society going to address these problems? It's not easy, it's very difficult."

"They're trying to improve the buildings, more business investment, education … but because of the type of work I do, it's just in my face.... I can wear make-up, that is an improvement, but will I change on the inside? Make-up is a superficial change."

Miriam did not want to give up on East-Docks: "With the help of others, I want to improve the area."

But by the end of 2000, feeling overwhelmed by the problems, she and her family had decided to move away.

Diane

Diane had had to spend a lot of time off work since the first interview as a result of ill-health. She speculated that this might be why she now felt the neighbourhood was getting worse: "I don't know if it's because I felt low coming out of hospital or not, and spent more time at home so I saw what's going on...".

"The problem of drugs in the area has increased. There are a lot of youngsters in the street and I know they're taking drugs. A lot of cars that have been stolen, smashed up, dumped or burnt. You hear a lot more rows in the street. Young people, alcohol-induced rows."

Diane said that groups of drug users had been seen in her back alleyway: "Sometimes you'll hear voices – it's noise and it just makes you edgy." She had also had the terrible shock of a relative in the area being killed during a burglary.

Some of the families had had contradictory experiences, and their feelings about the area were very mixed. It was possible to feel both positive and negative at the same time, as each of the following testimonies illustrates.

Cynthia

Cynthia had felt that West-City was getting better in the first interview. She still identified some continuing and important improvements, but was very concerned about a gang that had recently established a strong presence:

"We've got this private housing [management contractor] – now we can actually see the estate looks better ... collecting the rubbish. Before, you could never enter the lift on a Saturday morning. The back of the building looks cleaner now...."

"[But] they are breaking the lights downstairs – what can you do? I just watch and I feel terrible about it. And I think about my daughter growing up – some of them are girls."

"I think the kids need something to keep them going – like boys' club or something. If they are improving the area, yes they've worked on the renovation fine, but what about something for the children?"

Eve

Eve said she could see continuing improvements in West-City. But she was concerned at the worsening crime problem (particularly mugging) and the impact of improvements to other blocks of flats on her own block, which was one of the few remaining without a secure door-entry system:

> "It's really changed – for the bad a bit. Some of the buildings, they've got the security alarms. So with our one and other ones that haven't got security ... between 7 and 8pm there are about 12 boys by the lift. It's frightening."

> "And there have been quite a few muggings which involves the police – especially on the old people round the post office.... Pertaining to the crime, it's getting worse. But with the renovations and that side, it's getting better."

Rachel

Rachel no longer felt safe in East-Docks, her family having experienced four crimes in the space of nine-and-a-half months. The crimes were serious; her teenage son was mugged twice, once at knife-point, the family's car was stolen, and they also suffered the theft of a visitor's vehicle from outside their house. She commented how previously crime did not affect her, but now she was aware of the crime rate just rising:

> "There's always been theft, but before it never personally affected me. Now I don't feel as secure – now given the choice I think I would like to move out of the area. Although my job is here, so I wouldn't want to leave because of that."

She continued to see the positive changes taking place in East-Docks, and indeed had experienced some positive changes directly herself, including moving into employment:

> "In general it is improving – more local people are being approached in terms of decision making locally. Local people are working more with local businesses to improve education [through the Education Action Zone]. The finishing of [the Underground] has brought a lot of changes as well – you tend to think you're more on the map. A lot of people tend to know where East-Docks is now. [That's also due to the Dome.] The kids enjoyed it. There's so much criticism about it – I don't think you can say anything until you've experienced it."

Eight families who had said their area was getting worse at the first interview, still felt it was getting worse at the second interview. The fears of one mother, living in an area near East-Docks, had been compounded:

> "I'm almost definitely planning to move out because I regard this place as a prison. It's not a home anymore, it's a little box, it's a prison. My [primary-age] daughter can't go out to play or even go to school

on her own. All that's finished with. She was assaulted in the lift by a young lad who was just visiting, shouldn't even have been here. You can just push the door and get in.... There's some sort of ... I don't know what you'd call it ... a breakdown.... I can't really put my finger on it.... I feel I just want to pack my bags and go – it's got that bad." (Marie)

In December 1999, Tina had said that, even though there were many things she liked about West-City, she thought it was getting worse "because it is not as safe as I would like it to be". She had had her fears confirmed by the second interview, in September 2000:

"I've had my bag stolen and my car stolen. So I have to say it's probably got worse – to me personally, anyway."

Many positive changes were undermined by a desire to shield children from 'trouble'; and buttress their role as mothers by living in a more predictable and more controlled social environment.

Individual family dynamics

Alongside and intertwined with the complexities of shifts in neighbourhood conditions are the dynamics of family life. We have seen how personal experiences in the local environment can impact on views of the neighbourhood. There are many other family experiences that may be less clearly linked to a specific shift in attitude, but which all affect a family's relationship with their immediate surroundings. For example, spending more time at home through the birth of a child or the loss of a job; getting to know more people locally through joining a course of study; having your child start school which introduces you to a whole new world of obligations, fears, supports and opportunities for social contact.

Tables 10.17 and 10.18 illustrate some of the changes in family composition, and in work or study, between our two interviews. There were many other changes, such as children starting or leaving school, new friends, and so on which influence family life and which we do not record here.

There were a few changes in resident partnerships over the 12 months or so between interviews; two

Table 10.17: Changes in family composition between the first and second interviews

Type of change	Number of families
Birth	4
Pregnancy	1
Dependent child moved out	1
Non-dependent child moved in	1
Non-dependent child moved out	2
Extended family member moved out	2
Resident partnership formed	2
Marriage of cohabiting couple	1
Total	12 families, 14 changes

parents gained a new resident partner, one cohabiting couple got married, and there were no partnership break-ups. Six families had a family member move in or out, usually a child or another relative, and there were four births. In all, 12 families experienced at least one change in their composition. Table 10.17 shows these changes.

There were many more changes in work and study, with 31 families experiencing at least one change in their work/study arrangements. This includes changes experienced by any family member. We look specifically at the employment changes undergone by mothers and fathers in Chapter Five. There was a significantly greater increase than decrease in paid and voluntary work activity. Eleven people increased their work activity, compared with four reducing it. Table 10.18 shows all these changes.

Table 10.18: Changes in work/adult study arrangements between the first and second interviews

Type of change	Number of people experiencing change
Study	19
Started studying	6
Completed course and stopped studying	4
Transferred to higher level course	3
Gained qualifications within existing job	1
Stopped course before it finished eg for health reasons	5
Work	
More activity	11
Gained paid job	3
Increased hours/number of paid jobs	3
Started voluntary work	2
Gained apprenticeship	1
Returned to paid job following maternity leave	2
Less activity	4
Lost paid job	2
Now on long-term sick leave	1
Stopped voluntary work	1
Other	4
Changed paid job	4
Total	38 changes, 31 families

Limited impact of the neighbourhood?

A small number of mothers commented that they spent very little time outside their home, around the neighbourhood, and so they found questions about how it might have changed very difficult to answer. But 'locking yourself in' in itself suggests that the neighbourhood is having an oppressive impact:

> "I lock myself in so you don't realise what is going on out there."
> (Single mum, Clare, living near East-Docks, talking about crime)

> "It's alright. My neighbours are OK. But I don't go out often. I'm always indoors, I can't be bothered." (Belinda)

Neighbourhood quality can also be completely overshadowed by personal problems that dominate a family's whole sense of well-being. For example, one mother's every waking moment was dominated by ongoing and extremely serious domestic violence. Several of the families we spoke to are asylum-seekers, awaiting decisions from the Home Office. Snejana described how, although generally happy with her area, this decision hung over the family all the time and she just did not know what would happen in the future:

> "It's very good. It's quiet here. We didn't have problem at all since we moved here.... [Yet] we are like ... until the Home Office decide what to do with us ... we are very depressed. You don't know how long you're going to live here. I wish the Home Office could decide something more quickly. You have to wait so many years. We are not secure about this."

Snejana's uncertainty was exacerbated by the situation in her own country; the war was over, but living conditions were still desperate, and likely to remain so for the foreseeable future. It was very difficult for her to work out what was in the best interests of her child – and that was her overriding priority:

> "I [would] like to go badly [back to] my country. I feel alone. I miss my parents and my family there. But if you have financial problems and when I think of my baby, I don't know."

This mother hints at one of the underlying problems in these neighbourhoods. Many things are uncertain or feel beyond the control of individual families.

Summary and conclusions

When we first interviewed the families, nearly half thought that the areas were improving. By the second visit, 27% still thought the areas were improving but a third had mixed views, better in some ways, worse in others, up from just 7% in the earlier interviews.

The main improvements were to the physical environment, social provision, economic progress and service delivery. Physical and social changes were the most conspicuous. On the other hand, crime, disorder, more general social problems and some aspects of physical conditions and services earned more negative comments. Particularly in East-Docks, ethnic and immigration tensions also created some mixed or negative feelings.

These changes were visible to newer and older residents alike, but newer families were more likely to become more aware of problems over time while more established families became aware of improvements over time, despite problems.

Change can be positive, but an uncertain direction can be deeply undermining. Too many of the families felt insecure at too many different levels. And yet the progress, the positive signs, the upbeat atmosphere could surely provide a foundation for providing some missing ingredients. More positive policing of crime, more active support for parents, a different style of management for council estates, more care of basic conditions, control of nuisances and the enforcement of public standards seem to us the missing ingredients in these neighbourhoods. Families would then be more confident of the positive changes they see and feel more able to anchor their lives despite the negative changes that they see. If they could be more confident and therefore more anchored, then their family lives would become more secure and the neighbourhoods more stable. With less movement and less uncertainty, the more positive changes would possibly reduce the impact of the negative elements.

We have shown how much most of the families care about their community, how linked in they are to doing things in their neighbourhood. We have discussed the complicated pressures and feelings around rapid ethnic change. We have shown how mothers often come from a low-skill work background but gradually add to their skills and training. We have contrasted the poor neighbourhood services and conditions with the much higher standards elsewhere, reflected in the high levels of dissatisfaction. We have closely examined the experience of crime and disorder, revealing seriously destabilising levels of criminal activity and behaviour. No wonder many families have mixed views about neighbourhood change. Their attachments and commitments are strong but many elements of neighbourhood life make it feel like an uphill battle. It is not surprising that nearly two fifths of the families want to move out of the areas altogether. Unless something is done to tackle social problems, the poorest neighbourhoods will continue to lose the families who are able to go, leaving behind more precarious, more vulnerable communities.

Notes

[1] The government reports provide evaluations of overall impacts and government websites provide updated information. Research centres provide substantial clusters of information for the sub-debates. The Joseph Rowntree Foundation's extensive research and reviews of regeneration – at national and local level – provide both detail and overview (www.jrf.org.uk, see in particular JRF, 1999a, 1999b, 1999c, 1999d, 2000a, 2002b, 2002c). The ESRC 'Cities: Competitiveness and Cohesion' programme (which ended in June 2002; http://cwis.livjm.ac.uk/cities) provides detailed accounts and long-term evaluations of regeneration, and the ESRC Centre for Neighbourhood Research (www.neighbourhoodcentre.org.uk) provides much that sets these findings in comparative context. For discussions of the extent to which local people and their organisations have been able to engage with regeneration, see Stewart and Taylor 1995; Taylor, 1995; Hastings et al, 1996; PAT 2/SEU, 1999; Balloch and Taylor, 2001; Palgreave and Smith, 2001.

[2] Attrition does not explain the continuing generally positive view of area improvements. The eight families we lost between rounds 1 and 2 all thought their neighbourhood was getting better or staying the same; none thought it was getting worse.

ELEVEN

Conclusions

This book is about 100 families living in two low-income communities in the East End of London. It explains how it feels to bring up children in what are classed as 'severely deprived' areas. This concluding chapter examines the connections between the families, the communities and the neighbourhoods where they live, and the social conditions and housing problems they face. It shows the impact of wider social change on these very local areas. The views of mothers dominate as their role in the home and community building is still dominant.

Conditions in these neighbourhoods and for these families are often very difficult. The sample families are much more dissatisfied with almost all local services than residents in other areas. They are very worried about raising their children in inner-city neighbourhoods. Many of them survive on very low incomes and nearly half are lone parents, often making them feel vulnerable, pressurised and 'up against it'. They struggle with high levels of crime and a strong feeling of insecurity. They mostly live in council rented housing which offers very little control and are upset by the housing and environmental conditions that they consequently feel powerless to change.

Despite all these problems, and maybe in part because of them, a most fascinating and unexpected conclusion is that 'community' seems to matter a great deal to these families, and more so in these areas than in more privileged places. The attachment to the notion of community derives from strong local connections, a high level of contact in many of the families with other relatives, and almost daily contact with neighbours and friends living locally. The areas are rich in local social links, even though the communities are changing rapidly; many families move in and out, and many new groups are constantly forming within the East End. Kurds, West Africans and East Europeans are among recent arrivals into traditionally white working-class East End areas; the sample families reflect this diversity. Racial tensions are sometimes high and certainly almost all families, whatever their origins, are acutely conscious of the changing community, and the competition for space and for other resources, such as housing, schools, jobs and state benefits. However, even within the sometimes fraught arena of inter-racial communication, the idea of community is extremely important to over 90% of the families. Most mothers have friends from other ethnic backgrounds. It does not appear to be true, therefore, that attachment to community disintegrates in a global age, in a global city, with fast changing populations, strong cultural and ethnic differences and many alienating pressures. We ask the question, why not?

Families and community

'Community', in the words of the parents we talked to, is about local links between people who share common spaces and services. 'Community spirit', to which they attach great importance, is about the 'friendly relations' that make a community work. Families need their local area for many, or even most, activities relating to their children, particularly if there is no worker in the family. Living near other people and sharing the same spaces beyond the front door engenders frequent informal contact. These informal meeting-points form the basis of familiarity that leads to social interchange. Human beings are social animals and cities are the strongest, most complex, largest form of evidence of this.

In societies worldwide cities have emerged from the need to exchange, share and experiment. They act as giant suction and production centres for new ideas, new ways of doing things, new linkages. The very size and complexity of the city forces people to link up locally with other people, people who are the most familiar and who most often 'look out for you'. Most importantly, as mothers are tied for most waking hours to their children; for almost all the mothers the link with relatives, friends, neighbours, local organisations, schools and other children makes the burden of family responsibility lighter, more fun, and more manageable. Mothers without a partner have the added responsibility of making all key decisions alone, from the most trivial such as getting bread, to the most onerous such as moving or choosing schools. The need for someone to talk to, to run the occasional errand, to share local gossip and information, to pick up on danger points, activities and bargains, is strong. The sample families fill this need for social links through many local channels.

Proximity is everything. Many rely a great deal on other relatives, particularly their own mothers, and use the telephone as a vital link across distance where necessary. But for a majority, having a nearby community acquires special significance. Most are in almost daily contact with other local families. Most have someone very near that they can call on and trust, not necessarily to help with deep personal problems but certainly to share 'low-level', direct and often simple requests or offers of help. These community links develop among relative strangers because they are needed and they work because they are reciprocal: "We're there for each other". Social capital, the reciprocal trusting relationship that engenders shared goals and values, helping people to cooperate, flourishes at a micro-scale in these communities (Putnam et al, 1993).

Most mothers lament the more limited childhoods that they feel their children enjoy than they had, because of a more uncertain, more unstable sense of community. Young teenagers create particular worries because they often fall between stools – they are no longer tied so closely to their mothers, but are as yet unable to pay for, or organise, independent pursuits outside the immediate neighbourhood. This also makes mothers want more for their children, particularly more security, more green spaces, more street supervision and more organised activity. Community involvement and community activity help to compensate for the lack of freedom their children suffer because of where they live. A total of 85% of the families are connected directly into the neighbourhood through joining in local activities, work, voluntary involvement, and offering and getting support from their local community organisations.

Involvement by definition helps to create social links. This not only helps bridge racial barriers; it bridges the micro-communities people adhere to and the wider social organisation of the neighbourhood. It engages families positively and harnesses their energy to make things work better. Families feel better about their neighbourhood as a result of this engagement and their children grow up with a better chance of more positive attitudes as a result. People often link community and neighbourhood in this way – an important connection.

Community is a strong and real experience for many families, but it is vulnerable to wider pressures within the neighbourhoods and 'a spirit' that they cannot always find. Knowing that there are people nearby that you can rely on for crucial, if small, things becomes all important. Even knowing that someone will say hello, be friendly to your children, smile as they walk past, can transform feeling about life and its daily struggles.

It is logical that community should matter a lot to families with young children. Mothers, often marooned in their homes with their children, can be desperately lonely, isolated and unconfident. The pressures on young mothers were clearly recognised even in the 1950s in *Family and kinship in East London*, when the sense of community was by reputation stronger, and family links were certainly closer, more powerful and more stable. Michael Young concluded that a strong rationale for the continuing bonds that he observed between mother and daughter, between relatives and other residents, was the need mothers felt for social support, advice, information sharing and mutual aid. They helped and were helped by their local social networks (Young and Willmott, 1957). The sample mothers articulated this same need in many powerful ways. And they lamented the failures and inadequacies of communities deeply.

Community is an intangible idea, without clear boundaries or rules. It is not always confined to a specific location, and there are many wider communities influencing these neighbourhoods, such as ethnic or religious communities. However, for the sample families the idea of community is confined to very local areas within neighbourhoods. It is small-scale, informal and immediate – smiling and saying hello, meeting on the street or at the shop, exchanging small favours, knocking on the door to ask for or to offer something, watching out for older people or children – the 'banal encounters' that Ash Amin identifies as highly significant in inter-group relations (Amin, 2002). Those who feel part of a community value it highly and those who do not often regret its absence.

Surprisingly, community depends as much on simply being neighbours as it does on the length of time people have been in the neighbourhood. Community feelings develop through highly informal links between people who live near to each other, usually within a 5 or 10 minute walk, and who recognise each other as sharing common ground, quite literally. Today in fast-changing inner-city neighbourhoods residents often need these connections – having come from all corners of the world, and having often spent far less time in a neighbourhood than is common. In turn, this intensely local contact breeds familiarity, which generates friendliness, which then enables people to share what they know and what they can do for each other. Exchanging minute signs of 'feeling comfortable' together in those shared spaces and activities 'makes you feel better about yourself'.

An essential part of community relations in multi-ethnic neighbourhoods is the opportunity for people from different ethnic backgrounds to relate to each other. Here many complex factors come into play. On the one hand, competition for scarce resources, particularly housing and education, generates considerable tension. On the other hand, proximity and interdependence generate a level of contact and shared experiences that can create harmonious relations and a positive view of other groups. A crucial factor in sustaining cohesive community relations appears to be the chance to meet and create friendships. But unless this is coupled with a more transparent allocation of public resources, diverse groups will not understand how public services are shared out. The tenuous links at the local level can be broken by insensitive and misdirected public action. Women in community settings often feel powerless in the face of these wider pressures. Our evidence supports the idea that local community links have an intrinsic value that can aid inter-ethnic relations if supported more openly.

Community therefore matters a great deal to families with children because it binds people together when they need support, and it raises morale. Families, above all, are small social groupings. In this way they manage to survive in a harsh urban environment, where mothers often feel vulnerable to the unknown, the strangers, and the changes they neither drive nor control. Community brings strangers together and transforms a frightening sense of uncertainty into a more confident feeling towards the bigger world of the neighbourhood and beyond.

Families and neighbourhoods

In order to feel part of a community, no matter how local, families need to be part of a social structure anchored in the place where they live. But the neighbourhoods they live in are not neutral places, any more than the idea or feeling of community is. There is a big difference between people's sense of place or neighbourhood and people's sense of belonging or community, although the one depends greatly on the other.

The sample neighbourhoods generate both loyalty and alienation. Families are often attached to where they live and like many aspects of their home. For example, far more of the sample families rate their neighbourhood as friendly than the national average. They also view many of the changes going on as positive, and overall they tend to think that the neighbourhoods are getting better despite any problems. Physical improvements are the most popular and the most conspicuous. The government's many regeneration initiatives tend to show up on the ground as conspicuous and positive interventions. They do change things for the better. In particular, parents notice school improvements as more money, more effort, more activities, above all a stronger push on the basics of literacy and numeracy, take effect in every classroom. Some parents believe that children are learning more than they themselves did at school. The increasing efforts to involve parents in schools and in other local organisations encourage their sense of progress. Several mothers see schools, particularly primary schools, as achieving far more than when they were at school.

However, these positive views of neighbourhood change are tempered by the bigger problems of inadequate core services, lack of local supervision, litter, vandalism, and generally poor environments. The neighbourhoods are particularly difficult for families and for bringing up children because negative physical and social conditions can swamp any positive changes. Traffic, lack of space, poor policing, frightening 'no-man's-lands' between blocks of flats, along rundown streets or in damaged entrances, constrain and intimidate families. Threatening behaviour appears to be connected with poor physical conditions as signs of damage, disrepair and neglect generate an undefined feeling of beleaguered incapacity among families. Mothers often feel that they have little control over what happens in their area and this matters to them a great deal. In the face of visible decay, they avoid what they see as danger spots, and it is in these empty and unprotected areas that bad things then happen. Families are reluctant to let their children play outside and the streets and open spaces become a kind of vacuum into which trouble gravitates.

Well over a third of the families had experienced crime at close quarters in the previous year. Even fairly minor crime, such as car theft, had a deeply undermining influence on the victims, their neighbours and friends. The impact of crime fans out from its original target across community networks, creating a generalised sense of unease. Tales of much more serious crimes – attacks on children, stabbings, fights – spread like wildfire around these neighbourhoods. Many mothers had seen or directly knew about such terrifying events through friends. There is a lot more crime in these neighbourhoods than the London average, and people report far more rough and disorderly behaviour than is common elsewhere (Home Office, 2000). Families can end up feeling trapped within their homes, unwilling to let their children out, worried about unsupervised parks and play areas, and anxious to move away from trouble. Poor environments, inadequate services and sometimes racial tensions also play a part in these feelings. Nearly 40% of the families would move out if they could. This undermines the value of poor neighbourhoods and could eventually threaten the very existence of community on which families rely so heavily. So community and neighbourhood are distinct and yet interdependent.

There are several explanations for the dislocation between the need for community and the decline of inner-city neighbourhoods. Poorer services, conditions and environments drive service workers away in the same way as they drive families away. The pressures on doctors' surgeries crowded with families seeking help not only for health but also social problems, the frequent emergency high pitch, high speed screeches of police cars, the high turnover of teachers, all paint a picture of services under strain. Most worryingly to families, policing is in no way a match for the level of crime, particularly drug-related crime. In fact it is rare to see normal street policing at all as most time is spent on reactive calls and other functions invisible to the local community.

A vicious circle is set in train of highly concentrated financial, physical and social problems, intense pressure on services, frequent withdrawal of more able and more experienced staff to greener pastures in a situation where only high skills and commitment are a match for the scale of the problems. Families had special praise for 'trouble shooter' heads of schools and enterprising and dedicated staff who did make things better. Meanwhile, the poor conditions in several main parks in the neighbourhoods underline a more general service spiral. As a result of the gradual disappearance of most permanent park wardens and resident caretakers, parks and open spaces are less frequented, toilets and swings often broken and locked up, dog dirt uncontrollable, and threatening behaviour unchecked (DTLR Select Committee, 2002). Poor neighbourhood conditions undermine the idea of community by directly signalling that public areas are not publicly valued and cannot be reasonably managed or maintained. These are the very areas that families and children need to share safely and amicably if community relations are to survive.

Without constant informal supervision, low-level control and some way of brokering standards, we all tend to abdicate responsibility for wider conditions. This happens in acute form in inner-city neighbourhoods and the grip of decay becomes entrenched. This spiral generates a strong desire to escape trouble, creating constant turnover among local workers as well as families. When families move out because of problems, they leave behind social space for society's wider responsibilities. For this reason both areas are experiencing an influx of refugees from abroad, in large part because the supply of council housing within the areas is used as housing for extreme needs. They also house above-average proportions of other low-income groups, including many families dependent on state benefits.

The people who move in are usually poorer and more vulnerable than those leaving because they have less choice. Thus these already difficult areas carry more than their share of what are seen as the 'burdens' of society. Yet the internal resources of these neighbourhoods are extremely limited, and the amount the wider society is willing to pay to equalise conditions is far too constrained.

These neighbourhoods are trying to meet some of the world's major challenges – large-scale political upheaval, war and economic destitution in Africa, the Middle East, Eastern Europe, the Balkans and South Asia. International migration finds its way through to these neighbourhoods, homes, schools and streets. In this way, poor neighbourhoods are constantly replenished at the bottom of the wider society's hierarchy in a globalising world. At the same time gentrification pressures mean that higher-income residents take up much of the new and renovated housing as well as Right to Buy resale flats within some of the council blocks. This puts a double set of pressures on families with limited means who need affordable homes. In no way do current regeneration and neighbourhood renewal programmes (see www.neighbourhood.gov.uk) match the needs of the citizens carrying these responsibilities in their daily lives – the sample families and their children.

Families and social conditions

Families witness the spare energy and sense of frustration of youth who have not yet established quite how or where they belong. Young people fill the vacuum in supervision. They gravitate towards each other in the outdoor areas where few claims of ownership are made. Mothers often talked about 'gangs' of young men 'hanging about' and were worried about what they got up to. Almost all parents talked about their fears for their children as they grew up. Mothers hoped that their children would be strong enough to resist peer pressure, that they would stay away from drugs, that they would not be bullied or become part of a gang.

A lot of local crime and anti-social behaviour is committed by gangs of boys who fit somewhere within the neighbourhoods but do not seem to belong to any part of the community strong enough to hold them (Power and Tunstall, 1997). The families thought of their own children as the victims or targets of these unruly and menacing pressures, rather than as part of a more general 'youth problem'. Yet some families believed that boys they knew were bullied into joining in, intimidated into saying nothing about what they saw, frightened of 'grassing' and getting beaten up. In this way the children of the families we spoke to often hovered on the edge of trouble. In the poorest areas where social pressures are greatest, diverse and mobile populations have little opportunity to broker agreed standards beyond the immediate, local communities they are able to create. Thus whole neighbourhoods are at risk of decline and even collapse in conditions.

Many mothers simply hoped for the best for their children but were deeply unsure of what was really going on outside the home, or how their children might be influenced as they got older. Secondary schools come under far greater pressure than junior schools because they grapple with this difficult transition in children's lives. Sustaining parental involvement becomes more difficult, as teenagers begin to seek independence. Pushing up the children's ambitions and academic achievements is far harder, particularly for boys, when peer pressure favours 'rougher', more hostile and challenging behaviour (Power and Tunstall, 1997; SEU, 1998c, 1999a). Drugs at this point become a major worry for parents as they provide an alternative escape for the teenagers and many mothers were experiencing the impact – occasional needles lying in the street, dealing in hidden but public corners, shady comings and goings of unknown men and always youth hovering on the edge of the activity, obviously involved and therefore trying to intimidate and exclude from their sphere more innocent passers-by. Some mothers felt menaced and excluded themselves from these 'goings on', and therefore from parts of their neighbourhood. It was often this fear for their children as they grew up that made parents want to leave the neighbourhoods.

Trouble also loomed because parents were worried that their children might fail in school and face a lifetime of struggle. Jobs at the low-skill end of the job market were scarcer for boys than for girls, and acquiring higher skills required a clear long-term commitment, and strong parental and community support. For the boys and girls that 'do okay' many new opportunities are opening up, and some parents talked about the children staying on, getting qualifications, going to college. Others worked against all odds, just to show their children 'that's how you get on'. For the ones that 'aren't much good at learning' it's an uphill battle – too few rewards, too many failures and humiliations. By the age of 11 too often the 'street school' has taken over. Some parents were ambitious for their children and pushed hard. Most just wanted them to be happy and to stay out of trouble. Schools did not provide a solution to teenage gangs and drugs because too much 'went on' that schools couldn't control. The boys in trouble were too often simply not there, or not there regularly enough to benefit. Consequently, secondary schools are facing radical reforms in response to these failures.

Poor conditions, usually caused by poor services, low investment and high turnover, signal to disaffected, under-occupied, youth that damage, decay and destruction are 'fair game'. Low value generates low esteem, low controls and low ambitions. Damage and cheap gain at the expense of others become more satisfying than lack of any sense of direction or purpose. Nothing is worse than nothing to do, and many mothers talked frequently about there being 'nothing to do for young people'. They worried a great deal about their children 'getting drawn into trouble' on these grounds.

So who were the boys causing trouble if the mothers restricted the freedom of their own children so much? Were mothers and fathers actually able to constrain their children when they reached a certain age?

Only two of the mothers said that their own children were directly involved in crime or drugs, but most were familiar with the pervasive threat of illegal dealing, peer or gang pressures. They were acutely aware of drug dealing, illegal use and its direct connections with crime. Parents who lived in fear of such things, who experienced the harsh side of life too often, developed a strong protective instinct. No mother had completely given up on this struggle. We do not know how successful they were but we do know that the pressures felt were so intense and their children so vulnerable that some wanted to move away. They felt unsupported and often overwhelmed by the social conditions. Because tenants had very little control over their local housing conditions or choice, they often could not move more locally, which for many was a preferred option. This was the big destabilising factor in the neighbourhoods that cut into the sense of community.

Families and social breakdown

Poor behaviour and poor parental control within poor neighbourhoods are often seen as the cause of poor social conditions. Our core argument is that the causes of breakdown are far wider and deeper, that local communities in fact cannot single-handedly control the neighbourhood conditions they face, that the conditions are the result of many wider social changes, played out and concentrated heavily in the poorest communities.

So community, meaning most simply a feeling of belonging, and neighbourhood, meaning the place where home and environment help you put down roots, are often in tension with each other. Better neighbourhood conditions, implying better public and private services, would certainly help, as the families themselves suggest. But unless social conditions, sandwiched between community and neighbourhood, become more stable, then the sense of community, of neighbourliness, of security, will constantly break down. A sense of community stands high as something our families try to create. Neighbourhood conditions, on the other hand, are not something local families themselves can deliver or broker. They are driven by the wider city, and by elements of the wider local community that families feel they cannot control. Drug wealth and drug crime epitomise the wider reach of social problems. Therefore neighbourhoods, a physical and spatial reality, so closely tied to social conditions, foster or undermine a sense of community depending on the social pressures the wider world exerts on people at the bottom.

The small circles of highly informal neighbourhood-based community structures have no formal status or recognition, and play no formal part in overall neighbourhood conditions. More importantly there is no structure of responsibility for neighbourhoods, their social and physical conditions. Long gone are the days when community stability, kinship networks, known landlords, recognised public service workers and 'beat bobbies' made up a composite neighbourhood social structure that was strong enough and stable enough to withstand or absorb youthful deviance or serious crime – if in fact it ever was so. In Michael Young's East End of the 1950s, virtually all the families had been born there and had extended networks of kinship that generated and reinforced neighbourhood control. Among our sample families, one in five had lived there all their lives but around half had been there for under 10 years and many for under five. Very few services still had a fixed local base and many 'familiar faces' – the caretaker, the 'parkie', the 'beat bobbie' – had been withdrawn.

East End neighbourhoods are experiencing a breakdown in social conditions, despite a strong attachment to the notion of community and constant efforts by public bodies to engage with and support those communities. This is precisely because there is no mechanism within the neighbourhoods to control conditions, or to support highly localised community networks and neighbourhood-based organisations and services. Proximity can only help if there is sufficient stability and sufficient support to allow social networks to operate without fear.

The wider public, political and economic system view these neighbourhoods as intractable appendages to the wider social system – often easier to demolish and wipe out than to restore. As a counter to this, the sample families rely on the wider community, the city and society. They want the problems to be tackled. They want simple measures such as more street cleaning, more security, more greenery. They want more familiar local faces, more community stability, more buttresses and, above all, more opportunity. They believe that many of the problems they face come from outside, and have to be tackled by the wider community, not the highly local communities to which they belong. They may fear the removal of their housing from public control if they are council tenants because they do not know what it would do to their precarious hold on society.

If we see society as organised in layers from top to bottom, then these communities would normally be placed at the bottom, for they are among the most deprived and the most troubled. But they also accommodate and tackle their great diversity and need with a philosophy of community that allows relative strangers to help each other survive. In that sense these neighbourhoods are part of a much wider web of connections, and a web catches many different forms of life in its hold. If society is seen as a web with complex threads of contact rather than as a layered hierarchy with limited range on either side, then these families are at the very heart of that web – near the centre of a global city with huge wealth on its doorstep, and some of the world's poorest people gravitating in from the furthest reaches of the globe.

There are powerful reasons for the apparent contradiction between families adhering strongly to their local community, yet clearly articulating their fears, dissatisfaction and desire to move. Their micro-communities are neither big enough nor strong enough to contain the wider needs, fears and hopes they hold. So people are bound to try and escape to safer areas if they can, out of an instinctive desire to protect their children and to progress themselves. But people need community even more when things are difficult than when things are comfortable, so families in beleaguered neighbourhoods rely on the comfort of community, just as in wartime. These rapidly changing areas generate a surprising level of solidarity among neighbours despite serious undermining of the idea of community by sometimes intolerable social conditions. The result is both strong communities and weak neighbourhoods.

Families and housing

Many of our conclusions about community, neighbourhood and social conditions relate so directly to the East End housing system that we cannot ignore its all-pervasive impact. Over 70% of the housing in both East End neighbourhoods is publicly owned and rented. The supply of public housing guarantees and underwrites such poor communities in a high cost, high demand city, by providing low cost, affordable, subsidised homes for those in greatest need. At the same time, the public funding, the below market rent levels and the low incomes of many tenants determine the quality and standards of the housing, minimal and declining relative to the wider society. Housing standards have risen so far that council housing has become one of the biggest barriers to equalising social and physical conditions (SEU, 1998a). A council flat has become the equivalent of black and white television in a situation where most other people have colour (Hills, 1998). The majority of families would prefer to own.

Local councils have a duty to respond to acute housing needs, particularly of vulnerable families with children, by offering homes as they become vacant to the most needy or highest priority households. This is their raison d'être. So within the large stock of council housing it is impossible to allow families already in the stock to multiply and to stay close together, as children grow up or as elderly parents need more help, or as young mothers need more grandparents' support, without limiting the use of council housing to give community priority over outsiders. This has long since been outlawed as a landmark advance in tackling homelessness and establishing the principle of racial equality. Instead of filling up organically as flats become vacant with the families that already 'belong' or are in some way connected to these communities, they are used as a way of shouldering societal responsibility for the very poor. Several families felt deeply aggrieved that they were unable to be nearer to their parents, or that they were unable to move their parents closer to them as their need for mutual aid became stronger through children or ill-health. A few families were desperately cramped and simply could not get more space. An unforeseen consequence is to drive out many families as a result of the ensuing community instability; for it places a major block on housing progress within a neighbourhood. Many estates have too high a concentration of need to retain control over social conditions and too high a turnover of people to allow community roots to grow. Thus council housing can have a major impact on community and neighbourhood.

Cities expand and thrive on constant change, and London is doing just this. Many newcomers are more entrepreneurial, more ambitious and more positive about the neighbourhoods, community relations and the prospects for the future than some longer-standing families. This is a natural and helpful form of revitalisation. But unless families can couple their intense desire for security with an ability to improve their housing and social conditions within the neighbourhoods, they will continually try to move to where they can. And if only the most needy are allowed in, then the exclusion of communities that already exist and the excluded character of the new communities being created may become inevitable. Some better balance should be possible.

Housing, security and neighbourhood conditions are inextricably linked in the East End because council landlords are instrumental in how things work locally. They are seen as big, public and remote, not close enough to the communities they serve to understand neighbourhood dynamics or the fragile social networks on which they survive. Councils are responsible for the constant 'churning' of people. They are often unable or unwilling to allow even an element of choice and discretion in moving people around within neighbourhoods. They have too few local controls to create social conditions that are family-friendly. They can afford too little supervision to 'police' conditions and they often house drug dealers and other anti-social families, with behaviour that disrupts the peace and security of many others, because they are forced by public requirement to 'prevent homelessness' at the bottom of society. In this way the lack of viable ways of tackling the most serious societal problems is firmly displaced onto the communities under severest pressure through the mechanism of council housing, built in large communal estates to house families displaced by earlier slum clearance. Councils bear a heavy responsibility for the repeated disruption of East End communities, as Michael Young forecast in the 1950s.

If families could buy their way out of rented housing, many of them would. A few families do already own their homes within the neighbourhoods, seem to like them and feel more committed to them as a result. But most have no choice but to rent. The Right to Buy itself offers large discounts to existing families, but it has become unattainable even when offered at half price for low-income families as high valuations reflect the boom in house prices in London. So families will try to move in order to buy a home which they believe will give them some greater security, greater control, a better neighbourhood and probably a more stable community. Above all it will buy them out of social conditions created by the changing role of council housing into a last resort for desperate incomers.

Can the need for affordable rented housing in London and the housing needs of low-income families be reconciled with the needs of community? First, more housing would have to be produced within the very limited space of inner London neighbourhoods to reconcile these two needs, and some of this is happening in the more spacious old dock areas and the Thames gateway. Some of the families have moved into the new housing further East as owner-occupiers, and they like their homes. Nearer the City it is much more difficult because of intensely competitive housing pressures among higher earners, desperate to be near work and pushing up prices. An enlarged and therefore higher density mixed housing market is an absolute requirement if four very different and competing needs are to be met: the needs of vulnerable newcomers, often from a minority ethnic background; the needs of existing residents of many different ethnic backgrounds; the needs of their growing families; and essential service workers often excluded from council housing and priced out of the private market. The expectations and purchasing power of higher-income young City professionals who increasingly opt for living close to the city centre are raising the stakes in this intense competition for space. The combination may be possible but is not currently being delivered.

Second, special ways of helping lower-income families to buy into an enlarged housing market can be invented. At the moment the gap between Housing Benefit supported, low rent council housing and London's high value open housing market is too wide. So families move out if they can. Multiple routes into housing have to be found that distribute access more equitably between those already rooted in the community and those who want to move in, both very rich and very poor. At the moment the middle band of ordinary low-income families feel too badly squeezed by pressures from the lower and higher echelons of a deeply divided city.

Third, the often shocking social conditions have to be tamed in order to make low-cost housing work for low-income families. For inner-city neighbourhoods to work, we can no longer use them to dump societal problems. Nor can we 'gentrify' them out of existence. Some new mix must be found. Many special and acute needs have to be addressed differently. The families who do live there are all important to social stability, to community ownership and to bridge building. Making them feel that these are places where they can belong for the longer term, wherever they have come from, will transform the prospects for the future of cities.

Councils and government which together own most of the property in these areas should be less afraid of the exclusionary potential of giving those who live there a stake and more afraid of the exclusionary power of deep polarisation. The very simple idea of neighbourhood community spirit that the families propound is under threat because of their exclusion from their communities. If council housing drives out ordinary families, excluding those who would otherwise help to make it work, then we must surely look again at how we use this vital public resource. The very complexity of the task and its current unmanageability requires a different and smaller-scale of operation, one that matches people's sense of community. Council housing or its successor – community-based housing associations – and additional private housing could create more open, transparent access routes, based on a fairer distribution between competing social groups.

Families and change

Our conclusion is simple. People need both family *and* community, no matter how far they have travelled, how disrupted the community, how mixed, fast changing or problematic the wider society – and possibly because of all these things. Low-income families tied by young children need a highly localised network of community organisations and activities in order to guarantee basic security, some control, a sense of belonging and easy access to places where they can belong.

A sense of community or belonging which young families want and need is heavily dependent on both the physical spaces within any given community and on the social conditions that are visibly played out within these spaces. At the moment ordinary families are constantly displaced by society's extremes – the very poor and the very rich. 'Looking out for each other' (informal supervision) and neighbourhood services (more formal supervision) are vital keys to create neighbourhood conditions that are liveable.

Neighbourhood conditions change under the impact of much wider forces than any one small community can shape – migration, family circumstances, economy, property values, government and private investment, and housing and regeneration programmes. The poorer the neighbourhood, the more subject it is to external pressures because it is here that society concentrates its problems and creates entry points for newcomers. Families have great difficulty controlling or identifying the bigger forces with which they battle in their daily lives, even though the consequences are played out often 'in their face'. For both the wider social problems and the localised community spirit are in this sense physically located in the heart of poor neighbourhoods. The sample families from all ethnic groups witness the instability of the neighbourhoods, the pressures of incoming refugees and of gentrifiers squeezing opportunities for family members to stay close together as they grow up or grow old. Steeply rising property values in the areas caused by housing pressures on the rich and worsening social conditions as the areas become more extreme, make families feel that if they want better they have to move away. Thus community, the vital lifeline to families, is constantly weakened by the neighbourhoods acting as suction pumps, drawing people in, and as outflow traps, encouraging those who can to escape.

Many will leave, those who are unable to but want to will feel trapped, and newcomers will at the very least feel 'alien' and possibly unwelcome. As this jostling for exit and entrance goes on, many unwanted conflicts arise and the threat of breakdown in community relations becomes often all too real. Low-income European and American city neighbourhoods are also experiencing acute social dislocations, rapid ethnic change and an exodus of those that can. But the US experience is of a totally different order, precisely because wider efforts at equalising conditions and services have been almost non-existent rather than faint-hearted. The outcome is deep ghetto formation, intense poverty concentrations and social isolation. In spite of all this, detailed neighbourhood studies uncover complex social networks showing that parental care and community involvement are the best protectors for children growing up in such conditions (Brooks Gunn et al, 1997; F. Furstensburg, meeting with author, 8 May 2000).

Are there obvious things that can be done to enhance the function of community, to improve neighbourhood conditions, and to contain social breakdown? Would a wider and more integrated mix of housing allow more diverse and often competing groups to share the city?

There are multiple avenues for intervening to achieve this goal of sharing the city. More neighbourhood supervision would lead to higher standards of public care and maintenance, creating a much more secure environment. More family-friendly streets, parks and open spaces would lead to more social contact, more cohesion and more outlets for children and young people's energy. Wider, more community oriented access routes into social housing and greater ability to move within it would create more sustainable neighbourhoods. More rewards for teachers, health workers, police wardens and other public service employees who work in difficult neighbourhoods would compensate for higher housing costs and more challenging tasks. More childcare for mothers who want to work and more skill-based training for low-income adults who need to work would expand opportunities for front-line 'para-professional' jobs. More support and recognition for community links in multi-cultural areas of rapid change would strengthen people's natural desire to get on and slow the exodus of more successful families.

To do all this we must manage neighbourhood and social conditions. We have to create a local organisational framework to deliver on all the problematic details of neighbourhood management. Only public bodies can create this framework, but success will depend on recognising and tapping community resources. And all this will only work if the imperatives of law enforcement and crime control attract more active visible policing. If neighbourhood management works, then wider social and physical regeneration can follow on a scale that matches the problems the families face. Only a strong local handle on conditions will allow wider recovery.

Are families with children different from the childless households that increasingly occupy inner-city neighbourhoods? We argue that mothers with children do have special local needs, are particularly vulnerable to social pressures and have an overriding desire to experience a sense of local community. Their basic need for positive social contact is a barometer of neighbourhood life that reflects accurately what dominant local problems are. Through their eyes we can see what might make city neighbourhoods thrive. For surely if they do not work for families with children, they will not flourish for society as a whole. If we respond to these needs – for security, for safety, for services and social links – we will help cities work as places of the future, as surely they must in our over-crowded country.

Family and kinship in East London, written 50 years ago about family and social life in the East End, showed that while families wanted better social conditions, the vast majority wanted to stay in the East End. Today many say that they want to move out. Can we and should we attempt to reverse this trend? If we need more social anchorage to counter the intensifying social problems of inner cities, if we want to avoid the violent and destructive racial ghetto patterns of the USA, if we want to bridge the gap between poor and rich, if we believe we should protect human, social and environmental capital, then we have no choice but to apply stronger custodial care. For families, communities and neighbourhoods in the East End of our global capital encapsulate an undervalued resource in a crowded and deeply divided city. The fact that they increasingly mirror conditions around the globe only underlines the immensity of the challenge.

References

Amin, A (2002) *Ethnicity and the multicultural city: Living with diversity*, Report for the DTLR and ESRC Cities Initiative, Durham: University of Durham.

Amin, A., Massey, D. and Thrift, N. (2000) *Cities for the many not the few*, Bristol: The Policy Press.

Aston Community Involvement Unit (1996) *They don't understand us at all: Local views on regeneration*, London: Aston Community Involvement Unit.

Auer, M. (2002) 'The relationship between paid work and parenthood: a comparison of structures, concepts and developments in the UK and Austria', *Community, Work and Family*, vol 5, no 2, pp 203-18.

Balloch, S. and Taylor, M. (eds) (2001) *Partnership working: Policy and practice*, Bristol: The Policy Press.

Barber, A. (1995) *Parks at the heart: A parks and open spaces strategy for the London Borough of Newham*, Bristol: Stadium Leisure Ltd.

Bianchi, S.M. (1999) 'The feminization and juvenalization of poverty: trends, relative risks, causes and consequences', *Annual Review of Sociology*, vol 25, pp 307-33.

Bloch, H. (1995) *Newham Dockland*, Stroud: Tempus Publishing Limited.

Bloch, H. (1996) 'Historical introduction', in Aston Community Involvement Unit *They don't understand us at all: Local views on regeneration*, London: Aston Community Involvement Unit.

Bond, S. and Sales, J. (2001) 'Household work in the UK: an analysis of the British Household Panel Survey 1994', *Work, Employment and Society*, vol 15, no 2, pp 233-50.

Bottoms, A.E. (1994) 'Environmental criminology', in M. Maguire, R. Morgan and R. Reiner (eds) *The Oxford handbook of criminology*, Oxford: Clarendon Press.

Bourdieu, P. (ed) (1999) *The weight of the world: Social suffering in contemporary society*, Stanford, CA: Stanford University Press.

Bowman, H. (2001) *Talking to families in Leeds and Sheffield: A report on the first stage of the research*, CASE Report 19, London: CASE, London School of Economics.

Bridge, G. (2002) 'The neighbourhood and social networks', Centre for Neighbourhood Research (www.neighbourhoodcentre.org.uk).

Bramley, G., Pawson, H. and Third, H. (2000) *Low demand housing and unpopular neighbourhoods*, London: DETR.

Brighouse, T. (2002) Submission to the Independent Commission of Inquiry into Council Housing in Birmingham.

Brooks-Gunn, J., Duncan, G.J. and Aber, J.L. (eds) (1997) *Neighbourhood poverty: Context and consequences for children*, New York, NY: Russell Sage.

Burningham, K. and Thrush, D. (2001) 'The environmental concerns of disadvantaged groups', Findings 911, York: Joseph Rowntree Foundation.

Burnley Task Force (2001) Report of the Burnley Task Force, chaired by Lord Anthony Clarke of Hampstead, Burnley: Burnley Borough Council.

Burrows, R. and Rhodes, D. (1998) *Unpopular places? Area disadvantage and the geography of misery in England*, Bristol/York: The Policy Press/Joseph Rowntree Foundation.

Cairncross, L., Clapham, D. and Goodlad, R. (eds) (1990) *Participation: A tenants' handbook*, Salford: TPAS.

Cattell, V. and Evans, M. (1999) *Neighbourhood Images in East London: Social capital and social networks on two East London estates*, York: Joseph Rowntree Foundation.

Centre for Architecture and the Built Environment (2002) *Paving the way*, London: CABE, Thomas Telford, ODPM.

Chaskin, R.J. (1997) 'Perspectives on neighbourhood and community: a review of the literature', in *Social Service Review*, Chicago, IL: University of Chicago Press.

CRE (Commission for Racial Equality) (2001) 'Racial segregation in the North of England and its implications for our multi-racial society', Unpublished report, London: CRE.

Crompton, R. (1997) *Women and work in modern Britain*, Oxford: Oxford University Press.

Crompton, R. (ed) (1999) *Restructuring gender relations and employment: The decline of the male breadwinner*, Oxford: Oxford University Press.

Dale, A. et al (2002) 'The labour market prospects for Pakistani and Bangladeshi women', *Work, Employment and Society*, vol 16, no 1, pp 5-26.

Dasgupta, P. and Serageldin, I. (eds) (2000) *Social capital: A multi-faceted perspective*, Washington, DC: World Bank.

DETR (Department of the Environment, Transport and the Regions) (2000) *Our towns and cities: The future delivering an urban renaissance*, London: DETR.

Dorsett, R. (1998) *Ethnic minorities in the inner city*, Bristol/York: The Policy Press/Joseph Rowntree Foundation.

Drew, E., Emerck, R. and Mahon, E. (eds) (1998) *Women, work and family in Europe*, Basingstoke: Routledge.

DTLR (Department for Transport, Local Government and the Regions) (2001) *Housing in England 99/00: A report of the 1999/00 Survey of English Housing*, London: The Stationery Office.

DTLR (2002) *Green spaces better places*, London: DTLR.

DTLR Select Committee (2002) *Public spaces: The role of PPG 17 in the urban renaissance*, Report, together with proceedings of the Committee, London: House of Commons.

DTLR/DEFRA (Department for Environment, Fisheries and Rural Affairs) (2002) 'Byers and Meacher launch abandoned car crackdown', Press Release (www.motoring.gov.uk/news/abandoned_cars.html).

Duffy, B. (2000) *Satisfaction and expectations: Attitudes to public services in deprived areas*, CASE Paper 45, London: CASE, London School of Economics.

Duffy, B. (2001) 'Can't get no satisfaction?', *New Start*, 9 March.

Duncan, S. and Edwards, R. (1999) *Lone mothers, paid work and gendered moral rationalities*, Basingstoke: Macmillan.

Dunnett, N., Swanwick, C. and Wooley, H. (2002) *Improving urban parks, play areas and green spaces*, London: DTLR.

East-Docks SRB Partnership (1996) *East-Docks Single Regeneration Budget: agreed year one delivery plan 1996-1997*, London: East-Docks Partnership.

Equal Opportunities Commission (1997) *Work and parenting*, Manchester: Equal Opportunities Commission.

Etzioni, A. (1993) *The spirit of community: Rights, responsibilities and the communitarian agenda*, New York, NY: Crown.

Evans, H. (2001) *Sprouting seeds: Outcomes from a community-based employment programme*, CASE Report 7, London: CASE, London School of Economics.

Fetherolf Loutfi, M. (ed) (2001) *Women, gender and work*, Geneva: International Labour Organisation.

Frazer, E. and Lacey, N. (1993) *The politics of community: A feminist critique of the liberal-communitarian debate*, Hemel Hempstead: Harvester.

Gatens, M. and MacKinnon, A. (eds) (1999) *Gender and institutions: Welfare, work and citizenship*, Cambridge: Cambridge University Press.

Gehl, J. (1996) *Life between buildings: Using public space*, Copenhagen: Arkitektens Forlag.

Gehl, J. and Gemzoe, L. (2001) *New city spaces*, Copenhagen: Danish Architectural Press.

Goffman, E. (1972) *Encounters*, Harmondsworth: Penguin.

Gordon, D. and Pantazis, C. (eds) (1997) *Breadline Britain in the 1990s*, Aldershot: Ashgate.

Greenhalgh, L. and Worpole, K. (1995) *Park life: Urban parks and social renewal*, London/Stroud: Demos/Comedia.

Gregg, P. and Wadsworth, J. (1996) *Mind the gap please?: The changing nature of entry jobs in Britain*, Discussion Paper no 303, London: Centre for Economic Performance, London School of Economics.

Hales, J., Roth, W., Barnes, M., Millar, J., Lessof, C., Gloyer, M. and Shaw, A. (2000) *Evaluation of the New Deal for Lone Parents*, DSS Research Report No 109, London: The Stationery Office.

Halperin, R.H. (1998) *Practising community: Class, culture and power in an urban neighbourhood*, Austin, TX: University of Texas Press.

Harloe, M. (1995) *The people's home?: Social rented housing in Europe and America*, Oxford: Blackwell.

Hanna, B. (2001) Contribution to Conference on Sustainable Growth and Development, Belfast City Council Conference, Belfast, 27 September.

Hastings, A., McArthur, A. and McGregor, A. (eds) (1996) *Less than equal? Community organisations and estate regeneration partnerships*, Bristol/York: The Policy Press/Joseph Rowntree Foundation.

Hedges, B. and Clemens, S. for the DETR (1994) *Housing Attitudes Survey*, London: HMSO.

Hills, J. (1995) *Inquiry into income and wealth, Vol 2: A summary of the evidence*, York: Joseph Rowntree Foundation.

Hills, J. (1998) Presentation to CASE/Social Exclusion Unit Seminar held at the National Tenants' Resource Centre, Trafford Hall on 'Tackling Difficult Estates', March.

Hills, J. and Lelkes, O. (1999) 'Social security, selective universalism and patchwork redistribution', in R. Jowell, J. Curtice, A. Park and K. Thomson (eds) *British Social Attitudes: The 16th report*, Aldershot: Ashgate Publishing Ltd.

HM Treasury (2002) *Comprehensive Spending Review*, London: HM Treasury.

Holman, B. (1999) *Faith in the poor*, Oxford: Lion Publishing.

Home Office (2000) *British Crime Survey 2000*, London: Home Office.

Home Office (2001) *Community cohesion: A report of the Independent Review Team chaired by Ted Cantle*, London: Home Office.

Hope, T. and Foster, J. (1991) *Conflicting forces: Changing the dynamics of crime and community on a problem estate*, London: Home Office.

IIED (1997-2002) *Case studies in environment and urbanization 1997-2002*, Stevenage: Earthprint.

Jacquier, C. (1991) *Voyage dans dix quartiers Européens en crise*, Paris: l'Harmattan.

Jargowsky, P.A. (1997) *Poverty and place: Ghettos, barrios and the American city*, New York, NY: Russell Sage Foundation.

Jarvis, H. (1999) 'The tangled webs we weave: household strategies to co-ordinate home and work', *Work, Employment and Society*, vol 13, no 2, pp 225-47.

JRF (Joseph Rowntree Foundation) (1998) *The role of mutual aid and self-help in combating exclusion*, York: JRF.

JRF (1999a) *Neighbourhood images in East London*, York: JRF.

JRF (1999b) *Neighbourhood images in Liverpool*, York: JRF.

JRF (1999c) *Neighbourhood images in Nottingham*, York: JRF.

JRF (1999d) *Neighbourhood images in Teesside*, York: JRF.

JRF (1999e) *Young Caribbean men and the labour market: A comparison with other ethnic groups*, York: JRF.

JRF (2000a) 'Key steps to sustainable area regeneration', Foundations D10, York: JRF.

JRF (2000b) *Community participants' perspectives on involvement in area regeneration programmes*, York: JRF.

JRF (2000c) *Strengthening community leaders in area regeneration*, York: JRF.

JRF (2000d) *A man's place in the home: Fathers and families in the UK*, York: JRF.

JRF (2000e) *The secret of CASPAR*, York: JRF.

JRF (2001) *Experiences of lone and partnered working mothers in Scotland*, York: JRF.

JRF (2002a) *A new approach to assessing community strengths*, York: JRF.

JRF (2002b) *The groundwork movement: Its role in neighbourhood renewal*, York: JRF.

JRF (2002c) *The Commission on Poverty, Participation and Power: An evaluation*, York: JRF.

JRF CASPAR reports online at (www.jrf.org.uk/housingtrust/caspar/default.asp).

Katz, B. (2002) *Smart growth: the future of the American Metropolis*, CASE Paper 58, London: CASE, London School of Economics.

Kelling, G.L., Coles, C.M. and Wilson, J.Q. (1996) *Fixing broken windows*, New York, NY: Simon & Schuster.

Kelling, G.L. (1996) *Restoring order and reducing crime in our communities*, New York, NY: Simon & Schuster.

Kempson, E. (1996) *Life on a low income*, York: Joseph Rowntree Foundation.

Kiernan, K. (1996) 'Lone motherhood, employment and outcomes for children', *International Journal of Law, Policy and Family*, vol 3, no 3, pp 233-49.

Kleinman, M. (1998) *Include me out? The new politics of place and poverty*, CASE Paper 11, London: CASE, London School of Economics.

Konttinen, S. (1983) *Byker*, London: Jonathan Cape.

Labour Force Survey (1998) London: ONS.

Labour Market Trends (1998) London: The Stationery Office.

Layte, R. (1999) *Divided time: Gender, paid employment and domestic labour*, Aldershot: Ashgate.

LPAC (London Planning Advisory Committee) (1994) *Advice on strategic planning guidance for London*, London: LPAC.

LPAC (1995) *State of the environment, Report for London*, London: LPAC.

Lupton, R. (2000) Descriptive profile of West-City (Hackney), Accompanying document to *Places apart?*, the initial report of CASE's Areas Study, London: CASE, London School of Economics.

Lupton, R. (2000a) Descriptive profile of East-Docks (Newham), Accompanying document to *Places apart?*, the initial report of CASE's Areas Study, London: CASE, London School of Economics.

Lupton, R. (2003, forthcoming) *Poverty street: Spatial inequality and neighbourhood problems*, Bristol: The Policy Press.

Lupton, R., Wilson, A., May, T., Warburton, H. and Turnbull, P.J. (2002) *A rock and a hard place: Drug markets in deprived neighbourhoods*, Home Office Research Study 240, London: Home Office.

MacDonald, M. (1999) Seminar on Neighbourhood Renewal, Trafford Hall, Chester, Unpublished proceedings.

McKnight, A. (2002) 'Low paid work drip feeding the poor', in J. Hills, J. Legrand and D. Piachaud (eds) *Understanding social exclusion*, Oxford: Oxford University Press.

McLaverty, A. (ed) (2002) *Public participation and innovations in community governance*, Aldershot: Ashgate.

Maguire, M. (1994) 'Crime statistics, patterns, and trends: changing perceptions and their implications', in M. Maguire, R. Morgan and R. Reiner (eds) *The Oxford handbook of criminology*, Oxford: Clarendon Press.

Malpass, P. and Murie, A. (1994) *Housing policy and practice*, Basingstoke: Macmillan.

Mander, D. (1996) *More light, more power*, Stroud: Sutton Publishing Limited.

Massey, D. and Denton, N. (1993) *American apartheid: Segregation and the making of the underclass*, Cambridge, MA: Harvard University Press.

Middleton, C. (2002) 'New brooms', The *Guardian Society*, 20 February.

Millar, J. and Rowlingson, K. (eds) (2001) *Lone parents employment and social policy: Cross-national comparisons*, Bristol: The Policy Press.

Mirrlees-Black, C. and Allen, J. (1998) *Concern about crime: Findings from the 1998 British Crime Survey*, Research Findings No 83 London: Home Office Research, Development and Statistics Directorate.

Mitton, R. and Morrison, E. (1972) *A community project in Notting Dale*, London: Allen Lane Penguin Press.

Modood, T., Berthoud, R., Lakey, J., Nazroo, J., Smith, P., Virdee, S. and Beishon, S. (1997) *Ethnic minorities in Britain: Diversity and disadvantage*, London: Policy Studies Institute.

Mumford, K. (2001) *Talking to families in East London: A report on the first stage of the research*, London: CASE, London School of Economics.

Mumford, K. and Power, A. (2003) *Boom or abandonment*, Coventry: CIH.

Murray K. and Evans R. (2002) 'Winners and losers', *Inside Housing*, 2 August.

NCSR (National Centre for Social Research) (2001) *Survey of English Housing 1999-00*, London: DTLR.

NPFA (National Playing Fields Association) (1995) *Report on school playgrounds and children*, London: NPFA.

NPFA (2001) *The six acre standard*, London: NPFA.

Nevin, B., Lee, P., Goodson, L., Murie, A. and Phillimore, J. (2001) *Changing housing markets and urban regeneration in the M52 corridor*, Birmingham: CURS, University of Birmingham.

Newham Education (1999) 'DfEE Form 7 primary schools data on pupil ethnicity', January.

Newson, J. and Newson, E. (1968) *Four years old in an urban community*, London: Allen and Unwin.

Newson, J. and Newson, E. (1976) *Seven years old in the home environment*, London: Allen and Unwin.

Oldham Independent Review (2001) Panel report, 11 December, 'One Oldham, one future', chaired by David Ritchie, Manchester: Government Office for the North West.

OPCS (Office of Population Censuses and Surveys) Social Division (2000) *Survey of English Housing 1999-2000*, Essex: University of Essex, Data Archive.

Padfield, D (ed) (1999) *Hidden lives: Stories from the East End*, London: Eastside Community Heritage.

Palgreave, J. and Smith, J. (eds) (2001) *Rebuilding community: Policy and practice in urban regeneration*, Basingstoke: Palgrave.

Park, A., Curtice, J., Thomson, K., Jarvis, L. and Bromley, C. (2001) *Bristish social attitudes, the 18th Report: Public policy, social ties*, London: Sage Publications.

PAT 1/SEU (2000) *Jobs for all: A report of Policy Action Team 1*, London: DfEE.

PAT 14/SEU (1999) *Access to financial services: A report of PAT 14*, London: HM Treasury, November, to the Social Exclusion Unit.

PAT 2/SEU (1999) *Skills for neighbourhood renewal: A report of Policy Action Team 2*, London: DfEE.

PAT 7/SEU (1999) *Unpopular housing: A report of Policy Action Team 7*, London: DETR.

Power, A. (1987) *Property before people*, London: Unwin Hyman.

Power, A. (1991) *Housing management: A guide to quality and creativity*, London: Longman.

Power, A. (1993) *Hovels to high rise: State housing in Europe since 1850*, London: Routledge.

Power, A. (1996) 'Area-based poverty and resident empowerment', *Urban Studies*, vol 33, no 9, pp 1535-64.

Power, A. (1999) *Estates on the edge: The social consequences of mass housing in Northern Europe*, London: Macmillan.

Power, A. and Bergin, E. (1999) *Neighbourhood management*, CASE Paper 31, London: CASE, London School of Economics.

Power, A. and Mumford, K. (1999) *The slow death of great cities? Urban abandonment or urban renaissance*, York: York Publishing Services.

Power, A. and Tunstall, R. (1995) *Swimming against the tide*, York: Joseph Rowntree Foundation.

Power, A. and Tunstall, R. (1997) *Dangerous disorder: Riots and violent disturbances in thirteen areas of Britain 1991-92*, York: Joseph Rowntree Foundation.

Prime Minister (2001) 'Improving your local environment', Speech, 24 April, available online at www.number-10.gov.uk/output/page2938.asp.

Priority Estates Project (1980-89) Reports to the DoE on priority estates, unpublished.

Putnam, D., Leonardi, R. and Nanetti, R.Y. (1993) *Making democracy work: Civic traditions in modern Italy*, Princeton, NJ: Princeton University Press.

Putnam, R.D. (2000) *Bowling alone: The collapse and revival of American community*, New York, NY: Simon & Schuster.

Ratcliffe, P., Harrison, M., Hogg, R., Line, B., Phillips, D., Tomlins, R. and Power, A (2001) *Breaking down the barriers: Improving Asian access to social rented housing*, Coventry: CIH.

Reich, R.B. (1992) *The work of nations: Preparing ourselves for 21st century capitalism*, New York, NY: Vintage Books.

Robson, B., Peck, J. and Holden, A. (2000) *Regional agencies and area-based regeneration*, Bristol/York: The Policy Press/Joseph Rowntree Foundation.

Rogers, R. and Power, A. (2000) *Cities for a small country*, London: Faber and Faber.

Rowe, P.G. (1997) *Civic realism*, Boston, MA: MIT Press.

Russell, H. (1999) 'Friends in low places: gender, unemployment and sociability', *Work, Employment and Society*, vol 13, no 1, pp 205-24.

Sampson, A., Shepherd, J. and Vaz, M. (2000) *Towards an understanding of racial violence and harassment and its prevention*, London: Centre for Institutional Studies, University of East London.

Schuller, T., Baron, S. and Field, J. (eds) (2001) *Social capital: Critical perspectives*, Oxford: Oxford University Press.

SEU (Social Exclusion Unit) (1998a) *Bringing Britain together: A national strategy for neighbourhood renewal*, London: SEU.

SEU (1998b) *Rough sleeping*, London: SEU.

SEU (1998c) *Truancy and school exclusion*, London: SEU.

SEU (1999a) *Bridging the gap: New opportunities for 16-18 year olds not in education, employment or training*, London: SEU.

SEU (1999b) *Review of the Social Exclusion Unit*, London: SEU.

SEU (1999c) *Teenage pregnancy*, London: SEU.

SEU (2000a) *Minority ethnic issues in social exclusion and neighbourhood renewal: A guide to the work of the Social Exclusion Unit and the Policy Action Teams so far*, London: SEU.

SEU (2000b) *National strategy for neighbourhood renewal: A framework for consultation*, London: SEU.

SEU (2000c) *National strategy for neighbourhood renewal: Policy Action Team report summaries: A compendium*, London: SEU.

SEU (2001a) *A new commitment to neighbourhood renewal: National strategy action plan*, London: SEU.

SEU (2001b) *Consultation report on young runaways*, London: SEU.

SEU (2001c) *National strategy for neighbourhood renewal: Policy Action Team audit*, London: SEU.

SEU (2001d) *Preventing social exclusion*, London: SEU.

SEU (2002a) *Making the connections: Transport and social exclusion interim findings*, London: SEU.

SEU (2002b) *Reducing re-offending by ex-prisoners*, London: SEU.

Simmons, J. et al (2002) *Crime in England and Wales 2001/2002*, London: RDS/Home Office.

Smith, G. (2001) *Employability and other issues*, London: Aston-Mansfield Community Involvement Unit for the East-Docks Partnership.

Stewart, M. and Taylor, M. (1995) *Empowerment and estate regeneration: A critical review*, Bristol: The Policy Press.

Tam, H.B. (1998) *Communitarianism: A new agenda for politics and citizenship*, Basingstoke: Macmillan.

Taylor, M. (1995) *Unleashing the potential: Bringing residents to the centre of estate regeneration*, York: Joseph Rowntree Foundation.

Thompson, F. (1990) *Cambridge social history*, Cambridge: Cambridge University Press.

Travis, A. (2001) 'Largest fall in crime for 20 years', *The Guardian*, 26 October.

Turok, I. and Edge, N. (1999) *The jobs gap in Britain's cities: Employment loss and labour market consequences*, Bristol/York: The Policy Press/Joseph Rowntree Foundation.

UNCHS (2001) *Cities in a globalising world: Global report on human settlements*, London: Earthscan Publications.

UPF (Urban Parks Forum) (2002) *Parks and greenspace: Engaging the community – A local authority guide*, Caversham: UPF.

Urban Task Force (1999) *Towards an urban renaissance*, Final report of the Urban Task Force, London: The Stationery Office.

Utting, D. (1996) *Families and parenting*, Conference Report, London: Family Policy Studies Centre.

van Kempen, R. and Ozuekren, A.S. (1998) 'Ethnic segregation in cities: new forms and explanations in a dynamic world', Paper presented at Metropolis Inter Conference 'Divided Cities and Strategies for Undivided Cities', Gothenburg, 25-26 May.

van Vliet, W. (1990) *International handbook of housing policies and practises*, London: Greenwood Press.

Warren, T., Rowlingson, K. and Whyley, C. (2001) 'Female finances: gender gaps and gender assets gaps', *Work, Employment and Society*, vol 15, no 3, pp 465-88.

Weissberg, R. (1999) *The politics of empowerment*, Westport, CN: Praeger.

West-City New Deal Trust (1999) *Baseline resident survey: Detailed report*, London: USER Research.

West-City New Deal Trust (2000a) *New Deal for West-City: Phase 2 Delivery plan*, London: West-City New Deal Trust.

West-City New Deal Trust (2000b) New Deal Trust Newsletter, June.

West-City New Deal Trust (2000c) New Deal Trust Newsletter, August.

Whitehead, C. and Smith, L. (1998) *Evaluation of the Single Regeneration Budget Challenge Fund: Key results from the residents' baseline social surveys*, Cambridge: Department of Land Economy, University of Cambridge.

Wilson, A. (2001) Unpublished report on East-Docks as part of ongoing research about local drug markets for the Home Office.

Wilson, W.J. (1996) *Are American ghetto trends emerging in Europe*, London: London School of Economics.

Wilson, J. and Kelling, G. (1982) 'Broken windows', *Atlantic Monthly*, March.

Wilson, W.J. (forthcoming) *The roots of racial tensions: Urban ethnic neighborhoods*.

Windebank, J. (2001) 'Dual-earner couples in Britain and France: gender divisions of domestic labour and parenting work in different welfare states', *Work, Employment and Society*, vol 15, no 2, pp 269-90.

Young, M. and Willmott, P. (1957) *Family and kinship in East London*, Middlesex: Penguin Books.

Appendix 1: Interviewees

'Name'	Family relationship	Ethnicity	Age	Number of children resident	Occupation[a]	Length of residence in area[b]
Adeola	Married mum	Black African	20s	1	Not in paid work	1 year
Alice	Married mum	White UK	30s	2	Childminder	11 years
Aliya and Said	Married couple	Other	30s	3	Husband occasional computer engineer, wife not in paid work	5 years
Aminia	Married mum	Black African	30s	2	Not in paid work	3 years
Andaiye	Single mum	Black African	40s	2	School assistant	14 years
Andrea	Mum in couple	White UK	40s	1	Teacher	Whole life
Annie	Married mum	Black British, with mixed race children	30s	3	School assistant	Whole life
Audrey	Single mum	Black African	30s	1	Nurse	1 year
Barbara	Married mum	White UK, with mixed race children	40s	3	Administrative assistant	20 years
Becca	Single mum	Black African	30s	4	Not in paid work	4 years
Belinda	Single mum	Black African	30s	4	Not in paid work	10 years
Carrie	Married mum	White UK	30s	4	Home-worker	25 years
Chanika	Married mum	Black African	–	2	Not in paid work	4 years
Chantel	Married mum	Black African	40s	5	Home-working	11 years
Charley	Mum in couple	White UK, with mixed race children	30s	3	Not in paid work	3 years
Clare	Single mum	White UK, with mixed race children	20s	2	Not in paid work	7 years
Constance and Grace	Grandmother/ granddaughter	Black Caribbean	60s/ teen	1	Retired	29 years/ whole life
Cynthia	Married mum	Black African	30s	2	Cleaning	13 years
Debra and Alan	Married couple	White UK, mixed race and white children	30s	3	Not in paid work	8 years
Delilah	Mum in couple	Black African	30s	4	Occasional social care work	9 years
Desiree	Single mum	Black African	40s	2	Not in paid work	2 years
Diane	Married mum	White UK	40s	1	School assistant	Whole life
Dionne	Married mum	Irish	30s	1	Not in paid work	15 years

'Name'	Family relationship	Ethnicity	Age	Number of children resident	Occupation[a]	Length of residence in area[b]
Dominique	Mum in couple	Black African	30s	1	Domestic work	6 years
Ece and Onur	Married couple	Turkish	30s	1	Not in paid work	6 years
Ellie	Married mum	White UK	50s	1	Foster-carer	29 years
Emily	Mum in couple	White Jewish	20s	1	Casual sales work	3 years
Eve	Mum in couple	Black African	30s	2	Care work	5 years
Faye	Single mum	Black Caribbean	30s	3	Occasional shop work	Whole life
Felicity	Married mum	White UK	30s	1	Not in paid work	3 years
Flowella	Single mum	Black Caribbean	20s	1	Occasional childcare assistant	Whole life
Fran	Single mum	White UK	20s	2	Not in paid work	Whole life
Frances	Single mum	Black African	30s	2	Support worker	5 years
Gillian	Mum in couple	White UK	40s	1	School assistant	Whole life
Gloria	Single mum	Black African	30s	2	Not in paid work	9 years
Hannah	Single mum	Black African	40s	4	Public service officer	8 years
Helat and Aziz	Married couple	Kurdish	30s	1	Own their own business	7 years
Hulya	Married mum	Turkish	20s	2	Not in paid work	5 years
Jackie	Single mum (two friends also contributed to second interview)	White UK	30s	3	Not in paid work	Whole life
Jane	Married mum	White UK	30s	2	Not in paid work	11 years
James	Father	White UK	30s	1	Not in paid work	2 years
Jelka	Married mum	Kosovan	20s	1	Not in paid work	1 year
Jess	Single mum	White UK	20s	2	Not in paid work	20 years
Jessica	Mum in couple	White UK	20s	2	Not in paid work	Whole life
Joan	Single mum	White UK	40s	1	Foster-carer	19 years
Joanne	Married mum	White UK	30s	4	Editor	9 years
Joyce	Single mum	White UK	40s	2	Administrator	9 years
Justine	Single mum	White UK	30s	1	Sales assistant	Whole life
Kate	Mum in couple	White UK	20s	2	Not in paid work	5 years
Kathleen	Married mum	White other	40s	2	Not in paid work	13 years
Katja	Single mum	Eastern European	20s	2	Not in paid work	3 years
Kessie	Single mum	Black British	30s	4	Not in paid work	4 years
Kebire	Married mum	Turkish	30s	2	Not in paid work	4 years
Kerim	Married mum	Kurdish	20s	3	Not in paid work	Less than 1 year

'Name'	Family relationship	Ethnicity	Age	Number of children resident	Occupation[a]	Length of residence in area[b]
Kezban and Mustafa	Married couple	Kurdish	20s	1	Not in paid work	5 years
Kim	Single mum and daughter	White UK	Teen	1	Not in paid work	14 years
Lesley	Mum in couple	White UK	30s	3	Not in paid work	Whole life
Linda	Mum in couple	White UK	20s	2	Occasional hairdressing	2 years
Liz	Single mum	White UK	30s	2	School assistant	Whole life
Louise	Married mum	Black Caribbean	30s	5	Supervisor, cleaning services	20 years
Madeleine	Married mum	White UK	30s	1	Nursery nurse	7 years
Marie	Single mum	White with mixed race children	50s	1	Not in paid work	6 years
Marilyn	Married mum	White UK	30s	3	Secretarial	Whole life
Megan	Single mum	White UK	20s	1	Childminder	2 years
Millie	Married mum	–	30s	2	Childminder	17 years
Mina	Married mum	Asian	20s	6	Not in paid work	Less than 1 year
Miriam	Married mum	Black	30s	3	Nurse	4 years
Nadia	Married mum	White with mixed race children	30s	2	Teacher	3 years
Naomi	Mum in couple	Black African	30s	2	Cleaning services	6 years
Narin	Married mum	Kurdish	30s	2	Not in paid work	4 years
Natasha	Single mum	White UK	30s	1	Not in paid work	5 years
Natalie	Single mum	Mixed race	20s	2	Not in paid work	Whole life
Niamh	Married mum	Irish	40s	1	Childminder	18 years
Nicola	Single mum	White UK with mixed race children	30s	2	Childcare	Whole life
Nora	Single mum	Black Caribbean	30s	5	School assistant	21 years
Oni	Single mum	Black African	20s	1	Within legal profession	3 years
Peggy	Single mum and grandmother	White UK	50s	1	School assistant	Whole life
Rachel	Mum in couple	White UK	30s	3	School assistant	14 years
Refika	Daughter and sister	Turkish	Teen	2	Youth work	Whole life

'Name'	Family relationship	Ethnicity	Age	Number of children resident	Occupation[a]	Length of residence in area[b]
Renata	Married mum	Brazilian	20s	1	Not in paid work	1 year
Rose	Married mum	White UK	30s	3	Not in paid work	15 years
Rosemary	Married mum	White UK	20s	1	School assistant	Whole life
Sade	Single mum	Black African	20s	2	Not in paid work	6 years
Sarah	Mum in couple	White UK	20s	4	Play worker	5 years
Sasha	Single mum	Black African	30s	3	Childcare worker	8 years
Selda	Single mum	Turkish	30s	2	Not in paid work	20 years
Shushan	Married mum	Black African	30s	1	Financial sector	2 years
Sinead	Single mum	Irish	30s	1	Teacher	12 years
Snejana	Married mum	Kosovan	20s	2	Not in paid work	1 year
Sola	Married mum	Black Caribbean	40s	1	Care-worker	19 years
Sonia	Single mum	White UK	30s	2	School assistant	Whole life
Sophie	Single mum	Black British	20s	1	Not in paid work	19 years
Tessa	Single mum	White UK	30s	3	School assistant	17 years
Theresa	Mum in couple	White UK	20s	1	Not in paid work	Whole life
Tina	Mum in couple	White UK	30s	3	Sports instructor	Whole life
Yetunda	Single mum	Black Caribbean	40s	1	Financial sector	20 years
Yinka	Single mum	Black African	40s	1	Not in paid work	8 years
Yonca	Married mum	Turkish	40s	1	Not in paid work	9 years
Zena	Single mum	Asian	30s	4	Not in paid work	7 years
Zoe	Single mum	Mixed race	30s	1	Not in paid work	10 years

Notes: [a] We have deliberately described occupations in slightly more general terms here than in the chapters about work. [b] At time of first interview (1999). All other information in the table relates to the interviewee's circumstances at the time of second interview, if they took part in the second round.

Appendix 2: Characteristics of the neighbourhoods, families interviewed, and comparisons with local authority, regional and national averages[a] (%)

	West-City	50 West-City families	East-Docks	50 East-Docks families	Hackney	Newham	Inner London	Greater London	Great Britain[b]
Tenure % in social housing	82	72	75 (1996)[c]	78	59 (1991)	37 (1991)	43 (1991)	29 (1991)	23 (1993, E&W)
Ethnicity[d] Proportion of 'white' children	32[e] (56, 1991)	64 (0-18)	61[f] (76, 1991)	34 (0-18)	54 (1991)	42 (1991)	59 (1991)	70 (1991)	91 (1991)
Lone parents Proportion of lone-parent families (as a % of all families with dependent children)	42[g] (1991)	28	46[h] (1991)	62	41 (1991)	29 (1991)	37 (1991)	25 (1991)	19 (1991)
Proportion of lone parents working (full- or part-time)	26	29	18[h] (1991)	47	29 (1991)	25 (1991)	30 (1991)	32 (1991)	35 (1991)
Work poverty Proportion of working-age population not in work, study or training	39 (16+)	42 (18+)	42 (1991)	33 (18+)	36 (1991)	36 (1991)	30 (1991)	26 (1991)	25 (1991)

Notes: [a] All figures 99/00 unless specified. [b] Or England and Wales (E&W) where marked. [c] East-Docks Partnership, 1996. [d] The Census category of 'white' includes Irish, Greek, Turkish and other European groups (Karn, 1997). We counted these groups separately. For the purposes of comparison, we included them in the white totals for the family sample shown in this table. A more detailed breakdown is shown in Table 16. [e] Derived from pupil ethnicity data for 9 West-City primary schools. [f] Derived from pupil ethnicity data for 5 primary schools and 2 secondary schools. [g] This figure represents the average for the four wards, parts of which are included within the area, based on the 1991 Census. [h] These figures are the average for the three neighbouring wards that represent the closest fit to the area, based on the 1991 Census.

Sources: All West-City figures are based on the 1999 NDC 10% sample, unless specified. East-Docks figures are based on the 1991 census for three wards, unless specified. The national tenure figure is from Malpass and Murie (1994). All other figures are based on the 1991 Census.

Our neighbourhood study involving families is linked to CASE's '12 Areas Study', which is researching twelve low-income areas across England and Wales. This study is tracking the areas back to 1991 and forward to 2007. Each of our 'areas' is made up of a series of levels: (i) regional; (ii) local authority; (iii) areas of approximately 20,000 people; and (iv) estate/small group of streets. The study aims to find out why some areas recover while others do not, and to assess the effectiveness of different interventions, including large government-driven regeneration schemes. To do this, Ruth Lupton is collecting a wide range of data, including: interviews with staff at all levels; health indicators; educational performance; housing indicators (such as empty property rates, turnover, stock condition); crime statistics; and a record of the aims and progress of the special initiatives being tried in each area.

The areas are in: Hackney, Newham, Knowsley, Nottingham, Newcastle upon Tyne, Sheffield, Blackburn, Birmingham, Caerphilly, Redcar and Cleveland, Leeds and Thanet (Glennerster et al, 1999).

The fieldwork for the study began to get underway in November 1998, and has already unearthed a wealth of information, providing a rich context in which to set the neighbourhood study.

The Centre for Analysis of Social Exclusion (CASE) is running a survey of 200 families with children (under the ages of 18) in four low-income areas in England, of which *East Enders* is a part. Through successive rounds of interviews we are trying to understand how area conditions and area changes affect people who live locally. Our aim is to find out about and document the ways in which areas improve or decline as local families see it.

The Neighbourhood Study in Leeds and Sheffield is funded by the Nuffield Foundation and is the second part of the neighbourhood study started in two areas of London in 1999 (Mumford, 2001). The two areas of Leeds and Sheffield are also part of CASE's 12 Areas Study (R. Lupton, discussion with author, 4 June 2001). Once the fieldwork was underway in East London the Nuffield Foundation agreed to fund the parallel Neighbourhood Study in Leeds and Sheffield. This work started in May 2000. The researcher for this post is based in Leeds.

Appendix 4: Mothers' work patterns in different work trajectories

1. Consistent career (8 mothers)
(a) Professional (6 mothers)

Qualifications (highest)	Summary of work experience
1. BEd	Casual work abroad → bar work/waitressing → teacher training → teacher
2. A-levels and nursing certificate	Teaching assistant → nurse training → qualified nurse
3. Degree	Voluntary work → access course → degree → prison officer
4. Nursing diploma	Office work/secretary → nurse training → qualified nurse
5. Law degree	Law student and working at solicitors → lawyer (completing exams)
6. Degree	Marketing (outside UK) → marketing (UK) → banker

(b) Other (2 mothers)

Qualifications (highest)	Summary of work experience
1. NNEB	Nursery nurse → playgroup leader → gap of two years with baby → temporary nursery nurse → permanent nursery nurse (in school)
2. None	Tailor (self-employed)

2. Unsteady career (2 mothers)

Qualifications (highest)	Summary of work experience
1. Degree and postgraduate qualifications	University student → PA → gap with family → editor
2. Degree	Civil servant (non-UK) → catering → access course → degree → occasional social care work through agency to fit in with children

3. Career progression (10 mothers)

Qualifications (highest)	Summary of work experience
1. City & Guilds Specialist teaching	Sales assistant → manageress → PA → at home with children Volunteer in school → dinner lady → reading assistant → learning support → specialist teaching assistant
2. None	Office junior → receptionist → six years at home taking care of children → dinner lady → welfare assistant → school secretary
3. CSEs and RSAs (typing etc)	Office junior → receptionist → 20 years at home taking care of family → teacher's assistant → special support assistant
4. Degree and PGCE	Finance clerk → youth work → adult education manager
5. Degree	Various cash-in-hand → agency work → learning support assistant
6. GCSEs	Various office/shop/administration → assistant manager → doctor's receptionist
7. O-levels and pharmacy course	Shop (chemist) → gap with children → bar work → gap with children → chemist shop → pharmacist assistant

8. O-levels and sports instructor qualifications	Secretary → unemployed for 1½ years after being made redundant → shop → leisure centre crèche → sports instructor
9. A-levels	Partially completed degree → admin assistant → eight years at home with family → lunch-time supervisor → adult education teacher
10. GCSEs and City & Guilds	Waitressing → five years bringing up children → cleaning → play worker

4. Career shrinkage (1 mother)

Qualifications (highest)	Summary of work experience
1. NNEB (nursery nursing)	Nursery nursing → volunteer coordinator of community project → paid manager of community project → left because wanted a change, but could not get back into nursery nursing field → carer (very satisfied with)

5. Mixed jobs (20 mothers)
(a) Good, fairly continuous (3 mothers)

Qualifications (highest)	Summary of work experience
1. GCSEs and City & Guilds	Apprentice hairdresser → cleaning supervisor (briefly) → freelance hairdresser
2. Not recorded	Data entry in a series of different companies, including periods of temping of up to six years → accounts administrator
3. Hairdressing diploma	Hairdressing → school office clerk and lunch-time supervisor

(b) Good, not continuous (3 mothers)

Qualifications (highest)	Summary of work experience
1. A-levels	Jobs have included library assistant, crèche work, and classroom assistant
2. O-Levels (non-UK) Secretarial (UK)	Bank worker (non-UK) → cleaning and waitressing → bank clerk → one year gap because wanted a career change → education assistant
3. O-Levels and RSAs (office)	Office junior → secretary → two years travelling → clerk (full-time then part-time when had children)

(c) Low paid, fairly continuous (3 mothers)

Qualifications (highest)	Summary of work experience
1. Childcare course	YTS → office clerk → short break with child (one year) → driver → childminding
2. None	Domestic work → factory work → cook (some breaks with children) → childminding
3. CSEs	YTS → office junior → receptionist → public transport worker → childminding

(d) Low paid, steady with gap (4 mothers)

Qualifications (highest)	Summary of work experience
1. None	Sales assistant → 12 years bringing up family (plus voluntary work and occasional temping) → childminding
2. O-Levels (non-UK) RSAs	Laundry worker → domestic (left due to redundancy and pregnancy) → four years taking care of family → laundry worker
3. None	Factory work → bakery → eight years at home bringing up children → lunch-time supervisor
4. Not recorded	Machinist → 12 years bringing up children → sales assistant (redundancy) → two year gap → foster carer

(e) Low paid, unsteady (6 mothers)

Qualifications (highest)	Summary of work experience
1. O-Levels City & Guilds	Office work (redundancy) → three years at home with children (+ some cleaning work) → cleaner → office worker → taking care of children → cleaner (redundancy) → two year gap → cleaner → supervisor
2. A-Level City & Guilds	Hairdressing → office work → bringing up children → office work (sacked) → sales assistant → full-time babysitting
3. Not recorded	Office work (sacked) → office work (redundancy) → various short-term jobs → office work → caring for children → homeworker
4. Foundation course Childcare course	YTS → office junior (left) → one year unemployed, one year with baby → office work → sales assistant → nine years bringing up family → leader of children's club
5. NNEB	Sales assistant → full-time student (NNEB) → occasional work (including crèche work) combined with bringing up children
6. NVQ	Cashier (non-UK) → three years not working (UK) → catering → two years taking care of children → carer

(f) Mix of good and low paid, with gaps (1 mother)

Qualifications (highest)	Summary of work experience
1. NVQ	Five separate breaks from labour market to either give birth or care for existing children. Mix of jobs – including factory work and being a head chef for five years.

Appendix 5a: Career histories of all non-working interviewees

Previous work trajectory and number of mothers		Individual details	
Qualifications (highest)	Previous work experience includes:	Time since last job	Why left last job

1 Consistent career *(2 mothers, 0 seeking work)*

1 Teaching	Teacher	1 year	Children
2 Hairdressing diploma	Hairdresser	10 years	Children

2 Unsteady career *(3 mothers, 1 looking for funding to start own business)*

1 O-Levels	Accounts management (now resident activist)	5 years	Children
2 Masters degree	Office work, teaching English	14 years	Children
3 A-levels	Administrator, different organisations	1 year	Children

3a Mixed jobs: good, fairly continuous *(6 mothers, 1 seeking work currently, 1 has no work permit)*

1 None	Office/typist	11 years	Children
2 None	Telephonist/receptionist	6 years	Children
3 –	School assistant	3 years	Marriage
4 O-Levels	Cash supervisor, currently support group coordinator (voluntary)	3 years	Debt, childcare problems, child support agency problems
5 1 CSE	Shop manageress	6 years	Children
6 Secretarial and O-Levels (non-UK)	Secretary	9 years	To come to UK

3b Mixed jobs: good, not continuous *(2 mothers, 1 actively seeking work, 1 studying)*

1 Basic	Childcare, auxiliary nursing	16 years	Children
2 None	Retail management, security	4 years	Children (some temping since)

3c Mixed jobs: low paid, fairly continuous *(9 mothers, 0 seeking work currently)*

1 Secretarial (non-UK)	Cleaning	10 years	Children
2 None	Factory, play, cleaning	6 years	–
3 GCEs	Cleaning, catering	6 years	Children
4 None	Factory work	11 years	Children
5 None	Farm work	5 years	Came to UK
6 Catering	Catering, bar, certificates beauty	3 years	Marriage
7 A-levels, City & Guilds	Shop assistant, nanny	5 years	Children

Previous work trajectory and number of mothers		Individual details	
Qualifications (highest)	**Previous work experience includes:**	**Time since last job**	**Why left last job**
8 Secretarial (non-UK)	'Sweat-shops'	–	–
9 'A-Levels' (non-UK)	Factory work, cafes	2 years	–

3d Mixed jobs: low paid, unsteady *(7 mothers, 3 seeking work, 1 of whom also studying, 2 further mothers studying)*

1 None	Waitressing/shop work (currently hospital volunteer)	6 years	–
2 O-levels and City &Guild	Chamber-maiding	7 years	Health/children
3 YTS in childcare	Childcare assistant/factory work	6 years	Children
4 O-levels	Cleaning and catering	4 years	–
5 Basic (but studying NVQ II)	Cleaning (currently volunteer coordinator of community group)	2 years	–
6 Degree	Sales assistant	12 years	–
7 Foundation course	Waitress/dinner lady	1 year	To go to college

4a Slender work experience: no previous paid work experience *(5 mothers, 0 currently seeking work, 1 does not have a work permit)*

1 School-level	None (age 22)	–	–
2 Was part-way through university in Turkey	None (age 28)	–	–
3 Was training to be a nurse – forced to leave	None (age 29)	–	–
4 School-level and basic English qualifications	None (age 37)	–	–
5 –	None (age 33)	–	–

4b Slender work experience: hardly any paid work experience *(2 mothers, 0 seeking work)*

1 None	Factory work	10 years	Children
2 None	Factory work	6 years	Children

4c Slender work experience: no formal work experience, but some informal *(2 mothers, 0 seeking formal work)*

1 NVQ II	Cash-in-hand, 'bits and pieces' eg market	–	–
2 None	Fairly continuous cash-in-hand jobs for last seven years	–	–

5b: The circumstances of the mothers at home who did not want paid work

	Couple status	Not worked	Previous work experience	Reason left last paid job	Reason do not want paid work currently (age of youngest child in brackets)
In couple, partner working					
1	Married, partner in f-t work	1 year	Qualified teacher	To spend more time with child before started f-t school	About to move out of London (pre-school)
2	Married, partner in f-t work	1 year	Continuous employment – a series of permanent jobs with art-oriented companies	To have her child	Baby to look after (pre-school)
3	Married, partner in f-t work	2 years	Periods of factory work and in catering industry	Had more children	Children to look after (pre-school)
4	Couple, partner in f-t work	3 years (some p-t work since)	Hairdressing – fairly continuous employment/ self-employment	Shop sold, continued on a freelance basis infrequently	Children to look after (pre-school)
5	Couple, partner in f-t work	3 years	Finance officer (continuous)	Because she realised she would be financially better off on benefits	Currently caring for new baby (pre-school)
6	Married, partner in f-t work	3 years	Mainly hotel jobs, catering (continuous)	To get married	Child to look after (pre-school) Cost of childcare and transport
7	Couple, partner in f-t work	6 years	Periods of childcare and factory work	Could not find childcare	Children to look after (pre-school)
8	Couple, partner in f-t work	6 years	Office/admin work – mixture of different jobs, including temping (fairly continuous)	Became pregnant	Children to look after (pre-school)
9	Couple, partner in f-t work	10 years	Hairdressing (continuous)	To have children	Children to look after (pre-school)

	Couple status	Not worked	Previous work experience	Reason left last paid job	Reason do not want paid work currently (age of youngest child in brackets)
10	Married, partner in f-t work	14 years	Mixture of different jobs (continuous employment) including office work, teaching English	To have children	Children to look after (primary age)
11	Married, partner's work fluctuates	–	Medical doctor (although not qualified to work in UK)	To have children	Children to look after (pre-school)

In couple, partner not working

	Couple status	Not worked	Previous work experience	Reason left last paid job	Reason do not want paid work currently (age of youngest child in brackets)
12	Married, partner not working	6 years	Factory work (for under a year)	To have child	Children and extended family to look after (primary age)
13	Couple, partner not working	n/a	Cash-in hand work, eg cleaning, market (fairly continuous, still ongoing)	n/a	Child to look after (pre-school)
14	Married, partner not working	Never	None	n/a	Children to look after (pre-school) Earnings versus childcare expenses Language barrier
15	Married, partner not working	Never	None	n/a	Child to look after (pre-school)
16	Married, partner not working	Never	None	n/a	Child to look after (pre-school)

Lone

	Couple status	Not worked	Previous work experience	Reason left last paid job	Reason do not want paid work currently (age of youngest child in brackets)
17	Lone	6 years	Intermittent – waitressing/retail	–	Child with special needs to look after (primary age) Responsibility for paying rent would be too much
18	Lone	10 years	Factory work – for a year, on and off	Got married and had children	Children to look after (primary age)

	Couple status	Not worked	Previous work experience	Reason left last paid job	Reason do not want paid work currently (age of youngest child in brackets)
19	Lone	10 years	Cleaning (continuously employed)	To have children	Children to look after (pre-school)
20	Lone	11 years	Factory work	To have child	Children to look after, including one with special needs (primary age)
21	Lone	16 years	Care (intermittent)	Left a year before had first child	Problem of work not making you better off than being on benefits Also children to look after (primary age)
22	Lone	Never	None	n/a	Children to look after (pre-school)

5c: The kind of paid work that the mothers and one lone father wanted

	Couple status	Age of youngest child	Preferred job	Previous work experience includes:	Maximum distance would travel	Take-home pay aiming for[a]	Lowest take-home pay would accept	Time since last worked	Current job-search activity/preparation
1	Couple, partner works f-t	Primary	Involving computers/office	Factory, play, cleaning	Local	£200 per week	–	6 years	Waiting for a computer course to come up
2	Lone	Pre-school	Classroom assistant (hours so that can drop off and pick up from school)	Cleaning, catering	Don't mind but need to collect children	–	–	6 years	–
3	Couple, partner works p-t	Pre-school	Computer operator, but willing to be admin officer (full-time)	Sales assistant (does not want to return this, or typing or lifting, as is not what has trained for)	Even 2 hours!	£14,000pa gross (£225 per week net)	£10,000pa gross (£173 per week net)	7 years	Sending in applications/attended interview
4	Lone	Pre-school	Nursery worker/office/sales assistant	Cleaning/catering (does not want to return to this)	1 hour, but after 9am	£200 per week	£180 per week	3 years (not sure)	Currently studying computers, and has applied for nursery course with placement
5	Lone	Primary	Office job (full-time) (not factory job/house-keeping as has back problem)	Cleaning	Within 5 miles	£200 per week	£200 per week	2 years	Currently studying full-time
6	Lone	Primary	Care	Factory work	–	£200 per week	£200 per week	7 years	Got leaflet to restart courses

	Couple status	Age of youngest child	Preferred job	Previous work experience includes:	Maximum distance would travel	Take-home pay aiming for[a]	Lowest take-home pay would accept	Time since last worked	Current job-search activity/preparation
7	Lone	16+	Admin job	Secretarial (non-UK)	Local (though depends on pay)	£150 per week	£120 per week	9 years	Trying to get asylum application sorted – not allowed to work yet
8	Lone	Pre-school	Security/lorry driving	Security/driving	1 hour	£300–£350 per week	£250/wk	2 years	Childcare obstacle at present
9	Lone	Primary	Not clear, needs to be within school hours 10am–2pm (not dinner lady or cleaning job)	Office work	The City	If part-time £60 per week If full-time £200 per week	£60 per week (p-t) £200 per week (f-t)	11 years (some p-t casual, irregular work since)	No action at present
10	Married, partner not working	Pre-school	Own website business	Accounts management	Would work from home	–	–	5 years	Looking for funding to set up own business
11	Lone	Pre-school	Teacher's assistant (part-time to start with)	Shop assistant/nanny	30 minutes	£150–£200 for full-time week	–	4 years	Nothing yet – plans to in nine months when child starts part-time school
12	Lone	Pre-school	Social worker (full-time)	Social care work	45 minutes	£11 per hour (£440 per week)	£8 per hour (£320 per week)	2 years (some p-t work since)	Studying Masters in Social Work
13	Married, partner works p-t	Pre-school	Will depend on how children will cope with getting to school	Secretarial (non-UK), sweat-shops	About 1 hour	Don't know	Don't know	–	Planning to start an English language course, and possibly a computer course

	Couple status	Age of youngest child	Preferred job	Previous work experience includes:	Maximum distance would travel	Take-home pay aiming for[a]	Lowest take-home pay would accept	Time since last worked	Current job-search activity/preparation
14	Couple, partner not working	Pre-school	Carer (full-time)	Waitressing/mid-day supervisor	About an hour	Don't know	Don't know	1 year	Studying health and social care, looking for p-t job to do while studying – can't find one
15	Lone	Primary	Retail/childminding (10am-2pm to fit school)	Shop manageress (does not want to return to managing because "it's too demanding")	10 minutes on bus	£250 per week	£250 per week	7 years	Plans to enrol on a computer course
16	Lone	Pre-school	Driving instructor (full-time) (not office job)	Retail management, cashier	Anywhere	£450 per week	£280 per week	4 years (some versus casual work since)	Applied for career development loan (not yet successful), made contact with driving company
17	Married, partner works f-t	Pre-school	Many things – sales assistant, receptionist (part-time)	School assistant	30 minutes	Over £5 per hour (£200 per week)	£5 per hour (£200 per week)	3 years	Is registered at job centre, has enquired in local shops
18	Married, partner not working	Pre-school	–	Farm work	–	–	–	5 years	Nothing yet, feels needs to learn English first

[a] Where people specified an amount by hour or by year, we have shown this, but then indicated in brackets what the net weekly equivalent would be, assuming a full-time working week of 40 hours, to enable comparison. People often did not specify full-time or part-time; we have noted where they did, and also whether they talked about other restrictions, such as not starting work until after they had dropped their children off at school.

Source: Round 2 interviews.

Index

Page references for boxes, figures and tables are in *italics*; those for notes are followed by n

service sector 98, *99*
services 165-8
  negative changes 238-9, *238*, 249, *249*
  positive changes 232, *232*, 236, *236*, 240,
    240, 245-7, *246*, *249*, 250, 262
Sheffield 19
shops 167-8, 175
Single Regeneration Budget 26, 242, 250
slender work histories 120, *121*, 123, 124,
    124, *301-4*
Smith, J. 263n
Smith, L. 16, 197, *198*, 209
Smith, M. 13
social breakdown 273-4
social capital 7n, 56
social conditions 271-2
  negative changes 237-8, *237*, 248-9, *248*,
    249-50, *249*, 262, 263, 273-4
  positive changes 232, *232*, 234, 235, *235*,
    240, *240*, 243-4, *243*, *249*, 250, 262
social contact *37*, 38-40
Social Exclusion Unit (SEU) 3, 6n, 7n, 58,
    95, 115n, 145, 165, 176n, 263n, 271, 275
social housing *18*, 75, 172, *295*
  East-Docks 25
  West-City 20
  see also council housing; housing
    associations
stealing 198, *198*
step-fathers *see* fathers
Stewart, M. 263n
street litter *see* litter
Sunday Times 225
supermarkets 167-8, 175
support 51, 53-4
Sure Start 26
Survey of English Housing (SEH) 16, 72,
    147, 169-71, *170*, *171*, 176, 176n, *198*,
    208, *210*, *224*, *230*
Sutton *184*

T

take-home pay 137-8, 140, 142
Tam, H.B. 35
Taylor, M. 263n
Thompson, F. 41
Thrush, D. 164
transport 27
  journeys to work 105-6, *105*
  positive changes 240-1
  satisfaction 147, *148*, 154-6, *170*, 175
Travis, A. 198, 201
Treasury 7n
trees 184, *184*, 195
Tunstall, R. 2, 7n, 189, 215, 220, 271
Turks 60

community spirit 38, 43
non-working mothers' work histories
    123-4, *124*
Turok, I. 114, 116n, 140

U

UNCHS 7n
Underground 22, 27, 105, 154, 169, 240-1
unemployment 21, 26, 113
  see also employment
unfriendliness 39, *39*, 170
  see also friendliness
unsteady careers 99, *101*
  non-working mothers 99, *121*, 122, *124*,
    300
  working mothers 100, *100*, 102, *297*
Urban Green Spaces Task Force 188
Urban Task Force 178
Utting, D. 143n

V

van Kempen, R. 7n, 91
van Vliet, W. 7n
vandalism 197, *198*, 207, 209-11, *210*, 212
  importance of problem 163, *170*, *171*
  negative changes 230
Victoria Park 185, 193, *194*
voluntary roles *see* responsible voluntary
    roles

W

Wadsworth, J. 120
wages 137-8, 140, 142
Warren, T. 115n
Weissberg, R. 6n
West Africans 265
West-City 9, 19-20, *20*, 21, 29, *226*
  in 2002 20-2
  activities and services 22
  change 230, *230*, *231*, 232, *232*
  community garden *179*
  families' descriptions *23*
  finding families 15-19, *17*, *18*, *291-4*
  housing 75, *233*
  negative changes 237-40, *237*, *238*,
    249-51, *249*
  neighbourhood 10-11, *11*, *295*
  neighbourhood environment 28, *28*
  population *19*
  positive changes 232-6, *232*, *233*, *235*, *236*,
    249-51, *249*
  research approach 12-15, *12*, *14*
West-City New Deal Trust 20, 21, 22, 95,
    203, *203*, 204, 207, 240

Also available from The Policy Press

Managing community practice
Principles, policies and programmes
Edited by Sarah Banks, Hugh Butcher, Paul Henderson and Jim Robertson
Paperback £17.99 US$28.00
ISBN 1 86134 356 6
234 x 156mm 208 pages
March 2003

Achieving community benefits through contracts
Law, policy and practice
Richard MacFarlane and Mark Cook
Paperback £13.95
ISBN 1 86134 422 4
2976 x 210mm 56 pages
December 2002
In association with the
Joseph Rowntree Foundation

Best practice in regeneration
Because it works
Tony Trott
Paperback £11.95
ISBN 1 86134 455 4
297 x 210mm 32 pages
November 2002
In association with the
Joseph Rowntree Foundation

Approaches to community governance
Models for mixed tenure communities
Edited by Martin Knox, David Alcock, Anna Roderick and John Iles
Paperback £13.95
ISBN 1 86134 461 9
297 x 210mm 56 pages
November 2002
In association with the
Joseph Rowntree Foundation

For further information about these and other titles published by The Policy Press, please visit our website at:
www.policypress.org.uk

To order titles, please contact:
Marston Book Services
PO Box 269 • Abingdon
Oxon OX14 4YN • UK
Tel: +44 (0)1235 465500
Fax: +44 (0)1235 465556
E-mail: direct.orders@marston.co.uk